PIECES OF
THE FRAME

BY JOHN MC PHEE

PIECES OF THE FRAME

John McPhee

FARRAR, STRAUS AND GIROUX NEW YORK

818.5
M

The articles in this book originally appeared in the following periodicals: "Pieces of the Frame" (1970) in *The Atlantic;* "Josie's Well" (1970) in *Holiday;* "Centre Court" (1972) in *Playboy;* "Travels in Georgia" (1973), "Reading the River" (1970), "The Search for Marvin Gardens" (1972), "From Birnam Wood to Dunsinane" (1970), "Basketball and Beefeaters" (1963), "Firewood" (1974), "Ranger" (1971), and "Ruidoso" (1974) in *The New Yorker.*

Library of Congress Cataloging in Publication Data
McPhee, John A.
    Pieces of the frame.
    I. Title.
AC8.M267   081   75–4960

For Yolanda

CONTENTS

Travels in Georgia

I ASKED FOR THE GORP. Carol passed it to me. Breakfast had been heavy with cathead biscuits, sausage, boiled eggs, Familia, and chicory coffee, but that was an hour ago and I was again hungry. Sam said, "The little Yankee bastard wants the gorp, Carol. Shall we give him some?" Sam's voice was as soft as sphagnum, with inflections of piedmont Georgia.

"The little Yankee bastard can have all he wants this morning," Carol said. "It's such a beautiful day."

Although Sam was working for the state, he was driving his own Chevrolet. He was doing seventy. In a reverberation of rubber, he crossed Hunger and Hardship Creek and headed into the sun on the Swainsboro Road. I took a ration of gorp—soybeans, sunflower seeds, oats, pretzels, Wheat Chex, raisins, and kelp—and poured another ration into Carol's hand. At just about that moment, a snapping turtle was hit on the road a couple of miles ahead of us, who knows by what sort of vehicle, a car, a pickup; run over like a manhole cover, probably with much the same sound, and not crushed, but gravely wounded. It remained still. It appeared to be dead on the road.

Sam, as we approached, was the first to see it. "D.O.R.," he said. "Man, that is a big snapper." Carol and I both sat forward. Sam pressed hard on the brakes. Even so, he was going fifty when he passed the turtle.

Carol said, "He's not dead. He didn't look dead."

Sam reversed. He drove backward rapidly, fast as the car would go. He stopped on the shoulder, and we all got out. There was a pond beyond the turtle. The big, broad head was shining with blood, but there was, as yet, very little blood on the road. The big jaws struck as we came near, opened and closed bloodily—not the kind of strike that, minutes ago, could have cut off a finger, but still a strike with power. The turtle was about fourteen inches long and a shining horn-brown. The bright spots on its marginal scutes were like light bulbs around a mirror. The neck lunged out. Carol urged the turtle, with her foot, toward the side of the road. "I know, big man," she said to it. "I know it's bad. We're not tormenting you. Honest we're not." Sam asked her if she thought it had a chance to live and she said she was sure it had no chance at all. A car, coming west, braked down and stopped. The driver got out, with some effort and a big paunch. He looked at the turtle and said, "Fifty years old if he's a day." That was the whole of what the man had to say. He got into his car and drove on. Carol nudged the snapper, but it was too hurt to move. It could only strike the air. Now, in a screech of brakes, another car came onto the scene. It went by us, then spun around with squealing tires and pulled up on the far shoulder. It was a two-tone, high-speed, dome-lighted Ford, and in it was the sheriff of Laurens County. He got out and walked

toward us, all Technicolor in his uniform, legs striped like a
pine-barrens tree frog's, plastic plate on his chest, name of
Wade.

"Good morning," Sam said to him.

"How y'all?" said Sheriff Wade.

Carol said, "Would you mind shooting this turtle for us,
please?"

"Surely, Ma'am," said the sheriff, and he drew his .38. He
extended his arm and took aim.

"Uh, Sheriff," I said. "If you don't mind . . ." And I asked
him if he would kindly shoot the turtle over soil and not over
concrete. The sheriff paused and looked slowly, with new
interest, from one of us to another: a woman in her twenties,
good-looking, with long tawny hair, no accent (that he could
hear), barefoot, and wearing a gray sweatshirt and brown
dungarees with a hunting knife in the belt; a man (Sam)
around forty, in weathered khaki, also without an accent, and
with a full black beard divided by a short white patch at the
chin—an authentic, natural split beard; and then this incongruous little Yankee bastard telling him not to shoot the road.
Carol picked up the turtle by its long, serrated tail and carried
it, underside toward her leg, beyond the shoulder of the highway, where she set it down on a patch of grass. The sheriff
followed with his .38. He again took aim. He steadied the
muzzle of the pistol twelve inches from the turtle. He fired,
and missed. The gun made an absurdly light sound, like a
screen door shutting. He fired again. He missed. He fired
again. The third shot killed the turtle. The pistol smoked. The
sheriff blew the smoke away, and smiled, apparently at himself. He shook his head a little. "He should be good," he said,
with a nod at the turtle. The sheriff crossed the road and got
into his car. "Y'all be careful," he said. With a great screech of
tires, he wheeled around and headed on west.

Carol guessed that the turtle was about ten years old. By the tail, she carried it down to the edge of the pond, like a heavy suitcase with a broken strap. Sam fetched plastic bags from the car. I found a long two-by-ten plank and carried it to the edge of the water. Carol placed the snapper upside down on the plank. Kneeling, she unsheathed her hunting knife and began, in a practiced and professional way, to slice around the crescents in the plastron, until the flesh of the legs—in thick steaks of red meat—came free. Her knife was very sharp. She put the steaks into a plastic bag. All the while, she talked to the dead turtle, soothingly, reassuringly, nurse to patient, doctor to child, and when she reached in under the plastron and found an ovary, she shifted genders with a grunt of surprise. She pulled out some globate yellow fat and tossed it into the pond. Hundreds of mosquito fish came darting through the water, sank their teeth, shook their heads, worried the fat. Carol began to remove eggs from the turtle's body. The eggs were like ping-pong balls in size, shape, and color, and how they all fitted into the turtle was more than I could comprehend, for there were fifty-six of them in there, fully finished, and a number that had not quite taken their ultimate form. "Look at those eggs. Aren't they beautiful?" Carol said. "Oh, that's sad. You were just about to do your thing, weren't you, girl?" That was why the snapper had gone out of the pond and up onto the road. She was going to bury her eggs in some place she knew, perhaps drawn by an atavistic attachment to the place where she herself had hatched out and where many generations of her forebears had been born when there was no road at all. The turtle twitched. Its neck moved. Its nerves were still working, though its life was gone. The nails on the ends of the claws were each an inch long. The turtle draped one of these talons over one of Carol's fingers. Carol withdrew more fat and threw a huge hunk into the pond. "Wouldn't it be fun to analyze *that* for pesticides?" she said. "You're fat as a pig, Mama. You sure lived high off the hog." Finishing the job—it took forty minutes—Carol found frog bones in the turtle. She put more red meat into plastic sacks and divided the eggs. She kept half for us to eat. With her knife she carefully buried the remaining eggs, twenty-eight or so, in a sandbank, much as the mother turtle might have been doing at just that time. Carol picked away some leeches from between her fingers. The leeches had come off the turtle's shell. She tied the sacks and said, "All right. That's all we can say grace over. Let's send her back whence she came." Picking up the inedible parts—plastron, carapace, neck, claws—she heaved them into the pond. They hit with a slap and sank without bubbles.

As we moved east, pine trees kept giving us messages— small, hand-painted signs nailed into the loblollies. "HAVE YOU WHAT IT TAKES TO MEET JESUS WHEN HE RETURNS?" Sam said he was certain he did not. "JESUS WILL NEVER FAIL YOU." City limits, Adrian, Georgia. Swainsboro, Georgia. Portal, Georgia. Towns on the long, straight roads of the coastal plain. White-painted, tin-roofed bungalows. Awnings shading the fronts of stores—prepared for heat and glare. Red earth. Sand roads. Houses on short stilts. Sloping verandas. Unpainted boards.
"D.O.R.," said Carol.
"What do you suppose that was?"
"I don't know. I didn't see. It could have been a squirrel."
Sam backed up to the D.O.R. It was a brown thrasher. Carol looked it over, and felt it. Sam picked it up. "Throw him far off the road," Carol said. "So a possum won't get killed while eating him." Sam threw the bird far off the road. A stop for a D.O.R. always brought the landscape into detailed focus. Pitch coming out of a pine. Clustered sows behind a fence. An automobile wrapped in vines. A mailbox. "Donald Foskey." His home. Beyond the mailbox, a set of cinder blocks and on the cinder blocks a mobile home. As Sam regathered speed, Carol turned on the radio and moved the dial. If she could

find some Johnny Cash, it would elevate her day. Some
Johnny Cash was not hard to find in the airwaves of Georgia.
There he was now, resonantly singing about his Mississippi
Delta land, where, on a sharecropping farm, he grew up. Carol
smiled and closed her eyes. In her ears—pierced ears—were
gold maple leaves that seemed to move under the influence of
the music.

"D.O.R. possum," Sam said, stopping again. "Two! A grown
one and a baby." They had been killed probably ten minutes
before. Carol carried the adult to the side of the road and left
it there. She kept the baby. He was seven inches long. He was
half tail. Although dead, he seemed virtually undamaged. We
moved on. Carol had a clipboard she used for making occasional notes and sketches. She put the little possum on the clipboard and rested the clipboard on her knees. "Oh, you sweet
little angel. How could anybody run over *you?*" she said. "Oh,
I just love possums. I've raised so many of them. This is a great
age. They are the neatest little animals. They love you so much.
They crawl on your shoulder and hang in your hair. How
people can dislike them I don't understand." Carol reached
into the back seat and put the little opossum into a container
of formaldehyde. After a while, she said, "What mystifies me
is: that big possum back there was a male."

Bethel Primitive Baptist Church. Old Canoochee Primitive
Baptist Church. "THE CHURCH HAS NO INDULGENCES." A town
every ten miles, a church—so it seemed—every two. Carol
said she frequently slept in church graveyards. They were, for
one thing, quiet, and, for another, private. Graham Memorial
Church of the Nazarene.

Sam and Carol both sat forward at the same moment, alert,
excited. "D.O.R. Wow! That was something special. It had a
long yellow belly and brown fur or feathers! Hurry, Sam. It's a
good one." Sam backed up at forty miles an hour and strained
the Chevrolet.

"What is it? What is it?"

"It's a piece of bark. Fell off a pulpwood truck."

The approach to Pembroke was made with a sense of infiltration—Pembroke, seat of Bryan County. "Remember, now, we're interested in frogs," Sam said, and we went up the steps of Bryan County Courthouse. "We understand there is a stream-channelization project going on near here. Could you tell us where? We're collecting frogs." It is hard to say what the clerks in the courthouse thought of this group—the spokesman with the black-and-white beard, the shoeless young woman, and their silent companion. They looked at us—they in their pumps and print dresses—from the other side of a distance. The last thing they might have imagined was that two of the three of us were representing the state government in Atlanta. The clerks did not know where the channelization was going on but they knew who might—a woman in town who knew everything. We went to see her. A chicken ran out of her house when she opened the screen door. No, she was not sure just where we should go, but try a man named Miller in Lanier. He'd know. He knew everything. Lanier was five miles down the track—literally so. The Seaboard Coast Line ran beside the road. Miller was a thickset man with unbelievably long, sharp fingernails, a driver of oil trucks. It seemed wonderful that he could get his hands around the wheel without cutting himself, that he could deliver oil without cutting the hose. He said, "Do you mind my asking why you're interested in stream channelization?"

"We're interested in frogs," Sam said. "Snakes and frogs. We thought the project might be stirring some up."

Miller said, "I don't mind the frog, but I want no part of the snake."

His directions were perfect—through pine forests, a right, two lefts, to where a dirt road crossed a tributary of the Ogeechee. A wooden bridge there had been replaced by a culvert. The stream now flowed through big pipes in the culvert. Upriver, far as the eye could see, a riparian swath had been cut by chain saws. Back from the banks, about fifty feet on each side, the overstory and the understory—every tree, bush, and sapling—had been cut down. The river was under revision. It had been freed of meanders. It was now two yards wide between vertical six-foot banks; and it was now as straight as a ditch. It had, in fact, become a ditch—in it a stream of thin mud, flowing. An immense yellow machine, slowly backing upstream, had in effect eaten this river. It was at work now, grunting and belching, two hundred yards from the culvert. We tried to walk toward it along the bank but sank to our shins in black ooze. The stumps of the cut trees were all but covered with mud from the bottom of the river. We crossed the ditch. The dredged mud was somewhat firmer on the other side. Sam and I walked there. Carol waded upcurrent in the stream. The machine was an American drag-line crane. The word "American" stood out on its cab in letters more than a foot high. Its boom reached up a hundred feet. Its bucket took six-foot bites. As we approached, the bucket kept eating the riverbed, then swinging up and out of the channel and disgorging tons of mud to either side. Carol began to take pictures. She took more and more pictures as she waded on upstream. When she was fifty feet away from the dragline, its engine coughed down and stopped. The sudden serenity was oddly disturbing. The operator stepped out of the cab and onto the catwalk. One hand on the flank of his crane, he inclined his head somewhat forward and stared down at Carol. He was a stocky man with an open shirt and an open face, deeply tanned. He said, "Howdy."

"Howdy," said Carol.

"You're taking some pictures," he said.

"I sure am. I'm taking some pictures. I'm interested in the

range extension of river frogs, and the places they live. I bet you turn up some interesting things."

"I see some frogs," the man said. "I see lots of frogs."

"You sure know what you're doing with that machine," Carol said. The man shifted his weight. "That's a *big* thing," she went on. "How much does it weigh?"

"Eighty-two tons."

"Eighty-two *tons?*"

"Eighty-two tons."

"Wow! How far can you dig in one day?"

"Five hundred feet."

"A mile every ten days," Sam said, shaking his head with awe.

"Sometimes I do better than that."

"You live around here?"

"No. My home's near Baxley. I go where I'm sent. All over the state."

"Well, sorry. Didn't mean to interrupt you."

"Not 't all. Take all the pictures you want."

"Thanks. What did you say your name was?"

"Chap," he said. "Chap Causey."

We walked around the dragline, went upstream a short way, and sat down on the trunk of a large oak, felled by the chain saws, to eat our lunch—sardines, chocolate, crackers, and wine. Causey at work was the entertainment, pulling his levers, swinging his bucket, having at the stream.

If he had been at first wary, he no doubt had had experience that made him so. All over the United States, but particularly in the Southeast, his occupation had become a raw issue. He was working for the Soil Conservation Service, a subdivision of the United States Department of Agriculture, making a "water-resource channel improvement"—generally known as stream channelization, or reaming a river. Behind his dragline, despite the clear-cutting of the riverine trees, was a free-flowing natural stream, descending toward the Ogeechee in bends and eddies, riffles and deeps—in appearance somewhere between a trout stream and a bass river, and still handsomely so, even though it was shaved and ready for its operation. At the dragline, the recognizable river disappeared, and below the big machine was a kind of reverse irrigation ditch, engineered to remove water rapidly from the immediate watershed. "How could anyone even conceive of this idea?" Sam said. "Not just to do it, but even to *conceive* of it?"

The purpose of such projects was to anticipate and eliminate floods, to drain swamps, to increase cropland, to channel water toward freshly created reservoirs serving and attracting new industries and new housing developments. Water sports would flourish on the new reservoirs, hatchery fish would proliferate below the surface: new pulsations in the life of the rural South. The Soil Conservation Service was annually spending about fifteen million dollars on stream-channelization projects, providing, among other things, newly arable land to farmers who already had land in the Soil Bank. The Department of Agriculture could not do enough for the Southern farmer, whose only problem was bookkeeping. He got money for keeping his front forty idle. His bottomland went up in value when the swamps were drained, and then more money came for not farming the drained land. Years earlier, when a conservationist had been someone who plowed land along natural contours, the Soil Conservation Service had been the epicenter of the conservation movement, decorated for its victories over erosion of the land. Now, to a new generation that had discovered ecology, the S.C.S. was the enemy. Its drainage programs tampered with river mechanics, upsetting the relationships between bass and otter, frog and owl. The Soil Conservation Service had grown over the years into a bureau of fifteen thousand people, and all the way down at the working point, the cutting edge of things, was Chap Causey, in the cab of his American dragline, hearing nothing but the pounding of his big Jimmy diesel while he eliminated a river, eradicated a swamp.

After heaving up a half-dozen buckets of mud, Causey moved backward several feet. The broad steel shoes of the crane were resting on oak beams that were bound together in pairs with cables. There were twelve beams in all. Collectively, they were called "mats." Under the crane, they made a temporary bridge over the river. As Causey moved backward and off the front pair of beams, he would reach down out of the sky with a hook from his boom and snare a loop of the cable that held the beams. He snatched them up—they weighed at least half a ton—and whipped them around to the back. The beams dropped perfectly into place, adding a yard to Causey's platform on the upstream side. Near the tree line beyond one bank, he had a fuel tank large enough to bury under a gas station, and every so often he would reach out with his hook and his hundred-foot arm and, without groping, lift the tank and move it on in the direction he was going. With his levers, his cables, his bucket, and hook, he handled his mats and his tank and his hunks of the riverbed as if he were dribbling a basketball through his legs and behind his back. He was deft. He was world class. "I bet he could put on a baby's diapers with that thing," Sam said.

Carol said, "See that three-foot stump? I sure would like to see him pull *that* out." She gestured toward the rooted remains of a tree that must have stood, a week earlier, a hundred and fifty feet high. Causey, out of the corner of his eye, must have seen the gesture. Perhaps he just read her mind. He was much aware that he was being watched, and now he reached around behind him, grabbed the stump in his bucket, and ripped it out of the earth like a molar. He set it at Carol's feet. It towered over her.

After a modest interval, a few more buckets of streambed, Causey shut off the dragline and stopped for an adulation break. Carol told him he was fabulous. And she meant it. He was. She asked him what the name of the stream was. He said, "To tell you the truth, Ma'am, I don't rightly know."

Carol said, "Do you see many snakes?"

"Oh, yes, I see lots of snakes," Causey said, and he looked at her carefully.

"What kinds of snakes?"

"Moccasins, mainly. They climb up here on the mats. They don't run. They never run. They're not afraid. I got a canoe paddle in the cab there. I kill them with the paddle. One day, I killed thirty-five moccasins. People come along sometimes, like you, visitors, come up here curious to see the digging, and they see the dead snakes lying on the mats, and they freeze. They refuse to move. They refuse to walk back where they came from."

If Causey was trying to frighten Carol, to impress her by frightening her, he had picked the wrong person. He might have sent a shot or two of adrenalin through me, but not through Carol. I once saw her reach into a semi-submerged hollow stump in a man-made lake where she knew a water snake lived, and she had felt around in there, underwater, with her hands on the coils of the snake, trying to figure out which end was the front. Standing thigh-deep in the water, she was wearing a two-piece bathing suit. Her appearance did not suggest old Roger Conant on a field trip. She was trim and supple and tan from a life in the open. Her hair, in a ponytail, had fallen across one shoulder, while her hands, down inside the stump, kept moving slowly, gently along the body of the snake. This snake was her friend, she said, and she wanted Sam and me to see him. "Easy there, fellow, it's only Carol. I sure wish I could find your head. Here we go. We're coming to the end. Oh, damn. I've got his tail." There was nothing to do but turn around. She felt her way all four feet to the other end. "At last," she said. "How are you, old fellow?" And she lifted her arms up out of the water. In them was something like a piece of television cable moving with great vigor. She held on tight and carried her friend out of the lake and onto the shore.

At Carol's house, Sam and I one night slept in sleeping bags on the floor of her study beside Zebra, her rattlesnake. He was an eastern diamondback, and he had light lines, parallel, on his dark face. He was young and less than three feet long. He lived among rocks and leaves in a big glass jar. "As a pet, he's ideal," Carol told us. "I've never had a diamondback like him before. Anytime you get uptight about anything, just look at him. He just sits there. He's so great. He doesn't complain. He just waits. It's as if he's saying, 'I've got all the time in the world. I'll outwait you, you son of a bitch.' "

"He shows you what patience is," Sam said. "He's like a deer. Deer will wait two hours before they move into a field to eat."

In Carol's kitchen was the skin of a mature diamondback, about six feet long, that Sam and Carol had eaten in southwest Georgia, roasting him on a stick like a big hot dog, beside the Muckalee Creek. The snake, when they came upon him, had just been hit and was still alive. The men who had mortally wounded the snake were standing over it, watching it die. A dump truck full of gravel was coming toward the scene, and Carol, imagining the truck running over and crushing the diamondback, ran up to the men standing over it and said, "Do you want it?" Surprised, they said no. "No, *Ma'am!*" So she picked up the stricken snake, carried it off the road and back to the car, where she coiled it on the floor between her feet. "Later, in a gas station, we didn't worry about leaving the car unlocked. Oh, that was funny. We do have some fun. We ate him that night."

"What did he taste like?" I asked her.

"Taste like? You know, like rattlesnake. Maybe a cross between a chicken and a squirrel."

Carol's house, in Atlanta, consisted of four small rooms, each about ten feet square—kitchen, study, storage room, bedroom. They were divided by walls of tongue-and-groove boards, nailed horizontally onto the studs. A bathroom and vestibule were more or less stuck onto one side of the building. She lived alone there. An oak with a three-foot bole stood over the house like an umbrella and was so close to it that it virtually blocked the front door. An old refrigerator sat on the stoop. Around it were the skulls of a porpoise, a horse, a cow, and a pig. White columns adorned the façade. They were made of two-inch iron pipe. Paint peeled from the clapboard. The front yard was hard red clay, and it had some vestigial grasses in it (someone having once tried a lawn) that had not been mowed for possibly a decade. Carol had set out some tomatoes among the weeds. The house stood on fairly steep ground that sloped through woods to a creek. The basement was completely above grade at the rear, and a door there led into a dim room where Carol's red-tailed hawk lived. He was high in one corner, standing on a pipe. I had never been in the immediate presence of a red-tailed hawk, and at sight of him I was not sure whether to run or to kneel. At any rate, I could not have taken one step nearer. He was two feet tall. His look was incendiary. Slowly, angrily, he lifted and spread his wings, reached out a yard and a half. His talons could have hooked tuna. His name was Big Man. His spread-winged posture revealed all there was to know about him: his beauty —the snowy chest, the rufous tail; his power; his affliction.

One of his wings was broken. Carol had brought him back from near death. Now she walked over to him and stood by him and stroked his chest. "Come on, Big Man," she said. "It's not so bad. Come on, Big Man." Slowly, ever so slowly—over a period of a minute or two—the wide wings came down, folded together, while Carol stroked his chest. Fear departed, but nothing much changed in his eyes.

"What will he ever do?" I asked her.

She said, "Nothing, I guess. Just be someone's friend."

Outside the basement door was a covered pen that housed a rooster and a seagull. The rooster had been on his way to Colonel Sanders' when he fell off a truck and broke a drumstick. Someone called Carol, as people often do, and she took the rooster into her care. He was hard of moving, but she had hopes for him. He was so new there he did not even have a name. The seagull, on the other hand, had been with her for years. He had one wing. She had picked him up on a beach three hundred miles away. His name was Garbage Belly.

Carol had about fifteen ecosystems going on at once in her twenty-by-twenty house. In the study, a colony of dermestid beetles was eating flesh off the pelvis of an alligator. The beetles lived in a big can that had once held forty pounds of mincemeat. Dermestids clean bones. They do thorough work. They all but simonize the bones. Carol had obtained her original colony from the Smithsonian Institution. One of her vaulting ambitions was to be able to identify on sight any bone that she happened to pick up. Also in the can were the skulls of a water turkey, a possum, and a coon.

The beetles ate and were eaten. Carol reached into the colony, pulled out a beetle, and gave it to her black-widow spider. The black widow lived in a commercial mayonnaise jar. Carol had found her in the basement while cleaning it up for Big Man. The spider's egg was getting ready to hatch, and when it did thousands like her would emerge into the jar. Efficiently, the black widow encased the beetle in filament gauze that flowed from her spinnerets.

Carol then fed dermestids to her turtles. She had three galvanized tubs full of cooters and sliders, under a sunlamp. "They need sun, you know. Vitamin D." She fed dermestids to her spotted salamander, and to her gray tree frog. Yellow spots, polka dots, on black, the salamander's coloring was so simple and contrasting that he appeared to be a knickknack from a gift shop, a salamander made in Japan. The tree frog lived in a giant brandy snifter, furnished with rocks and dry leaves. With his latex body and his webbed and gummy oversize hands, he could walk right up the inside of his brandy snifter, even after its shape began to tilt him backward, then lay a mitt over the rim and haul himself after and walk down the outside. He could walk straight up a wall; and he did that, while digesting his beetle. He had been with Carol three years. He was a star there in her house. No mayonnaise jar for him. He had the brandy snifter. It was all his and would be as long as he lived.

Notebooks were open on Carol's desk, a heavy, kneehole desk, covered with pens, Magic Markers, brushes, pencils, drawing materials. The notebooks had spiral bindings and were, in part, diaries.

17 April. Okefenokee. Caught two banded water snakes, one skink. . . .

18 April. To King's Landing. Set three line traps baited with peanut butter, caught a rather small moccasin AGKISTRODON coming from under shed. Put out ninety-five set hooks baited with pork liner. To gator hole. Tried to use shocker, after putting up seines across exit. No luck!

19 April. D.O.R. *Natrix rigida,* glossy water snake; *Farancia abacura,* mud snake; *Elaphe guttata guttata,* corn snake. . . .

21 April. S.W. Georgia. D.O.R. vulture, ½ mi. E. Leary, Hwy 62, Calhoun County. Fresh. Possum D.O.R. nearby. . . .

The notebooks were also, in part, ledgers of her general interests.

Dissolve mouse in nitric acid and put him through spectrophotometer—can tell every element.

A starving snake can gain weight on water.

Gray whales are born with their bellies up and weigh a ton, and when they are grown they swim five thousand miles to breed in shallow lagoons and eat sand and stand on their tails and gravity-feed on pelagic crabs.

And the notebooks were, in part, filled with maps and sketches. Making a drawing of something—a mermaid weed, the hind foot of an opossum, the egg case of a spotted salamander, a cutaway of a deer's heart—was her way of printing it into her memory. The maps implied stories. They were of places too specific—too eccentric, wild, and minute—to show up as much of anything on other maps, including a topographical quadrangle. They were of places that Carol wanted to remember and, frequently enough, to find again.

12 May. Caught *Natrix erythrogaster flavigaster*, red-bellied water snake 9:30 A.M. Saw quite a large gator at 9:35. Ten feet. Swarm of honeybees 25 feet up cypress at edge of creek. Large—six-foot—gray rat snake in oak tree over water. *Elaphe obsoleta spiloides*. Tried unsuccessfully to knock it into canoe. Finally climbed tree but snake had gone into hole in limb. . . .

26 June. Sleep on nest where loggerhead laid eggs Cumberland Island, to protect eggs from feral hogs. Return later find that hog has eaten eggs. Shoot hog. . . .

27 August. Oconee River. Saw *Natrix* wrestling with a catfish in

water. *Natrix* was trying to pull fish out on bank. Snake about 2½ feet. Fish 8 inches. Snake finally won. Didn't have heart to collect snake as he was so proud of fish and wouldn't let go even when touched. Camped by railroad bridge. Many trains. Found catfish on set hook, smoked him for supper. . . .

The rods of the vertebrate eye provide scotopic vision—sight in dim light. Nocturnal animals that also go out in daylight need slit eyes to protect the rods. Crocodiles. Seals. Rattlesnakes. Cottonmouths.

13 June. North Georgia. Oh, most glorious night. The fireflies are truly in competition with the stars! At the tops of the ridges it is impossible to tell them apart. As of old, I wished for a human companion. On the banks of a road, a round worm was glowing, giving off light. What a wonderful thing it is. It allows us to see in the darkness.

Above the desk, tacked to a wall, was the skin of a bobcat— D.O.R. two miles west of Baxley, Highway 341. "I was excited out of my mind when we found him," Carol said. "He was the best D.O.R. ever. It was late afternoon. January. He was stiff, but less than a day old. Bobcats move mostly at night. He was unbloody, three feet long, and weighed twenty-one pounds. I was amazed how small his testicles were. I skinned him here at home. I tanned his hide—salt, alum, then neat's-foot oil. He had a thigh like a goat's—so big, so much beautiful meat. I boiled him. He tasted good—you know, the wild taste. Strong. But not as strong as a strong coon."

Zebra lifted his head, flashed his fangs, and yawned a pink yawn. This was the first time in at least a day that Zebra had moved. Carol said the yawn meant he was hungry. Zebra had had his most recent meal seven weeks before. Carol went over to the gerbil bin to select a meal for Zebra. "Snakes just don't eat that much," she said, shaking her head in dismay over the exploding population of gerbils. She tossed one to a cat. She picked up another one, a small one, for Zebra. "Zebra eats every month or two," she went on. "That's all he needs. He doesn't do anything. He just sits there." She lifted the lid of Zebra's jar and dropped the gerbil inside. The gerbil stood still, among the dry leaves, looking. Zebra did not move. "I'm going to let him go soon. He's been a good friend. He really has. You sometimes forget they're deadly, you know. I've had my hand down inside the jar, cleaning it out, and suddenly realized, with cold sweat, that he's poisonous. Ordinarily, when you see a rattlesnake you are on guard immediately. But with him in the house all the time I tend to forget how deadly he is. The younger the snake, the more concentrated the venom."

The gerbil began to walk around the bottom of the big glass jar. Zebra, whose body was arranged in a loose coil, gave no sign that he was aware of the gerbil's presence. Under a leaf, over a rock, sniffing, the gerbil explored the periphery of Zebra's domain. Eventually, the gerbil stepped up onto Zebra's back. Still Zebra did not move. Zebra had been known to refuse a meal, and perhaps that would happen now. The gerbil walked along the snake's back, stepped down, and continued along the boundary of the base of the jar, still exploring. Another leaf, another stone, the strike came when the gerbil was perhaps eight inches from Zebra's head. The strike was so fast, the strike and the recovery, that it could not really be followed by the eye. Zebra lanced across the distance, hit the gerbil in the heart, and, all in the same instant, was back where he had started, same loose coil, head resting just where it had been resting before. The gerbil took three steps forward and fell dead, so dead it did not even quiver, tail out straight behind.

Sam had once told me how clumsy he thought rattlesnakes were, advising me never to walk through a palmetto stand third in a line, because a rattlesnake, said Sam, takes aim at the first person, strikes at the second, and hits the third. After watching Zebra, though, I decided to go tenth in line, if at all. Carol seemed thoughtful. "I've had copperheads," she said. "But I'm not really that much on snakes. I'm always worrying that someday I'll come home and find the jar turned over and several dead cats lying around on the floor." That night, on the floor in my sleeping bag, I began to doze off and then imagined rolling over and knocking Zebra out of his jar. The same thought came to me when I started to doze off again. I spent most of the night with my chin in my hands, watching him through the glass.

There was a baby hawk in a box in the kitchen, and early in the morning he began to scream. Nothing was going to quiet him except food. Carol got up, took a rabbit out of the refrigerator, and cut it up with a pair of scissors. It had been a rabbit D.O.R. The rabbit was twice the size of the hawk, but the hawk ate most of the rabbit. There followed silence, bought and paid for. In the freezer, Carol had frogs' legs, trout, bream, nighthawk, possum, squirrel, quail, turtle, and what she called trash fish. The trash fish were for Garbage Belly. The destiny of the other items was indistinct. They were for the consumption of the various occupants of the house, the whole food chain—bird, amphibian, beast and beetle, reptile, arachnid, man. A sign over the kitchen sink said "EAT MORE POSSUM," black on Chinese red.

In the bedroom was a deerskin. "I saw blood on the trail," Carol said. "I knew a deer wouldn't go uphill shot, so I went down. I found it. It wasn't a spike buck, it was a slickhead. It had been poached. I poached it from the poacher." On the walls were watercolors and oils she had done of natural scenes, and three blown-up photographs of Johnny Cash. A half-finished papier-mâché head of Johnny Cash was in her bedroom as well, and other pieces of her sculpture, including "Earth Stars," a relief of mushrooms. Carol looked reverently at the photographs and said that whenever she had had depressing and difficult times she had turned to Johnny Cash, to the reassurances in the timbre of his voice, to the philosophy in his lyrics, to his approach to life. She said he had more than once pulled her through.

Carol grew up in Rochester, New York, until she was twelve, after that in Atlanta. Her father, Earl Ruckdeschel, worked for Eastman Kodak and managed the Atlanta processing plant. She was an only child. Animals were *non grata* at home, so she went to them. "You have to turn to something. There was a lot of comfort out there in those woods. Wild creatures were my brothers and sisters. That is why I'm more interested in mammals than anything else. They're warm-blooded. Fish are cold-blooded. You can't snuggle up with a fish." Her parents mortally feared snakes, but she never did. Her father once made her a snake stick. Her mother told her, many times a month and year, that it was not ladylike to be interested in snakes and toads. Carol went to Northside High in Atlanta. After high school, for five years, she worked at odd jobs—she fixed car radios, she wandered. Then she went to Georgia State University, studied biology, and married a biologist there. He was an authority on river swamps, an ecologist—a tall, prognathous, slow-speaking scientific man. His subspecialty was cottonmouths. He had found an island in the Gulf that had a cottonmouth under every palmetto, and he lived for a time among them. He weighed and measured them one by one. He was a lot older than Carol. She had taken his course in vertebrate zoology. The marriage did not really come apart. It evaporated. Carol kept going on field trips with him, and she stayed on at Georgia State as a biological researcher. The little house she moved into could not have been better: low rent, no class, high privacy, woods, a creek. And it was all her own. A cemetery was across the street. She could sleep there if she wanted to get out of the house. On Mother's Day, or whenever else she needed flowers, she collected bouquets from among the graves. From time to time, she wandered away. She had a white pickup truck and a German shepherd. His name was Catfish, and he was "all mouth and no brains." Carol and Catfish slept on a bale of hay in the back of the truck, and they went all over, from the mountains to the sea. They fished in the mountains, hunted in the sand hills, set traps in the Okefenokee Swamp. She began collecting specimens for the Georgia State University research collection. Most she found dead on the road. Occasionally, she brought new specimens into the collection, filling in gaps, but mainly she replenished exhausted supplies—worn-out pelts and skulls. There was always a need. An animal's skin has a better chance against a Goodyear tire than it does against the paws of a college student. She had no exclusive specialty. She wanted to do everything. Any plant or creature, dead or alive, attracted her eye.

She volunteered, as well, for service with the Georgia Natural Areas Council, a small office of the state government that had been established to take an inventory of wild places in Georgia worth preserving, proclaiming, and defending. While she travelled around Georgia picking up usable D.O.R.s for the university, she appraised the landscape for the state, detouring now and again into river swamps to check the range of frogs. Sam Candler, who also worked for the Natural Areas Council, generally went with her. Rarely, they flew in his plane. For the most part, they were on the road. Sam had a farm in Coweta County. He had also spent much of his life in the seclusion of Cumberland Island, off the Georgia coast. He was a great-grandson of the pharmacist who developed and at one time wholly owned the Coca-Cola Company, so he could have been a rampant lion in social Atlanta, but he would have preferred to wade blindfolded through an alligator swamp with chunks of horsemeat trussed to his legs. He wanted to live, as he put it, "close to the earth." He knew wilderness, he had been in it so much, and his own outlook on the world seemed to have been formed and directed by his observations of the creatures that ranged in wild places, some human, some not. Sam had no formal zoological or ecological training. What he brought to his work was mainly a sense of what he wanted for the region where he had lived his life. He had grown up around Atlanta, had gone to Druid Hills Grammar School and to Emory University and on into the Air Force. He had lived ever since on the island and the farm. His wife and their four children seemed to share with him a lack of interest in urban events. The Natural Areas Council had been effective. It had the weight of the government behind it. Georgia was as advanced in this respect as, say, Indiana, Illinois, Iowa, and New Jersey, where important conservancy work was also being accomplished on the state-government level, and far more advanced than most other states. There was much to evaluate. Georgia was, after all, the largest state east of the Mississippi River, and a great deal of it was still wild. Georgia forests, mountains, swamps, islands, and rivers—a long list of sites of special interest or value—had become Registered Natural Areas. Sam and Carol had done the basic work—exploring the state, following leads, assessing terrain, considering vegetation and wildlife, choosing sites, and persuading owners to register lands for preservation.

Sam had been a friend of mine for some years, and when he wrote to say that he was now travelling around the state collecting skulls and pelts, eating rattlesnakes, preserving natural areas, and charting the ranges of river frogs, I could not wait until I could go down there and see. I had to wait more than a year, though, while finishing up some work. I live in Princeton, New Jersey, so I flew from Newark when the day came, and I nearly missed the plane. Automobiles that morning were backed up at least a mile from the Newark Airport tollbooths (fourteen tollbooths, fourteen lanes), and the jam was just as thick on the paid side as it was on the unpaid side—thousands and thousands of murmuring cars, moving nowhere, nowhere to move, shaking, vibrating, stinking, rattling, *Homo sapiens* D.O.R. I got out of my car and left it there, left it, shamefully, with a high-school student who was accepting money to drive it home, and began to make my way overland to the terminal. I climbed up on bumpers and over corrugated fences and ducked under huge green signs. I went around tractor trailers and in front of buses. Fortunately, Sam had told me to bring a backpack. Carrying a suitcase through that milieu would have been like carrying a suitcase up the Matterhorn. Occasionally, I lost direction, and once I had to crawl under a mastodonic truck, but I did get through, and I ran down the cattle-pen corridors of the airport and, with a minute to go, up the steps and into the plane—relieved beyond measure to be out of that ruck and off to high ground and sweet air, taking my chances on the food. Sam and Carol met me, and we went straight to the mountains, stopping all the way for D.O.R.s. That night, we ate a weasel.

In a valley in north Georgia, Carol had a cabin that was made of peeled logs, had a stone fireplace, and stood beside a cold stream. We stayed there on the first night of a journey that eventually meandered through eleven hundred miles of the state—a great loop, down out of the river gorges and ravine forests of the mountains, across the granitic piedmont and over the sand hills and the red hills to the river swamps and pine flatwoods of the coastal plain. Sam had a canoe on the top of the car. We slept in swamps and beside a lake and streams. Made, in part, in the name of the government, it was a journey that tended to mock the idea of a state—as an unnatural subdivision of the globe, as a metaphor of the human ego sketched on paper and framed in straight lines and in riparian boundaries behind an unalterable coast. Georgia. A state? Really a core sample of a continent, a plug in the melon, a piece of North America. Pull it out and wildcats would spill off the high edges. Alligators off the low ones. The terrain was crisscrossed with geological boundaries, mammalian boundaries, amphibian boundaries—the range of the river frogs. The range of the wildcat was the wildcat's natural state, overlaying segments of tens of thousands of other states, one of which was Georgia. The State of Georgia. Governor Jimmy Carter in the mansion in Atlanta.

The first thing Sam and Carol wanted to assess on this trip was a sphagnum bog in Rabun County, off the north side of the Rabun Bald (4,696 feet). The place seemed marginal to me, full of muck and trout lilies, with swamp pinks in blossom under fringe trees and smooth alders, but Sam and Carol thought it ought to be registered, and they sought out the owner, a heavy woman, greatly slow of speech, with a Sears, Roebuck tape measure around her neck. She stood under a big white pine by the concrete front porch of her shingled house on a flinty mountain farm. Sam outlined the value of registering a natural area for preservation beyond one's years. She looked at him with no expression and said, "We treasure the bog." He gave her an application. ("Being aware of the high responsibility to the State that goes with the ownership and use of a property which has outstanding value in illustrating the natural history of Georgia, we morally agree to continue to protect and use this site for purposes consistent with the preservation of its natural integrity.") Perhaps she could consider it with her husband and his brothers and nephews when they came home. One day soon, he would stop back to talk again. She said, "We likes to hunt arrowheads. We treasure the bog."

The D.O.R.s that first day included a fan belt Sam took for a blacksnake—jammed on his brakes, backed up to see—and a banana peel that Carol identified, at first glimpse, as a jumping mouse. Eager was the word for them. They were so much on the hunt. "It is rare for specimens to be collected this way," Carol said. "Most people are too lazy. Or they're hung up on just frogs or just salamanders, or whatever, and they don't care about other things. Watching for D.O.R.s makes travelling a lot more interesting. I mean, can you imagine just *going* down the road?"

We went around a bend in a mountain highway and the road presented Carol with the find of the day. "D.O.R.!" she said. "That was a good one. That was a *good* one! Sam, hurry back. That was a weasel!"

Sam hurried back. It was no banana peel. It was exactly what Carol said it was: *Mustela frenata*, the long-tailed weasel, dead on the road. It was fresh-killed, and—from the point of view of Georgia State University—in fine condition. Carol was so excited she jumped. The weasel was a handsome thing, minklike, his long body a tube roughly ten by two, his neck long and slender. His fur was white and yellow on the underside and dark brown on his back. "What a magnificent animal!" Carol said. "And hard as hell to trap. Smell his musk. The scent glands are back here by the tail." While backing up after seeing him, she had hoped against hope that he would be a least weasel—smallest of all carnivores. She had never seen one. The least weasel diets almost exclusively on tiny, selected mice. This one would have eaten almost anything warm, up to and including a rabbit twice his size. Carol put him in an iced cooler that was on the back seat. The cooler was not airtight. Musk permeated the interior of the car. It was not disturbing. It was merely powerful. Carol said they had once collected a skunk D.O.R. They had put it in a plastic bag within a plastic bag within four additional plastic bags. The perfume still came through.

Carol's valley resisted visitors. It was seven miles from a paved road. It was rimmed with mountains. It was the coldest valley in Georgia. A trout stream cascaded out of the south end. Ridges pressed in from east and west. The north was interrupted by a fifty-five-hundred-foot mountain called Standing Indian. Standing Indian stood in North Carolina, showing Georgia where to stop. The valley was prize enough. Its floor was flat and green with pastureland and shoots of new corn. Its brooks were clear. Now, in May, there would be frost across the fields in the morning, heavy and bright, but blossoms were appearing on the dogwoods and leaves on the big hardwoods—only so far up the mountains, though; it was still winter on Standing Indian, stick-figure forests to the top. Sam had flown over this whole area, minutely, in his Cessna— Mt. Oglethorpe to the Chattooga River, Black Rock Mountain to the Brasstown Bald. He said there was no valley in Georgia like this one in beauty or remoteness. It was about two miles long and a half mile wide. Its year-round population was twelve. Someone else, somewhere else, would have called it by another name, but not here. Lyrical in its effrontery to fact, the name of the valley was Tate City. On our way in, we stopped to see Arthur and Mammy Young, its senior residents. Their house, until recently, had had so many preserves stacked on boards among the rafters that the roof sagged. Their outhouse straddled a stream. Their house, made of logs, burned to the ground one day when they were in town, eighteen miles away. Now they lived in a cinderblock hut with a pickup truck outside, fragments of machinery lying on the ground, hound dogs barking. The Youngs were approaching old age, apparently with opposite metabolisms, he sinewy, she more than ample, after sixty years of cathead biscuits. Inside, Arthur rolled himself a cigarette and sat down to smoke it beside his wood-burning stove. Near him was a fiddle. Sam said that Arthur was a champion fiddler. Arthur went on smoking and did not reach for the fiddle. He exchanged news with Carol. Christ looked down on us from pictures on each wall. The room had two kerosene lanterns, and its windows were patched with tape. "I always wished I had power, so I could iron," Mammy said. "When I had kids. Now I don't care." Dusk was near and Carol wanted time in the light, so we left soon and went on up the valley, a mile or so, to her log cabin.

A wooden deck reached out from the cabin on stilts toward the stream. The place had been cut out of woods—hemlock, ironwood, oak, alder, dogwood, rhododendron. A golden birch was standing in a hole in the center of the deck. Carol got out the weasel and set him, paws up, on the deck. Sam unpacked his things and set a bottle of The Glenlivet near the weasel, with three silver cups. I added a bottle of Talisker. Sam was no bourbon colonel. He liked pure Highland malt Scotch whisky. Carol measured the weasel. She traced him on paper and fondled his ears. His skull and his skin would go into the university's research collection. She broke a double-edged Gillette blade in half the long way. "Weasels are hard to come by, hard to scent, hard to bait," she said. "We've tried to trap a least weasel. We don't even have one. I hate to catch animals, though. With D.O.R.s, I feel great. We've got the specimen and we're making use of it. The skull is the most important thing. The study skin shows the color pattern."

With a simple slice, she brought out a testicle; she placed it on a sheet of paper and measured it. Three-quarters of an inch. Slicing smoothly through the weasel's fur, she began to remove the pelt. Surely, she worked the skin away from the long neck. The flesh inside the pelt looked like a segment of veal tenderloin. "I lived on squirrel last winter," she said. "Every time you'd come to a turn in the road, there was another squirrel. I stopped buying meat. I haven't bought any meat in a year, except for some tongue. I do love tongue." While she talked, the blade moved in light, definite touches. "Isn't he in perfect shape?" she said. "He was hardly touched. You really lose your orientation when you start skinning an animal that's been run over by a Mack truck." From time to time, she stopped for a taste of The Glenlivet, her hand, brown from sun and flecked with patches of the weasel's blood, reaching for the silver cup. "You've got to be careful where you buy meat anyway. They inject some animals with an enzyme, a meat tenderizer, before they kill them. *That* isn't any good for you." Where the going was difficult, she moistened the skin with water. At last it came away entire, like a rubber glove. She now had the weasel disassembled, laid out on the deck in cleanly dissected parts. "I used to love to take clocks apart," she said. "To see how they were built. This is the same thing. I like plants and animals and their relationship to the land and us. I like the vertebrates especially." The weasel's tailbone was still in the skin. She tugged at it with her teeth. Pausing for a sip, she said that sometimes you just had to use your mouth in her line of work, as once when she was catching cricket frogs. She had a frog in each hand and saw another frog, so she put one frog into her mouth while she caught the third. Gradually, the weasel's tailbone came free. She held it in her hand and admired it. "Some bones are real neat," she said. "In the heart of a deer, there's a bone. And not between the ventricles, where you'd expect it. Some animals have bones in their penises—raccoons, for example, and weasels." She removed the bone from the weasel's penis. It was long, proportionately speaking, with a hook at the penetrating end. It was called a baculum, she said, which meant "rod" in Latin. She would save it. Its dimensions were one way to tell the weasel's age. Baculums are also involved in keying differences in species. Sam said he kept a raccoon's baculum in his wallet because it made a great toothpick. He got out his wallet and displayed his great toothpick. Carol turned the pelt inside out and folded the forepaws in an X, standard procedure with a study skin. She covered it with a deep layer of salt and packed it away.

The dusk was deep then. Carol had finished working almost in the dark. The air was cold. It was on its way to thirty. Sam had a fire going, inside, already disintegrating into coals. The smell of burning oak was sweet. We went into the cabin. Carol put the weasel on the tines of a long fork and roasted it over the coals.

"How do you like your weasel?" Sam asked me.

"Extremely well done," I said.

Carol sniffed the aroma of the roast. "It has a wild odor," she said. "You *know* it's not cow. The first time I had bear, people said, 'Cut the fat off. That's where the bad taste is.' I did, and the bear tasted just like cow. The next bear, I left the fat on."

The taste of the weasel was strong and not unpleasant. It lingered in the mouth after dinner. The meat was fibrous and dark. "It just goes to show you how good everything is," said Carol. "People who only eat cows, pigs, sheep, chickens—boy, have those people got blinders on! Is that tunnelization! There's one poisonous mammal in the United States: the short-tailed shrew. And you can even eat that."

Sam built up the fire.

"How can you be sure that something is not too old?" I asked.

"My God, if you can't tell if it's bad, what's the difference?" said Carol.

Sam said, "If it tastes good, don't knock it."

"People don't make sense," Carol said. "They hunt squirrels, but they wouldn't consider eating a squirrel killed on the road. Only once have I ever had competition for a D.O.R. A man wanted a squirrel for his black servant, and we had a set-to in the road."

There were double-deck bunks in the corners of the room. The corners were cold. We pulled three mattresses off the bunks and put them down side by side before the fire. We

unrolled our three sleeping bags. It had been a big day; we
were tired, and slept without stirring. Sam dreamed in the
night that he was eating his own beard.

With a load of honey and cathead biscuits, gifts of Mammy
Young, we went down out of the valley in the morning, mile
after mile on a dirt road that ran beside and frequently
crossed the outlet stream, which was the beginnings of the
Tallulah River. Some twenty miles on down, the river had cut
a gorge, in hard quartzite, six hundred feet deep. Warner
Brothers had chosen the gorge as the site for the filming of a
scene from James Dickey's novel, *Deliverance*. This mountain
land in general was being referred to around the state as
"Deliverance country." The novel seemed to have been the
most elaborate literary event in Georgia since *Gone with the
Wind*. *Deliverance* was so talked about that people had, for
conversational convenience, labelled its every part ("the owl
scene," "the banjo scene"). It was a gothic novel, a metaphysi-
cal terror novel, the structural center of which involved four
men going through the rapids of a mountain river in canoes.
They were attacked. The action climax occurred when one of
the canoemen scaled the wall of a fantastically sheer gorge to
establish an ambush and kill a mountain man. He killed him
with a bow and arrow. Carol and Sam, like half the people in
Atlanta and a couple of dozen in Hollywood, called this "the
climb-out scene," and they took me to see where Warners
would shoot. The six-hundred-foot gorge was a wonder indeed, clefting narrowly and giddily down through the quartzite to the bed of the river that had done the cutting.
Remarkably, though, no river was there. A few still pools. A
trickle of water. Graffiti adorned the rock walls beside the
pools. There was a dam nearby, and, in 1913, the river had
been detoured through a hydropower tunnel. Steel towers
stood on opposite lips of the chasm, supported by guy wires. A

cable connected the towers. They had been built for perform-
ances of wire walkers, the Flying Wallendas. Nearby was
the Cliffhanger Café. A sign said, "Enjoy Coca-Cola. See it
here, free. Tallulah Gorge. 1200 feet deep." The Georgia
Natural Areas Council looked on. Too late to register that one.
The eye of the Warner Brothers camera would, however,
register just what it wanted to select and see, and it would
move up that wall in an unfailing evocation of wilderness. I
was awed by the power of Dickey. In writing his novel, he had
assembled "*Deliverance* country" from such fragments, restored
and heightened in the chambers of his imagination. The
canoes in his novel dived at steep angles down breathtaking
cataracts and shot like javelins through white torrents among
blockading monoliths. If a canoe were ten inches long and had
men in it three inches high, they might find such conditions in
a trout stream, steeply inclined, with cataracts and plunge
pools and rushing bright water falling over ledges and splay-
ing through gardens of rock. Dickey must have imagined
something like that and then enlarged the picture until the
trout stream became a gothic nightmare for men in full-size
canoes. A geologically maturer, less V-shaped stream would
not have served. No actual river anywhere could have served
his artistic purpose—not the Snake, not the Upper Hudson,
not even the Colorado—and least of all a river in Georgia,
whose wild Chattooga, best of the state's white-water rivers,
has comparatively modest rapids. The people of the *Deliverance* mountains were malevolent, opaque, and sinister. Arthur
and Mammy Young.

There were records of the presence of isolated cottonmouths
on Dry Fork Creek, in wild, forested piedmont country east of
Athens. Dry Fork Creek, a tributary of a tributary of the
Savannah River, was about halfway between Vesta and Rayle,
the beginning and the end of nowhere. We searched the
woods along the creek. It would not have been at all unusual

had we found the highland moccasin (the copperhead) there, for this was his terrain—*Agkistrodon contortrix contortrix*. What we were looking for, though, was the water moccasin (the cottonmouth), inexplicably out of his range. Cottonmouths belong in the coastal plain, in the rice fields, in the slow-moving rivers—*Agkistrodon piscivorus piscivorus*. Seeing a cottonmouth in a place like this would be a rare experience, and Carol fairly leaped into the woods. For my part, I regretted that I lacked aluminum boots. Carol was wearing green tennis shoes. Sam's feet were covered with moccasins. Carol rolled every log. She lifted anything that could have sheltered a newt, let alone a snake. By the stream, she ran her eye over every flat rock and projecting branch. Always disappointed, she quickly moved on. Sam sauntered beside her. The flood plain was beautiful under big sycamores, water oaks, maples: light filtering down in motes, wet leaves on the ground, cold water moving quietly in the stream. But the variety of tracks she found was disturbingly incomplete. "There, on that sandbar—those are possum tracks. Possums and coons go together, but that's just possum right there, no way about it. And that is not right. There shouldn't be a bar like that with no coon tracks on it, even if the water goes up and down every night. Possums can live anywhere. Coons can't. Coon tracks signify a healthy place. I don't much like this place. It's been cut over. There are no big dead trees." One big dead tree with a cottonmouth under it would have changed that, would have glorified Dry Fork Creek for Carol, coons or no coons—*piscivorus piscivorus* caught poaching, out of his territory, off the edge of his map, beyond his range. I felt her disappointment and was sorry the snakes were not there. "Don't be disappointed," she said. "When we go down the Cemocheckobee, cottonmouths will show us the way."

Buffalo disappeared from Georgia in early Colonial time. William Bartram noted this when he visited the colony and wrote *Travels in Georgia and Florida, 1773–74.* Bartram, from Philadelphia, was the first naturalist to describe in detail the American subtropics. After his book reached London, sedentary English poets cribbed from his descriptions (Wordsworth, for example, and Coleridge). Ten miles south of Dry Fork Creek, Sam, Carol, and I crossed Bartram's path. In Bartram's words, "We came into an open Forest of Pines, Scrub white Oaks, Black Jacks, Plumb, Hicory, Grapes Vines, Rising a sort of Ridge, come to a flat levill Plain, and at the upper side of this, levell at the foot of the hills of the great Ridge, is the great Buffiloe Lick, which are vast Pits, licked in the Clay, formerly by the Buffiloes, and now kept smoothe and open by Cattle, deer, and horses, that resort here constantly to lick the clay, which is a greesey Marle of various colours, Red, Yellow & white, & has a sweetish taste, but nothing saltish that I could perceive." Bartram was describing what is now Philomath, Georgia 30659—a one-street town consisting of thirty houses and a buffalo lick. Philomath was established, early in the nineteenth century, as a seat of learning—hence the name. The town was the address of an academy whose students, in time, vanished like the buffalo. Now it was a place of preeminent silence under big oaks, and as we glided into town we were the only thing that moved. Ninety blacks, fifty whites lived there, but no one was out in the midday shade. The almost idling engine was the only sound. In an L-shaped elegant clapboard house, built in 1795, lived Dorothy Daniel Wright. Sam and Carol, having read Bartram's description and having determined that the buffalo lick was still intact, wanted to see it and, they hoped, to register it as a Georgia Natural Area. Miss Wright was the person to see. It was her lick. She was in her upper sixties. Her hair was white and swept upward, and crowned with a braided gold bun. Her welcome was warm. She showed us the lick. Cattle and deer had licked it slick all through her girlhood, she said. Now it was covered

with grass, some hawthorn and sumac, and dominated by an
immense, outreaching laurel oak. Carol squatted flat-footed,
knees high, and dug with her hands for various colors of clay.
She ate some blue clay, and handed pieces to me and Sam. It
was sweet, bland, alkaline, slightly chewy. "My first thought
was 'soapy,'" she said. "I expected it to get stronger, but it
didn't. The final thought was 'sweetness.'" She put a bit more
in her mouth and ate it contemplatively. There was, apparently, no sodium chloride in this ground. Phosphate, sodium,
and calcium are what the buffalo licked. Where did they get
their salt? "Twelve miles away there was salt," Miss Wright
said. "Twelve miles is nothin' to a buffalo roamin' around.
Between the two licks, they got all the minerals they needed
for their bovine metabolism." Miss Wright had taught biology
and chemistry in various high schools for forty-three years. She
was eager to register the Great Buffalo Lick Natural Area,
which had once been a boundary-line landmark separating the
Georgia colony from the territory of the Creeks and Cherokees. She took us home to a lunch of salad and saltines. Into
the salad went mushrooms, violets, and trout lilies that Carol
had gathered in the mountains the day before.

Leaving Philomath, heading south, Sam commented how
easy and pleasant that experience had been and how tense
such encounters could sometimes be. He talked about a redneck peanut farmer in south Georgia, owner of a potential
Natural Area. This redneck had taken one look at Sam's beard
and had seemed ready to kill him then and there.

"What is a redneck, Sam?"

"You know what a redneck is, you little Yankee bastard."

"I want to hear your definition."

"A redneck is a fat slob in a pickup truck with a rifle across
the back. He hates 'niggers.' He would rather have his kids
ignorant than go to school with colored. I guess I don't like
rednecks. I guess I've known some."

"Some of my best friends are rednecks," Carol said.

D.O.R. blacksnake, five miles south of Irwinton—old and bloated. "I'll just get it off the road, so its body won't be further humiliated," Carol said. Across a fence, a big sow was grunting. Carol carried the snake to the fence. She said, "Here, piggy-poo, look what I've got for you." She tossed the snake across the fence. The sow bit off the snake's head and ate it like an apple.

"Interesting," Carol said, "that we can feed a rotten snake to something we in turn will eat."

I said I would rather eat the buffalo lick.

Carol said, "I'll tell you the truth, I've had better clay."

We were out of the piedmont and down on the coastal plain, into the north of south Georgia. The roadside ads were riddled with bullet holes. "PREPARE TO MEET JESUS CHRIST THE LORD." "WE WANT TO WIPE OUT CANCER IN YOUR LIFETIME." "WE CANNOT ACCEPT TIRES THAT HAVE BEEN CAPPED AS TRADE-INS."

Johnny Cash was back. Indians were now his theme. He was singing about a dam that was going to flood Seneca land, although the Senecas had been promised title to their land "as long as the moon shall rise." Cash's voice was deeper than ever. He sounded as if he were smoking a peace pipe through an oboe. Carol hugged herself. "As long . . . as the moon . . . shall rise . . . As long . . . as the rivers . . . flow."

"DON'T LOSE YOUR SOUL BY THE MARK OF THE BEAST."

We ate muskrat that night in a campsite on flat ground beside Big Sandy Creek, in Wilkinson County, innermost Georgia—muskrat with beans, chili powder, onions, tomatoes, and kelp. "I have one terrible handicap," Carol said. "I cannot follow a recipe." The muskrat, though, was very good. Carol had parboiled it for twenty minutes and then put it through a meat grinder, medium grind. Firewood was scarce, because the area was much used by fishermen who were prone to build fires and fish all night. Carol went up a tall spruce pine, and when she was forty feet or so above the ground she began to break off dead limbs and throw them down. She had to throw them like spears to clear the living branches of the tree. Pine burns oily, but that would not matter tonight. The muskrat was in a pot. Sam and I built up the fire. He pitched a tent.

To pass time before dinner, I put the canoe into the river and paddled slowly downstream. Carol called to me from the tree, "Watch for snakes. They'll be overhead, in the limbs of trees." She was not warning me; she was trying to raise the pleasure of the ride. "If you don't see the snake, you can tell by the splash," she went on. "A frog splash is a concentrated splash. A snake splash is a long splat." Gliding, watching, I went a quarter of a mile without a splash or a splat. It was dusk. The water was growing dark. I heard the hoot of a barred owl. Going back against the current, I worked up an appetite for muskrat.

After dinner, in moonlight, Sam and Carol and I got into the canoe and went up the river. A bend to the left, a bend to the right, and we penetrated the intense darkness of a river swamp that seemed to reach out unendingly. We could only guess at its dimensions. Upland swamps occur in areas between streams. River swamps are in the flood plains of rivers, and nearly all the streams in the Georgia coastal plain have them. They can be as much as six miles wide, and when the swamps of two or more big rivers connect, the result can be a vast and separate world. The darkness in there was so rich it felt warm. It was not total, for bars and slats of moonlight occasionally came through, touched a root or a patch of water. Essentially, however, everything was black: black water, black vegetation—water-standing maples, cypress—black on black. Columnar trunks were all around us, and we knew the channel only by the feel of the current, which sometimes seemed to be coming through from more than one direction. Here the black water sucked and bubbled, roiled by, splashed through the

roots of the trees. Farther on, it was silent again. Silent ourselves, we pushed on into the black. Carol moved a flashlight
beam among the roots of trees. She held the flashlight to her
nose, because the eye can see much more if the line of sight is
closely parallel to the beam. She inspected minutely the
knobby waterlines of the trees. Something like a sonic boom
cracked in our ears. "Jesus, what was that?"

"Beaver."

The next two slaps were even louder than the first. Carol
ignored the beaver, and continued to move the light. It
stopped. Out there in the obsidian was a single blue eye.

"A blue single eye is a spider," she said. "Two eyes is a frog.
Two eyes almost touching is a snake. An alligator's eyes are
blood red."

Two tiny coins now came up in her light. "Move in there,"
she said. "I want that one."

With a throw of her hand, she snatched up a frog. It was a
leopard frog, and she let him go. He was much within his
range. Carol was looking for river frogs, pig frogs, carpenter
frogs, whose range peripheries we were stalking. She saw
another pair of eyes. The canoe moved in. Her hand swept out
unseen and made a perfect tackle, thighs to knees. This was a
bronze frog, home on the range. Another pair of eyes, another
catch, another disappointment—a bullfrog. Now another shat-
tering slap on the water. Another. The beaver slapped only
when the canoe was moving upstream. The frog chorus, filling
the background, varied in pitch and intensity, rose and fell.
Repeatedly came the hoot of the barred owl.

Sam dipped a cup and had a drink. "I feel better about
drinking water out of swamps than out of most rivers," he
said. "It's filtered. No one ever says a good word for a swamp.
The whole feeling up to now has been 'Fill it in—it's too wet
to plow, too dry to fish.' Most people stay out of swamps. I
love them. I like the water, the reptiles, the amphibians. There

is so much life in a swamp. The sounds are so different. Frogs, owls, birds, beavers. Birds sound different in swamps."

"You see a coon in here and you realize it's his whole world," Carol said.

"It's a beautiful home with thousands of creatures," Sam said.

With all this ecological intoxication, I thought they were going to fall out of the canoe.

"Life came out of the swamps," Sam said. "And now swamps are among the last truly wild places left."

We went back downstream. Tobacco smoke was in the air over the river. Occasionally, on the bank, we saw an orange-red glow, momentarily illuminating a black face. Fishing lines, slanting into the stream, were visible against the light of small fires. The canoe moved soundlessly by, and on into the darkness. "The groids sure love to fish," Sam murmured. The moon was low. It was midnight.

Now, at noon, a hundred miles or so to the southeast and by another stream, we were sitting on the big felled oak, pouring out the last of the wine, with Chap Causey moving toward us a foot at a time in his American dragline crane. He swung a pair of mats around behind him and backed up a bit more, and as he went on gutting the streambed the oak began to tremble. It must have weighed two or three tons, but it was trembling and felt like an earthquake—time to move. Carol picked up a piece of dry otter scat. She bounced it in the palm of her hand and looked upcurrent at the unaltered stream and downcurrent into the new ditch. She said, "You can talk about coons' being able to go off into the woods and eat nuts and berries, because they're omnivores. But not this otter. He's finished." She broke open the scat. Inside it were fishbones and hair—hair of a mouse or hair of a young rabbit. There were fish otoliths as well, two of them, like small stones. She flung it all into the stream. "He's done for," she said, and waved goodbye to Chap Causey.

On down the dirt road from the stream-channelization project, we saw ahead a D.O.R.

"Looks like a bad one," Carol said.

Sam stopped. "Yes, it's a bad one," he said. "Canebrake. Do you want to eat him?"

Carol leaned over and looked. "He's too old. Throw him out of the road, the poor darlin'. What gets me is that some bastard is proud of having run over him. When I die, I don't want to be humiliated like that."

Sam threw the rattlesnake out of the road. Then we headed southwest through underdeveloped country, almost innocent of towns—Alma, Douglas, Adel, Moultrie, a hundred miles from Alma to Moultrie.

D.O.R. king snake, blue jay, sparrow hawk, wood thrush, raccoon, catbird, cotton rat. The poor darlin's. Threw them out of the road.

A.O.R. hobo—man with a dog. "Oh, there's a good guy," Carol said as we passed him. "He has a dog and a bedroll. What else do you need?"

D.O.R. opossum. Cook County. Three miles east of Adel. Carol spoke admiringly of the creature flexibility of the opossum. Among the oldest of mammals, the possum goes all the way back to Cretaceous time, she said, and, like people, it has never specialized, in a biological sense. "You can specialize yourself out of existence. Drain the home of the otter. The otter dies. The opossum, though, can walk away from an ecological disaster. So much for that. Try something else. He eats anything. He lives almost anywhere. That's why the possum is not extinct. That's why the possum has been so successful." One place this particular possum was never going to walk away from was Georgia Highway 76. Technology, for him the ultimate ecological disaster, had clouted him at seventy miles an hour.

Between Moultrie and Doerun, in the watershed of the Ochlockonee, was a lake in a pine grove surrounded by fifty acres of pitcher plants. They belonged to a couple named Barber, from Moultrie, who had read about the Natural Areas Council and had offered their pitcher plants to posterity. Sam and Carol, posterity, would accept. This was the largest colony of pitcher plants any of us was ever likely to see. Bright-green leaves, ruddy blooms, they glistened in the sun and nodded in the breeze and reached out from the lakeshore like tulips from a Dutch canal. Barber cut one off at the base and held up a leaf—folded upon itself like a narrow goblet, half full of water. The interior was lined with bristles, pointing downward. In the water were dozens of winged creatures, some still moving, most not. Barber had interrupted a handsome meal. His pitcher plants, in aggregate, could probably eat a ton of bugs a day. Sam said he sure was pleased to be able to make the pitcher plants a Georgia Natural Area. Carol saw a tiny water snake. She picked it up. It coiled in her hand and snapped at her. She talked gently to it until it settled down. "Are you going to be good now?" she said. She opened her hand, and the snake sat there, placidly, on her palm. The Barbers did not seem charmed. They said nothing and did not move. Carol set down the snake. It departed, and so did the Barbers. They went back to Moultrie in their air-conditioned car, leaving us their lake, their pines, their pitcher plants.

We jumped into the lake with a bar of soap and scrubbed ourselves up for dinner. In places, the lake was warm from the sun and in places cold from springs. We set up the tent and built a fire. The breeze was cool in the evening in the pines. Carol's stomach growled like a mastiff. She said that when she was hungry she could make her stomach growl on cue. It growled again. She had a tape recorder in the car. Sam got it and recorded the growls, which seemed marketable. He said they could scare away burglars. We fried beefsteaks and turtle steaks under a gibbous moon. We buried the fossils of pleasure: three cow bones and a bottle that had held The Glenlivet. Frogs were hooting. There were no owls. We slept like bears.

At six in the morning, we got into the canoe and moved slowly around the lake. Sam cast for bass. He could flick his lure seventy feet and drop it on a pine needle. He could lay it under stumps with the delicacy of an eyedropper, or drive it, if he wanted to, halfway down the lake. He caught two bass. One wrapped itself hopelessly into a big waterlogged multiple branch. We pulled the branch up out of the water. The bass had himself woven into it like a bird in a cage. Under the blue sky and star-burst clusters of longleaf pine—pitcher plants far as you could see, the lake blue and cool—we cooked the bass in butter and ate it with fried turtle eggs. Then we fried salt-risen bread in the bass butter with more turtle eggs and poured Tate City honey over the bread. Chicory coffee with milk and honey. Fish-crackling off the bottom of the pan.

The yolk of a turtle egg cooks readily to a soft, mushy yellow. The albumen, though, pops and bubbles and jumps around the pan, and will not congeal. No matter how blazing the heat beneath it may be, the white of the egg of the snapping turtle will not turn milky and set. It will jump like a frog and bounce and dance and skitter all over the pan until your patience snaps or the fire dies. So you give up trying to cook it. You swallow it hot and raw.

D.O.R. cat. D.O.R. dog. Near the Mitchell County line. Carol sighed, but no move was made to stop. We were heading west on 37 to check out a river that the Natural Areas Council had been told was like no other in Georgia. Florida was only forty miles away. The terrain was flat and serene between the quiet towns—Camilla, Newton, Elmodel. Cattle stood on light-green grassland under groves of dark pecans. Sometimes the road was a corridor walled with pines. Sometimes the margins opened out into farms, then closed down toward small cabins, more palisades of pine.

D.O.R. gray squirrel. "We could eat him," Carol said.

"We've got enough food," said Sam.

More pines, more pecans, more farms, a mild morning under a blue-and-white sky. Out of the sky came country music—the Carter Sisters, Johnny Cash, philosophy falling like hail: "It's not easy to be all alone, but time goes by and life goes on . . . for after night there comes a dawn. Yes, time goes by and life goes on."

D.O.R. fox squirrel. Baker County. He was as warm as in life, and he was in perfect shape. Kneeling in the road, Carol held out his long, feathery silver-gray tail so that it caught the sunlight. "There aren't many things prettier than that," she said. "Makes a human being sort of jealous not to have a pretty tail like that." Gently, she brushed the squirrel and daubed blood from his head. He looked alive in her hands. She put him in a plastic bag. The ice was low. We stopped at the next icehouse and bought twenty-five pounds.

D.O.R. nighthawk, fresh as the squirrel. Carol kept the hawk for a while in her lap, just to look at him. He could have been an Aztec emblem—wings half spread, head in profile, feathers patterned in blacks and browns and patches of white. Around the mouth were stiff bristles, fanned out like a radar screen, adapted for catching insects.

D.O.R. box turtle.

D.O.R. loggerhead shrike.

D.O.R. gas station. It was abandoned, its old pumps rusting; beside the pumps, a twenty-year-old Dodge with four flat tires.

D.O.R. cottonmouth. Three miles east of Bluffton. Clay County. Finding him there was exciting to Carol. We were nearing the Cemocheckobee, the river we had come to see, and the presence of one cottonmouth here on the road implied crowded colonies along the river. There was no traffic, no point in moving him immediately off the road. Carol knelt beside him. "He was getting ready to shed. He would have been a lot prettier when he had," she said. The skin was dull olive. Carol felt along the spine to a point about three-quarters of the way back and squeezed. The dead snake coiled. "That is what really frightens some people," she said. She lifted the head and turned it so that we could see, between the mouth and the nostrils, the deep pits, sensory organs, through which the striking snake had homed on his targets. Slowly, Carol opened the creature's mouth. The manuals of herpetology tell you not to do that, tell you, in fact, not to touch a dead cottonmouth, because through reflex action a dead one can strike and kill a human being. Now a fang was visible—a short brown needle projecting down from the upper jaw. "You have to be very careful not to scratch your finger on one of those," Carol said. She pressed with her fingertips behind the eyes, directly on the poison sacs, and a drop of milky fluid fell onto a stick she held in her other hand. Four more drops followed, forming a dome of venom. "That amount could kill you," she said, and she pressed out another drop. "Did you know that this is where they got the idea for the hypodermic syringe?" Another drop. "It has to get into the bloodstream. You could drink all you want and it wouldn't hurt you." She placed the cottonmouth off the road. Carol once milked honeysuckle until she had about two ounces, which she then drank. The fluid was so concentratedly sweet it almost made her sick.

Carol's purse fell open as we got back into the car, and out of it spilled a .22-calibre revolver in a case that looked much like a compact. Also in the purse was a Big Brother tear-gas gun, flashlight bulbs, chapstick, shampoo, suntan lotion, and several headbands. Once, when she was off in a swamp frogging and salamandering, a state trooper came upon the car and—thinking it might be an abandoned vehicle—rummaged through it. He found the purse and opened it. He discovered the pistol, the chapstick, the shampoo, et cetera, and a pink garter belt and black net stockings. He might have sent out a five-state alert, but Carol just then emerged from the swamp. She was on her way, she told him, to make a call on Kimberly-Clark executives in an attempt to get them to register some forest and riverbank land with the Natural Areas Council, and for that mission the black net stockings would be as useful as the pistol might be in a swamp or the chapstick in a blistering sun. "Yes, Ma'am." The visit to the Kleenex people was successful, as it happened, and the result was the Griffin's Landing Registered Natural Area, fifty acres—a series of fossil beds on the Savannah River containing by the many thousands *Crassostrea gigantissima,* forty-million-year-old oysters, the largest that ever lived.

Down a dirt road, across a railroad track, and on through woods that scraped the car on both sides, Sam worked his way as far as he could toward the river's edge. We took down the canoe, and carried it to the water. The Cemocheckobee was a rejuvenated stream. Widening its valley, long ago, it had formed relaxed meanders, and now, apparently, the land was rising beneath it, and the river had speeded up and was cutting deeply into the meanders. The current was strong—nothing spectacular, nothing white, but forceful and swift. It ran beneath a jungle of overhanging trees. The river was compact and intimate. The distance from bank to bank was only about thirty feet, so there could be no getting away from the trees. "I'd venture to say we'll see our share of snakes today," Carol exulted. "Let's go! This is cottonmouth country!" Carol shoved up the sleeves of her sweatshirt over her elbows. Sam went to the car and got a snakebite kit.

I had thought I might be apprehensive about this part of the journey. I didn't see how I could help but be. Now I realized that I was having difficulty walking toward the river. "Sam," I said, "wouldn't you prefer that I paddle in the stern?" I had put in many more hours than he had in canoes on rivers, so it seemed only correct to me that Sam should sit up in the bow and fend off branches and cottonmouths while I guided the canoe from the commanding position in the rear.

"I'll go in the stern," said Sam. "Carol will go in the middle to collect snakes. You go in the bow." So much for that. It was his canoe. I got in and moved to the bow. They got in, and we shoved off.

The canoe found the current, accelerated, went downstream fifty feet, and smashed into a magnolia branch. I expected cottonmouths to strike me in both shoulders and the groin. But the magnolia proved to be snakeless. We shot on through and downriver. We could not avoid the overhanging branches. The current was too fast and there were too many of them. Once or twice a minute, we punched through the leafy twigs reaching down from a horizontal limb. But I began to settle down. There weren't any snakes, after all—not in the first mile, anyway. And things Carol was saying made a difference. She said, for example, that snakes plop off branches long before the canoe gets to them. She also said that cottonmouths rarely go out onto branches. They stay back at the river's edge and in the swamps. Snakes on branches are, in the main, as harmless as licorice. Bands of tension loosened and began to drop away. I looked ahead. At the next bend, the river was veiled in a curtain of water oak. I was actually hoping to see a snake hit the surface, but none did. We slipped through and into the clear.

This was heavy current for a river with no white water, and when we rested the river gave us a fast drift. Scenes quickly changed, within the steep banks, the incised meanders, against backgrounds of beech and laurel, white oak, spruce pine, Venus maidenhair, and resurrection fern. We came upon a young coon at the foot of a tree. He looked at us with no apparent fear. We pulled in to the bank. "Hey, there, you high-stepper, you," Carol said. "Get up that tree!" The coon put a paw on the tree and went up a foot or two and looked around. "Why aren't you afraid?" Carol went on. "Are you O.K., cooner?" The raccoon's trouble—probably—was that he had never seen a human. He was insufficiently afraid, and Carol began to worry about him. So she got out of the canoe and went after him. The coon moved up the tree fifteen feet. The tree was a slender maple. Carol started up it like a rope climber. The coon stayed where he was. Carol said, "I'm not climbing the tree to make him jump out. I'll just go high enough to let him know he ought to be afraid of people." When she got near him, the coon scrambled to the high branches, where he hung on to one and swayed. Carol stopped about twenty feet up. "Hey, coon! We're no good. Don't you know that?" she called to him. Then she slid on down. "Let that be a lesson to you!" she called from the bottom.

We moved on downstream, passing blue-tailed skinks and salamanders, animal tracks on every flat. A pair of beavers dived into the water and went around slapping the surface, firing blanks. Carol saw the mouth of their den, and she got out of the canoe, climbed the bank, and stuck her head inside. She regretted that she had not brought a flashlight with her. We moved on. We passed a banded snake sitting on a limb. He produced mild interest. Fear was gone from me. It had gone off with the flow of the river. There was a light splash to the right—as if from a slide, not a dive. No one saw what made it. "Otter," Carol said. "Pull in to the opposite bank—over there. Quickly!" We stopped the canoe, and held on to bush stems of the riverbank and waited. Nothing happened. The quiet grew. "The otter will come up and look at us," Carol said. We waited. Smooth, the river moved—never the same, always the same. No otter. "He is an extraordinarily intelligent and curious animal," Carol said. "He could go off somewhere, if he wanted to, just to breathe. But he wants to see us. He will not be able to stand it much longer. He will have to come up." Up came a face, chin on the water—dark bright eyes in a dark-brown head, small ears, wide snout: otter. His gaze was direct and unflinching. He looked at us until he had seen his fill; then he went back under. "Wouldn't you like to live in this creek?" Carol said. "You'd never get lonely. Wouldn't you like to play with the otter?"

A waterfall, about twelve feet high, poured into the river from the left. Two hundred yards downstream, another fall dropped into the river from the right. The feeder streams of the Cemocheckobee were not cutting down as fast as the river itself, and these hanging tributaries poured in from above, all the way down. We now moved through stands of royal fern under big sycamores and big beeches, and past another waterfall. "This is otter, beaver, coon heaven," Carol said. Her only disappointment was the unexpected scarcity of snakes. She said she had seen more than her share of "magnolia-leaf snakes" that day. Her imagination, charged with hope and anticipation, could, and frequently did, turn magnolia leaves into snakes, green upon the branches. I found myself feeling disappointed, too. Only one lousy banded snake. The day was incomplete.

Sam said the threat to this river was the lumber industry.

Logging was going on in the forests on both sides, and he would try to persuade the lumbermen to register the river—and its marginal lands—before the day came when it would be too late. While he was speaking, I saw a snake on a log at the water's edge, and pointed to it, interrupting him.

"Is that a banded snake?"

"That is not a banded snake," Carol said.

"Is it a bad one?"

"It's a bad one, friend."

"Well, at last. Where have you been all day?"

He had been right there, of course, in his own shaft of sun, and the sight of a shining aluminum canoe with three figures in it was not going to cause him to move. Moving back was not in his character. He would stay where he was or go toward something that seemed to threaten him. Whatever else he might be, he was not afraid. He was a cottonmouth, a water moccasin. Carol was closer to him than I was, and I felt no fear at all. Sam, in the stern, was closest of all, because we were backing up toward the snake. I remember thinking, as we moved closer, that I preferred that they not bring the thing into the canoe, but that was the sum of my concern; we were ten miles downstream from where we had begun. The moccasin did not move. We were now right next to it. Sam reached toward it with his paddle.

"Rough him up a little to teach him to beware of humans," Carol said. "But don't hurt him."

Under the snake Sam slipped the paddle, and worked it a bit, like a spatula, so that the snake came up onto the blade. Sam lifted the cottonmouth into the air. Sam rocked the paddle. "Come on," he said. "Come on, there. Open your mouth so John can see the cotton."

"Isn't he magnificent?" Carol said. "Set him down, Sam. He isn't going to open his mouth."

Sam returned the moccasin to the log. The canoe moved on into a gorge. The walls of the gorge were a hundred feet high.

The Cemocheckobee was itself a feeder stream, ending in the Chattahoochee, there in southwestern Georgia, at the Alabama line. An appointment elsewhere with the Chattahoochee—a red-letter one for Sam and Carol—drew us back north. The Chattahoochee is Georgia's most prodigious river. Atlanta developed where railheads met the river. The Chattahoochee rises off the slopes of the Brasstown Bald, Georgia's highest mountain, seven miles from North Carolina, and flows to Florida, where its name changes at the frontier. It is thereafter called the Appalachicola. In all its four hundred Georgia miles, what seems most remarkable about this river is that it flows into Atlanta nearly wild. Through a series of rapids between high forested bluffs, it enters the city clear and clean. From parts of the Chattahoochee within the city of Atlanta, no structures are visible—just water, sky, and woodland. The circumstance is nostalgic, archaic, and unimaginable. It is as if an unbefouled Willamette were to flow wild into Portland— Charles into Boston, Missouri into Omaha, Hudson into New York, Delaware into Philadelphia, James into Richmond, Cuyahoga into Cleveland (the Cuyahoga caught fire one day, and fire engines had to come put out the blazing river). Atlanta deserves little credit for the clear Chattahoochee, though, because the Chattahoochee is killed before it leaves the city. It dies between Marietta Boulevard and South Cobb Drive, just below the Atlanta Water Intake, at the point where thirty-five million gallons of partially treated sewage and forty million gallons of raw sewage are poured into the river every day. A short distance below that stand two enormous power plants, whose effluent pipes raise the temperature of the river. A seven-pound brown trout was caught recently not far above the Water Intake. It is difficult to imagine what sort of fin-rotted, five-legged, uranium-gilled, web-mouthed monster could live in the river by Georgia Power. Seen from the air (Sam showed it to me once in his plane), the spoiling of the Chattahoochee is instant, from river-water blue to sewer ochre-brown, as if a pair of colored ribbons had been sewn together there by the city.

Now a sewer line was projected to run upstream beside the river to fresh subdivisions that would bloom beyond the city's perimeter highway. The sewer would not actually be in the water, but, unless it could be tunnelled or not built at all, it would cause the clear-cutting of every tree in a sixty-foot swath many miles long. A segment of the sewer was already under construction. The Georgia Natural Areas Council was among the leadership in an effort to put down this specific project and at the same time to urge a bill through the legislature that would protect permanently the river and its overview. Sam had asked Jimmy Carter to come get into a canoe and shoot the metropolitan rapids and see for himself the value and the vulnerability of the river. Carter was willing. So, in three canoes, six of us put in under the perimeter highway, I-285, and paddled into Atlanta.

Sam had Carter in his bow. Carter might be governor of Georgia but not of Sam's canoe. Carol and I had the second canoe. In the third was a state trooper, who had a pistol on his hip that could have sunk a frigate. In the stern was James Morrison, of the federal government, the Bureau of Outdoor Recreation's man in Atlanta. He wore wet-suit bootees and rubber kneepads and seemed to be ready to go down the Colorado in an acorn.

The current was strong. The canoes moved smartly downstream. Carter was a lithe man, an athletic man in his forties—at home, obviously enough, in boats. He was wearing a tan windbreaker, khaki trousers, and white basketball shoes. He had a shock of wind-tossed sandy hair. In the course of the day, he mentioned that he had grown up in Archery, Georgia, by a swamp of the Kinchafoonee and the Choctawhatchee. He and his friend A. D. Davis, who was black, had built a twelve-foot bateau. "When it rained and we couldn't work in the fields, we went down to the creek and set out set hooks for catfish and eels, and we drifted downstream in the bateau hunting ducks with a shotgun. We fished for bass and red-bellies, and we waded for jack. The bateau weighed eighty pounds. I could pick it up." Archery was three miles west of Plains, a crossroads with a short row of stores and less than a thousand people. Sam, Carol, and I had passed through Plains—in fifteen seconds—on our way north. An enormous red-lettered sign over the stores said, "PLAINS, GEORGIA, HOME OF JIMMY CARTER." Carter had played basketball at Plains High School, had gone on to Annapolis and into nuclear submarines, and had come back to Plains in 1953 to farm peanuts and to market them for himself and others, businesses he continued as he went on into the legislature and upward to become governor. The career of his boyhood friend had been quite different. The last Carter had heard of A. D. Davis, Davis was in jail for manslaughter.

Now, on the Chattahoochee, the Governor said, "We're lucky here in Georgia that the environment thing has risen nationally, because Georgia is less developed than some states and still has much to save." With that, he and Sam went into the largest set of rapids in the city of Atlanta. The rip was about a hundred yards long, full of Vs confusing to the choice, broad ledges, haystacks, eddies, and tumbling water. They were good rapids, noisy and alive, and strong enough to flip a canoe that might hit a rock and swing broadside.

In the shadow of a two-hundred-foot bluff, we pulled out on a small island to survey the scene. Carol said the bluff was a gneiss and was full of garnets. The Governor had binoculars.

With them, he discovered a muskrat far out in the river. The muskrat was gnawing on a branch that had been stopped by a boulder. "He's sniffin' around that little old limb on top of that rock," Carter said. "Maybe he's eating the lichens off it. Look, there's another. Who owns the land here?" "Various people," Morrison said. "Some are speculators. A lot of it is owned by Alfred Kennedy." "Kennedy?" "A director of the First National Bank," Carol said. "Is he a good guy, so far as conservancy goes?" "From what I hear, he's too busy making money." "Sometimes it's better to slip up on people like that," Carter told her. "Rather than make an issue of it right away." He spoke in a low voice, almost shyly. There was a touch of melancholy in his face that disappeared, as it did frequently, when he grinned. A trillium caught his eye. He asked her what it was, and she told him. "And what's that?" he said. "Dog hobble," Carol said. "*Leucothoë*. Look here." She pointed at the ground. "A coon track."

The canoes moved on, and the next stop was a visit with a fisherman who was casting from the bank. He was middle-aged and weathered, a classical, prototype fisherman, many years on the river. He was wreathed in smiles at sight of the Governor. I looked hard at Sam, but nothing in his face indicated that he had planted the man there. The fisherman, Ron Sturdevant, showed the Governor a Kodacolor print of a twenty-three-inch rainbow he had recently caught right here under this bluff. "I guess I'm glad I met you," Sturdevant said. "I'm glad you're taking this trip. I'm worried about the river." "I hope we can keep it this way," Carter said.

We climbed from the river through a deep wood of oaks and big pines to a cave in which families of Cherokees had once lived. It was about a hundred feet up. The view swept the river, no structures visible. "Who owns this place?"

Sam said, "Alfred Kennedy."

"And he hasn't even slept here," said Carol.

"Have you slept here, Carol?" the Governor asked her.

"Many times," she told him. "With a dog named Catfish."

Morrison said, "There's gold here, around the Indian cave. It's never been mined."

"That would be a good way to keep this place undisturbed," Carter said. "To announce that there was gold up here."

Back on the river, he used his binoculars while Sam paddled. He saw four more muskrats and an automobile, upside down in the water, near the far bank. He also saw a turtle.

"What kind is it?" Carol asked him.

"If I knew what kind it was, I could tell you." He handed the binoculars across to her, too late.

"I've been down through here and seen fifteen turtles with bullet holes in their shells," Carol told him.

"What kind?" Carter said.

"Cooters and sliders."

There was a racket of engines. Out of nowhere came two motorcyclists riding *in* the river. A mile or so later, we took out, beside an iron bridge. Carol said she had washed her hair any number of times under that bridge.

The Governor invited us home for lunch. The mansion was new—a million-dollar neo-Palladian Xanadu, formal as a wedding cake, and exquisitely landscaped. Carol and Sam and I were ropy from a thousand miles of mountains, rivers, and swamps. None of us had changed clothes in nearly a week, but we would soon be eating grilled cheese sandwiches at a twenty-foot table under a crystal chandelier. The Governor, for that matter, did not look laundered anymore—mud on his trousers, mud on his basketball shoes. We parked in back of the mansion. A backboard, hoop, and net were mounted there.

A ball sat on the pavement. Before going in, we shot baskets for a while.

"The river is just great," the Governor said, laying one in. "And it ought to be kept the way it is. It's almost heartbreaking to feel that the river is in danger of destruction. I guess I'll write a letter to all the landowners and say, 'If you'll use some self-restraint, it'll decrease the amount of legal restraint put on you in the future.' I don't think people want to incur the permanent wrath of the governor or the legislature."

"I've tried to talk to property owners," Carol said. "To get them to register their land with the Natural Areas Council. But they wouldn't even talk to me."

The Governor said, "To be blunt about it, Carol, why would they?"

The Governor had the ball and was dribbling in place, as if contemplating a property owner in front of him, one-on-one. He went to the basket, shot, and missed. Carol got the rebound and fed the ball to Sam. He shot. He missed, too.

Reading the River

UNTIL RECENTLY, the word "canoe" put an image in my mind of a light water craft with up-turned ends, open as a pod, and pointing symmetrically in two directions. I once knew every part of a canoe—ribs, half ribs, planking, bang plates, open gunwales, center thwart, stern thwart, stern quarter-thwart, and so on, until the whole boat was verbally disassembled and rebuilt. I more or less grew up in canoes—in summers, anyway—and slept under them, and capsized them for pleasure, rolling in still water and breathing the air that is trapped in them when they are upside down. There was an insurance factor in these games. I once turned over in wild water in a gorge on Otter Creek, in Vermont; one of my legs was caught by a thwart, and I survived by pulling my head up into the air space and riding out the rapid. The canoes I knew were E. M. Whites and Old Towns, keeled and keel-less, covered with

canvas, and alive with a timbre of their own. Among them—
hanging from rafters in a place called Keewaydin, and almost
never used, because of its fragility and symbolic value—was a
canoe covered with birch bark. This was the ingenious original
from which the generations of Whites and Old Towns had
come, and, in more recent times, despite hollow reverberations
and general yarelessness, the Grumman aluminums as well. I
had been long out of touch with developments in canoeing,
and, with the exception of a few descents in rented Grum-
mans, had completely lost touch with white water. Meanwhile,
that Indian birch remained for me the template, the standard,
the prototype canoe, with its apparently inevitable design,
conceived in the wilderness who knows how many hundreds
of years ago and valid into the technological present. I thought
of it as a basic shape, like a cone or a cube, immutable, invio-
lable, and I would never have thought to, or tried to, alter it,
not even with written permission from Hiawatha. I go into this
only to suggest the extent to which the rafters of my mind
were shaken, although the birch-bark canoe still hangs there,
when I went in early spring to the mountains of West Virginia
with a friend of mine from the National Park Service to ob-
serve the Potomac Highland and Middle States Wildwater
canoeing championships.

Beginnings of the Potomac come off the slopes of Spruce
Knob, just under five thousand feet high, and then the river
descends northward, eventually flowing almost to the Pennsylvania line before turning south toward Washington, which is
two hundred and eighty-five miles downriver from the source.
Near the headwaters, between Mouth of Seneca and Smoke
Hole Cavern (two West Virginia hamlets), run fourteen miles
of white water of varying degrees of difficulty, and in one
stretch these rapids drop through a narrow cut called Hopeville Canyon, the climactic segment of the racecourse. As we
looked over the river on the day before the races began, small

vessels came shooting out of the lower end of this defile, so snug to the water that the men paddling them appeared to be kneeling in the river, and I asked my friend what they were. "Canoes," he said. "Modern canoes. That's what they look like now."

Canoes? They were small, Fiberglas, modified cigars, streamline rounded at the gunwales and almost completely closed over, the only opening, in the singles category, being a small hole amidships in which the canoeman knelt. They were virtually watertight. A plastic spray skirt—drawn firm with rubber cords to the canoeman's waist and the cockpit combing—enabled the canoe to roll over without taking in water. When a canoeman became overheated from the vigor of the canyon, he would stop, in slow water, and lean over into the river until the entire upper half of his body was submerged and the canoe was all but upside down. Then he would flip upright again, soaking-cool, and move on downstream. When he got out of the river, he picked up his canoe in one hand, put it on his shoulder like a ski, and walked away.

I learned soon enough that these canoemen were pretty sensitive if someone suggested that what they were really paddling were kayaks. Kayaks were something else again, by their standards, and, in fact, there would be a complete and separate range of kayak races among the championship events. As for the antique canoes of my own experience, they would not even be permitted on the river in the major races. The rules required that all canoes be completely decked over.

The new canoes were developed in Europe—principally in Yugoslavia and Czechoslovakia—and only since the middle nineteen-sixties have they been brought to American rivers to replace the canoes the Indians invented here. Organized whitewater racing is fairly new in the world. The first international championships were held in 1950, in Czechoslovakia, and the first American championships came in 1958—in open canoes that were decked over with sheets of plastic. Unencumbered by Indian lore, the Europeans modified the canoe in the direction of the kayak to the point where the differences now are subtle and come in the form of regulated measurements. Canoes are a few inches shorter and a few inches wider, and, however unemphatically, the ends of canoes must be higher than the middles. But the real differences are these: a single-bladed paddle is used with a canoe, double with a kayak; paddlers sit with their legs forward in kayaks, but kneel in canoes. These differences do retain the essence of traditional American canoeing. The basic moves are much the same, but the craft—in both senses—is novel.

I once had a vision of an early canoeman that went with my vision of the archetypal canoe. He was a sinewy man with clear eyes, and he smoked a pipe as he sat in the stern of a twenty-four-foot canoe that was bulging with beaver skins and pemmican in packs under lashed-down canvas. He wore checked wool, and he worked for the Hudson's Bay Company, leaning hard on his long Canadian paddle as he steered his canoe down foaming white rapids where the spray curled up like smoke. Never mind that what he really wanted was a desk job at Company headquarters in Montreal. He was my man, and he was a far, far cry from these canoemen, in their little fourteen-foot tubes, in West Virginia. These little canoes wouldn't hold a beaver's sideburns. The men who paddle them wear plastic crash helmets, like hockey players or motor-cyclists. When they flip over and inconveniently crack their heads on submerged rocks, they come right back up. They are, nonetheless, serious canoemen. They wear wet-suits and go out and break ice on pools at the edge of the river to get into the fast water in winter. They read the journal of the American Whitewater Affiliation. To them, a lake is not a lake but "flat water." They make their own canoes. First they fashion a wooden plug, as they call it, and from this model cast Fiberglas molds—a deck mold and a hull mold. Bolts of Fiberglas—whose manufacturers thought they were making draperies—are then spread into the molds, layer upon layer, with liquid resin painted between. The result, conjoined, is ordinarily a "Czech" or a "Yugo"—referring to the wellspring nationalities of the two basic designs, which differ only slightly and have experienced so much crossbreeding that varieties are micromillimetrically infinite. In much the way that wallet cards can be sealed between layers of plastic, paper or fabric designs are often included between the deck laminations of the canoes, and one that I saw had a deck of beer-can labels, another appeared to be made of bricks, another was a garden of permanent blossoming flowers, and still another had a deck of red-and-yellow Paisley print, so that its owner appeared to be paddling a wet necktie. A man within one of these canoes is so fused with the river—in the compactness of the craft around him—that he almost appears to be standing waist-deep in the water rather than kneeling in a boat. An observer expects the canoeman to come walking out of the river with the canoe around his waist and thus to reveal it for what it really is, an epic codpiece, ventral and dorsal.

As many as five modern canoes will fit on top of a car, even a bug Volkswagen—singles canoes, doubles canoes, slalom canoes. All along a road that winds in and out of sight of the river, canoe- and kayak-covered vehicles clustered. They were so predominant in the traffic in the area that cars without boats on them attracted attention. License plates were from all over the East, South, and Middle West, from Wisconsin and Connecticut to Georgia. One Ford Econoline van had come, with three canoes on it, from California. Rigged up for sleeping and cooking, it was occupied by a nineteen-year-old with clear-rimmed, dark-brown eyeglasses and a full beard in two shades of brown. His name was John Evans. The word was that the C-1 (singles canoe) Middle States Wildwater championship race would be a question of beating John Evans, and that his principal competitor would be a hippily long-haired fellow, aged twenty-six, named Bob Waldrop, who learned his first strokes in Vermont, had been down the Canoe River in British Columbia, and worked in the District of Columbia as a representative of the Sierra Club. The canoemen, for the most part, were lean and not particularly tall, lightness and wiry strength being advantages in the sport. They spread in age from the teens to the forties, and they were not a forceful-looking group, but on the eve of the races they collected in a large schoolroom and watched with obvious pleasure movies of frail craft pounding across standing waves and smacking through walls of water, sometimes plunging into souse holes and cartwheeling end over end.

In a corridor outside the schoolroom, a man who makes and sells white-water canoes and equipment had set up a display of his wares. One of the doubles canoes he had had been built on order for my Park Service friend, John Kauffmann, who had come to West Virginia to pick it up. While Kauffmann was looking over his new boat, or C-2, Waldrop walked up and said to the salesman, "I need a new sixty-four/eight." Waldrop soon had in his hand a paddle in a style I had not seen before that day. Made of latticed and laminated Canadian spruce, it had a T-shaped grip and a blade that was square-tipped, like an oar. Its over-all length was sixty-four inches. The blade was enormous—eight inches wide and some two feet long. There is so much air in white water that a big blade is needed to find sufficient traction. The square tip gets a maximum bite in low water. Waldrop, rangy and loose, his hair flopping, walked away with his new paddle. Kauffmann's new canoe—which bore the trade name Berrigan—was not strictly a racer, having been designed to combine the streamlined advantages of the modern wild-water canoe with some storage space for tripping duffel, but Kauffmann had noticed that something called the Potomac Highland Wildwater C-2 championship race was in a non-expert category, open to all, so we had figured what the hell, and decided to enter. Trying to look rangy and loose, I asked the salesman if he happened to have a sixty/eight. "Fourteen dollars and twenty cents," he said, and I walked away with my first white-water paddle.

The canoemen sleep in motels, private houses, tents, their own cars, and, in some cases, in cabins and farmhouses they rent by the year so they can spend weekends and vacations on the river. (Incidentally, they refer to themselves as canoeists, but I may be unreformable on that one. From the age of eight, I was told that a canoeman was someone who knew how to handle a canoe anywhere, while a canoeist, typically, was someone flopping around ineptly in a sponson canoe on a lake in Central Park.) The canoemen, in their rooms and tents and farmhouses, after the movies, talked about the places they go to, their white-water circuit: Esopus Creek, at Phoenicia, New York; the Youghiogheny (*yok-a-gainy*) River at Ohiopyle, Pennsylvania; the Loyalsock, also in Pennsylvania ("If you flip, you might have to wash down a long way"); the Shenandoah Staircase, at Harper's Ferry (five miles of ledges); and, nearby in the West Virginia mountains, the Dry Fork of the Cheat ("When it's up, it just goes lickety-split. It was named that because men drowned and were cheated out of their lives running logs down the river").

Kauffmann and I stayed in a farmhouse owned by a man named Eston Yokum and accessible only by a cable-suspension footbridge that swayed and humped as you walked over the river. We were the guests of four canoemen, Yokum's tenants. From them I learned that white water is now classified in six categories on an International Scale, based on drop, water velocity, characteristics of the stream. Class I and Class II water are easily negotiable. Classes III ("small falls, numerous rapids," in the language of the International Scale) and IV

("high irregular waves with boulders directly in current, difficult broken water, eddies, and abrupt bends") call for experience and high skill. Class V has "long rocky rapids with
difficult and completely irregular broken water which must be
run head on"; and Class VI has "all previously mentioned
difficulties increased to the limit, cannot be attempted without
risk of life." The upper Hudson, not long after it pours out of
Lake Tear of the Clouds, is in places a Class VI river, and
segments of the Colorado are off the scale. The Potomac
between Mouth of Seneca and Smoke Hole Cavern is a Class
III and Class IV river, just right for general competition, being
tough but not too tough. The West River in Vermont, where
the national championships have often been held, was described as having less dramatic surroundings than the upper
Potomac—going through farmland instead of through West
Virginia's high sedimentary mountains—but having, as its
most attractive feature, an absolute reliability of water level.
Three miles up the West River from the canoe course is Bald
Mountain Dam. In close communication with the Army engineers at the dam, canoemen have the river turned up just so,
until it is flowing at a steady Class IV. While slalom gates are
being set, the river is turned off.

That is as nothing to the story of the Nantahala, a river in
North Carolina, where canoemen gather and stare fondly from
its banks at its homicidal gradient. One inconvenience is that
there is normally no water whatsoever in the riverbed. Upstream is a mammoth aluminum plant that impounds the
water in a reservoir and lets it out once a day. The canoemen
wait for that moment. They know it is coming because the
water is cold from the depths of the reservoir, and in the warm
North Carolina air it creates a cloud that hurtles and roils
along with it and can be seen long before the sound is heard of
the roar of the white water. Into the instant river the canoemen fly. They say that it is like going down the New Jersey

Turnpike in a fog. Shooting downriver and around bends, they desperately call out one another's names, trying to keep contact in the mists.

The man who told us about the Nantahala was Robert Harrigan, from Bethesda, Maryland, who, with a friend named John Berry, designed and first built the Berrigan canoe. Harrigan—tall and impressive, with gray edges on a shock of brown hair—also told about the time he took Secretary Udall down the upper Hudson. He implied that he was scared out of his mind by the rampaging, irregular broken water, while Udall sat upright in the bow like a taxidermal hawk, looking left and right, and saying, "Beautiful river, Bob. Beautiful river." Harrigan, in the stern, was desperately heaving himself flat out over the water in various directions against the conflicting currents, but Udall appeared not to notice and to be absolutely serene in the confidence that no canoe carrying the Secretary of the Interior was likely to flip.

When modern canoemen go down a river in a wild-water race, covering distance against a clock, the amplitude of what they can do is not so immediately apparent as it is when, at a time of leisure, they stop to enjoy a rapid. They can, for example, go zipping down a braided white torrent and suddenly stop dead in the middle of it, turn around, and hover, like trout in a stream. Facing the current, they will nose down behind a ledge and let the full force of the river pour upon their bows while they sit there contemplating. They will come schussing through a rip, crash through an eddy wall, rest a moment, poised and quiet, then peel off through the far line of the eddy and drop so fast that soon only their heads are visible from the place where they paused to rest. Darting into an eddy on one side of the river, they will sit steady, facing in the direction from which they came, then slice the canoe decisively into the main current, paddling hard upstream. The result of this maneuver, called a ferry, is that they go skidding sidewise directly across the river, despite its velocity, without moving six inches downstream. To them, the white water is not a chaos of flow and spray but a legible language, and they know how to read it. Its currents don't all flow in the same direction. Some tumble like barrels. Others, in eddies, flow gently upstream. Look for the tongue of water. Pick it. You pick the river. Lean away from the current. The fastest and deepest water is on the outside of a curve. Sometimes it's too vicious there; hug the inside. Don't go for quiet spots in the middle of turbulence—satin-water pillows are stuffed with rock. Watch yourself. Don't eddy out if you don't want to. Standing waves—haystacks—mark deep water. The man from the Hudson's Bay Company steered to the side of standing waves, but these men go right through them. His entire goal, like mine as a boy, was to get safely to the bottom of the rapid. These modern canoemen want to stop and play. They roll like Eskimos. Their slalom courses loop. Some gates are actually upriver from previous ones. I was taught the J stroke as the absolute denominator of canoemanship, but they almost never use it. It's inefficient. I was taught never to pry the bow of a moving canoe. They pry, and jump, like skiers, laterally, keeping parallel with the current. They may call themselves canoeists, but they are really fabulous.

John Evans, short, strong, and soft-spoken, had come from Los Angeles and was the son of a Hollywood assistant director. He learned and developed many of his techniques in swimming pools, and practiced morning after morning in Ballona Creek—the outer reaches of the Los Angeles storm sewers—which has high concrete banks, and saline water where it approaches the sea. For white water, he had to make long trips to the Sierra, where he was sometimes discouraged because he was always dumping over, cutting his hands, and fighting shy of standing waves. After his graduation from high school, in 1968, he became a full-time canoeman. He made his own canoes, as nearly everyone does, and he worked for a while in a Fiberglas factory. Like Waldrop, he built a C-1 in something of a delta shape, but his delta was far more pronounced, and the canoe could have been a wind-tunnel model for a supersonic airplane. An advantage in this, Evans felt, is that he minimized width around the cockpit and could put the paddle straight down into the water. The delta, as it widened out behind him, gave stability and also conformed to the regulations on minimal width (thirty-one and a half inches). Evans had beaten the man who was acknowledged to be the best wild-water boater in southern California, and, encouraged by that, he had come East to win all he could.

Crowds formed by all the important rapids in Hopeville Canyon—the Tree Rapid, the Cave Rapid, Table Rock Rapid —to see the C-1s go down the river. Starts were at one-minute intervals. Evans, in a field of twenty, was the seventh to begin, and Waldrop was the last. Using a fast, European, staccato stroke, between fifty and sixty per minute, Evans danced down through the rock gardens of the low river with a light and absolute touch, barely skirting eddy walls, finding the fast water, reading and absorbing the river. One after another, he caught and passed his predecessors—a Pittsburgh canoeman, one from Mifflin County, Pennsylvania, one from Morgantown, West Virginia—and when he crossed the finish line he had covered five miles in just under forty-nine minutes. Waldrop took second place, as expected. What was remarkable, though, was that Evans had beaten him by almost four minutes.

During the White Water Weekend, as the events agglomerately were called, Kauffmann and I had the luck to take a run with Bob Harrigan, who taught us all he could, except how to get out of the trough we capsized in, a humiliating development that gave us an ice-cold soaking. However, in the wild-water race for eager hacks, we found that the new

Berrigan seemed to know the river almost as well as its designer and to feel vertebrate beneath us and our paddles. We went the distance, nine miles, in an hour and thirty-one minutes. Forever after that trip, I'm here to tell you, an open, conventional canoe—aluminum, canvas, or birch-bark—will feel to me about as riverworthy as a rickshaw. We placed third, and were given engraved and ribboned medals. I couldn't care less whether Hiawatha would sanction all this. I, for one, will.

The Search for
Marvin Gardens

GO. I ROLL THE DICE—A SIX AND A TWO. Through the air I move my token, the flatiron, to Vermont Avenue, where dog packs range.

•

The dogs are moving (some are limping) through ruins, rubble, fire damage, open garbage. Doorways are gone. Lath is visible in the crumbling walls of the buildings. The street sparkles with shattered glass. I have never seen, anywhere, so many broken windows. A sign—"Slow, Children at Play"—has been bent backward by an automobile. At the lighthouse, the dogs turn up Pacific and disappear. George Meade, Army engineer, built the lighthouse—brick upon brick, six hundred thousand bricks, to reach up high enough to throw a beam twenty miles over the sea. Meade, seven years later, saved the Union at Gettysburg.

•

I buy Vermont Avenue for $100. My opponent is a tall, shadowy figure, across from me, but I know him well, and I know his game like a favorite tune. If he can, he will always go for the quick kill. And when it is foolish to go for the quick kill he will be foolish. On the whole, though, he is a master assessor of percentages. It is a mistake to underestimate him. His eleven carries his top hat to St. Charles Place, which he buys for $140.

•

The sidewalks of St. Charles Place have been cracked to shards by through-growing weeds. There are no buildings. Mansions, hotels once stood here. A few street lamps now drop cones of light on broken glass and vacant space behind a chain-link fence that some great machine has in places bent to the ground. Five plane trees—in full summer leaf, flecking the light—are all that live on St. Charles Place.

•

Block upon block, gradually, we are cancelling each other out—in the blues, the lavenders, the oranges, the greens. My opponent follows a plan of his own devising. I use the Hornblower & Weeks opening and the Zuricher defense. The first game draws tight, will soon finish. In 1971, a group of people in Racine, Wisconsin, played for seven hundred and sixty-eight hours. A game begun a month later in Danville, California, lasted eight hundred and twenty hours. These are official records, and they stun us. We have been playing for eight minutes. It amazes us that Monopoly is thought of as a long game. It is possible to play to a complete, absolute, and final conclusion in less than fifteen minutes, all within the rules as written. My opponent and I have done so thousands of times. No wonder we are sitting across from each other now in this best-of-seven series for the international singles championship of the world.

•

On Illinois Avenue, three men lean out from second-story windows. A girl is coming down the street. She wears dungarees and a bright-red shirt, has ample breasts and a Hadendoan Afro, a black halo, two feet in diameter. Ice rattles in the glasses in the hands of the men.

"Hey, sister!"

"Come on up!"

She looks up, looks from one to another to the other, looks them flat in the eye.

"What for?" she says, and she walks on.

•

I buy Illinois for $240. It solidifies my chances, for I already own Kentucky and Indiana. My opponent pales. If he had landed first on Illinois, the game would have been over then and there, for he has houses built on Boardwalk and Park Place, we share the railroads equally, and we have cancelled each other everywhere else. We never trade.

•

In 1852, R. B. Osborne, an immigrant Englishman, civil engineer, surveyed the route of a railroad line that would run from Camden to Absecon Island, in New Jersey, traversing the state from the Delaware River to the barrier beaches of the sea. He then sketched in the plan of a "bathing village" that would surround the eastern terminus of the line. His pen flew glibly, framing and naming spacious avenues parallel to the shore—Mediterranean, Baltic, Oriental, Ventnor—and narrower transsecting avenues: North Carolina, Pennsylvania, Vermont, Connecticut, States, Virginia, Tennessee, New York, Kentucky, Indiana, Illinois. The place as a whole had no name, so when he had completed the plan Osborne wrote in large letters over the ocean, "Atlantic City." No one ever challenged the name, or the names of Osborne's streets. Monopoly was invented in the early nineteen-thirties by Charles B. Darrow, but Darrow was only transliterating what Osborne had created. The railroads, crucial to any player, were the making of Atlantic City. After the rails were down, houses and hotels burgeoned from Mediterranean and Baltic to New York and Kentucky. Properties—building lots—sold for as little as six dollars apiece and as much as a thousand dollars. The original investors in the railroads and the real estate called themselves the Camden & Atlantic Land Company. Reverently, I repeat their names: Dwight Bell, William Coffin, John DaCosta, Daniel Deal, William Fleming, Andrew Hay, Joseph Porter, Jonathan Pitney, Samuel Richards—founders, fathers, forerunners, archetypical masters of the quick kill.

•

My opponent and I are now in a deep situation of classical Monopoly. The torsion is almost perfect—Boardwalk and Park Place versus the brilliant reds. His cash position is weak, though, and if I escape him now he may fade. I land on Luxury Tax, contiguous to but in sanctuary from his power. I have four houses on Indiana. He lands there. He concedes.

•

Indiana Avenue was the address of the Brighton Hotel, gone now. The Brighton was exclusive—a word that no longer has retail value in the city. If you arrived by automobile and tried to register at the Brighton, you were sent away. Brighton-class people came in private railroad cars. Brighton-class people had other private railroad cars for their horses—dawn rides on the firm sand at water's edge, skirts flying. Colonel Anthony J. Drexel Biddle—the sort of name that would constrict throats in Philadelphia—lived, much of the year, in the Brighton.

•

Colonel Sanders' fried chicken is on Kentucky Avenue. So is Clifton's Club Harlem, with the Sepia Revue and the Sepia

Follies, featuring the Honey Bees, the Fashions, and the Lords.

•

My opponent and I, many years ago, played 2,428 games of Monopoly in a single season. He was then a recent graduate of the Harvard Law School, and he was working for a downtown firm, looking up law. Two people we knew—one from Chase Manhattan, the other from Morgan, Stanley—tried to get into the game, but after a few rounds we found that they were not in the conversation and we sent them home. Monopoly should always be *mano a mano* anyway. My opponent won 1,199 games, and so did I. Thirty were ties. He was called into the Army, and we stopped just there. Now, in Game 2 of the series, I go immediately to jail, and again to jail while my opponent seines property. He is dumbfoundingly lucky. He wins in twelve minutes.

•

Visiting hours are daily, eleven to two; Sunday, eleven to one; evenings, six to nine. "NO MINORS, NO FOOD, Immediate Family Only Allowed in Jail." All this above a blue steel door in a blue cement wall in the windowless interior of the basement of the city hall. The desk sergeant sits opposite the door to the jail. In a cigar box in front of him are pills in every color, a banquet of fruit salad an inch and a half deep— leapers, co-pilots, footballs, truck drivers, peanuts, blue angels, yellow jackets, redbirds, rainbows. Near the desk are two soldiers, waiting to go through the blue door. They are about eighteen years old. One of them is trying hard to light a cigarette. His wrists are in steel cuffs. A military policeman waits, too. He is a year or so older than the soldiers, taller, studious in appearance, gentle, fat. On a bench against a wall sits a good-looking girl in slacks. The blue door rattles, swings heavily open. A turnkey stands in the doorway. "Don't you guys kill yourselves back there now," says the sergeant to the soldiers.

"One kid, he overdosed himself about ten and a half hours ago," says the M.P.

The M.P., the soldiers, the turnkey, and the girl on the bench are white. The sergeant is black. "If you take off the handcuffs, take off the belts," says the sergeant to the M.P. "I don't want them hanging themselves back there." The door shuts and its tumblers move. When it opens again, five minutes later, a young white man in sandals and dungarees and a blue polo shirt emerges. His hair is in a ponytail. He has no beard. He grins at the good-looking girl. She rises, joins him. The sergeant hands him a manila envelope. From it he removes his belt and a small notebook. He borrows a pencil, makes an entry in the notebook. He is out of jail, free. What did he do? He offended Atlantic City in some way. He spent a night in the jail. In the nineteen-thirties, men visiting Atlantic City went to jail, directly to jail, did not pass Go, for appearing in topless bathing suits on the beach. A city statute requiring all men to wear full-length bathing suits was not seriously challenged until 1937, and the first year in which a man could legally go bare-chested on the beach was 1940.

•

Game 3. After seventeen minutes, I am ready to begin construction on overpriced and sluggish Pacific, North Carolina, and Pennsylvania. Nothing else being open, opponent concedes.

•

The physical profile of streets perpendicular to the shore is something like a playground slide. It begins in the high skyline of Boardwalk hotels, plummets into warrens of "side-avenue" motels, crosses Pacific, slopes through church missions, convalescent homes, burlesque houses, rooming houses, and liquor stores, crosses Atlantic, and runs level through the bombed-out ghetto as far—Baltic, Mediterranean—as the eye can see. North Carolina Avenue, for example, is flanked at its beach end by the Chalfonte and the Haddon Hall (908 rooms, air-conditioned), where, according to one biographer, John Philip Sousa (1854–1932) first played when he was twenty-two, insisting, even then, that everyone call him by his entire name. Behind these big hotels, motels—Barbizon, Catalina—crouch. Between Pacific and Atlantic is an occasional house from 1910—wooden porch, wooden mullions, old yellow paint —and two churches, a package store, a strip show, a dealer in fruits and vegetables. Then, beyond Atlantic Avenue, North Carolina moves on into the vast ghetto, the bulk of the city, and it looks like Metz in 1919, Cologne in 1944. Nothing has actually exploded. It is not bomb damage. It is deep and complex decay. Roofs are off. Bricks are scattered in the street. People sit on porches, six deep, at nine on a Monday morning. When they go off to wait in unemployment lines, they wait sometimes two hours. Between Mediterranean and Baltic runs a chain-link fence, enclosing rubble. A patrol car sits idling by the curb. In the back seat is a German shepherd. A sign on the fence says, "Beware of Bad Dogs."

Mediterranean and Baltic are the principal avenues of the ghetto. Dogs are everywhere. A pack of seven passes me. Block after block, there are three-story brick row houses. Whole segments of them are abandoned, a thousand broken windows. Some parts are intact, occupied. A mattress lies in the street, soaking in a pool of water. Wet stuffing is coming out of the mattress. A postman is having a rye and a beer in the Plantation Bar at nine-fifteen in the morning. I ask him idly if he knows where Marvin Gardens is. He does not. "HOOKED AND NEED HELP? CONTACT N.A.R.C.O." "REVIVAL NOW GOING ON, CONDUCTED BY REVEREND H. HENDERSON OF TEXAS." These are signboards on Mediterranean and Baltic. The second one is upside down and leans against a boarded-up

window of the Faith Temple Church of God in Christ. There
is an old peeling poster on a warehouse wall showing a figure
in an electric chair. "The Black Panther Manifesto" is the title
of the poster, and its message is, or was, that "the fascists have
already decided in advance to murder Chairman Bobby Seale
in the electric chair." I pass an old woman who carries a
bucket. She wears blue sneakers, worn through. Her feet spill
out. She wears red socks, rolled at the knees. A white handkerchief, spread over her head, is knotted at the corners. Does she
know where Marvin Gardens is? "I sure don't know," she says,
setting down the bucket. "I sure don't know. I've heard of it
somewhere, but I just can't say where." I walk on, through a
block of shattered glass. The glass crunches underfoot like
coarse sand. I remember when I first came here—a long train
ride from Trenton, long ago, games of poker in the train—to
play basketball against Atlantic City. We were half black, they
were all black. We scored forty points, they scored eighty, or
something like it. What I remember most is that they had glass
backboards—glittering, pendent, expensive glass backboards,
a rarity then in high schools, even in colleges, the only ones we
played on all year.

I turn on Pennsylvania, and start back toward the sea. The
windows of the Hotel Astoria, on Pennsylvania near Baltic, are
boarded up. A sheet of unpainted plywood is the door, and in
it is a triangular peephole that now frames an eye. The plywood door opens. A man answers my question. Rooms there
are six, seven, and ten dollars a week. I thank him for the
information and move on, emerging from the ghetto at the
Catholic Daughters of America Women's Guest House, between Atlantic and Pacific. Between Pacific and the Boardwalk
are the blinking vacancy signs of the Aristocrat and Colton
Manor motels. Pennsylvania terminates at the Sheraton-
Seaside—thirty-two dollars a day, ocean corner. I take a walk
on the Boardwalk and into the Holiday Inn (twenty-three

stories). A guest is registering. "You reserved for Wednesday, and this is Monday," the clerk tells him. "But that's all right. We have *plenty* of rooms." The clerk is very young, female, and has soft brown hair that hangs below her waist. Her superior kicks her.

He is a middle-aged man with red spiderwebs in his face. He is jacketed and tied. He takes her aside. "Don't say 'plenty,' " he says. "Say 'You are fortunate, sir. We have rooms available.' "

The face of the young woman turns sour. "We have all the rooms you need," she says to the customer, and, to her superior, "How's that?"

•

Game 4. My opponent's luck has become abrasive. He has Boardwalk and Park Place, and has sealed the board.

•

Darrow was a plumber. He was, specifically, a radiator repairman who lived in Germantown, Pennsylvania. His first Monopoly board was a sheet of linoleum. On it he placed houses and hotels that he had carved from blocks of wood. The game he thus invented was brilliantly conceived, for it was an uncannily exact reflection of the business milieu at large. In its depth, range, and subtlety, in its luck-skill ratio, in its sense of infrastructure and socio-economic parameters, in its philosophical characteristics, it reached to the profundity of the financial community. It was as scientific as the stock market. It suggested the manner and means through which an underdeveloped world had been developed. It was chess at Wall Street level. "Advance token to the nearest Railroad and pay owner twice the rental to which he is otherwise entitled. If Railroad is unowned, you may buy it from the Bank. Get out of Jail, free. Advance token to nearest Utility. If unowned, you may buy it from Bank. If owned, throw dice and pay owner a total ten times the amount thrown. You are assessed for street repairs: $40 per house, $115 per hotel. Pay poor tax of $15. Go to Jail. Go directly to Jail. Do not pass Go. Do not collect $200."

•

The turnkey opens the blue door. The turnkey is known to the inmates as Sidney K. Above his desk are ten closed-circuit-TV screens—assorted viewpoints of the jail. There are three cellblocks—men, women, juvenile boys. Six days is the average stay. Showers twice a week. The steel doors and the equipment that operates them were made in San Antonio. The prisoners sleep on bunks of butcher block. There are no mattresses. There are three prisoners to a cell. In winter, it is cold in here. Prisoners burn newspapers to keep warm. Cell corners are black with smudge. The jail is three years old. The men's block echoes with chatter. The man in the cell nearest Sidney K. is pacing. His shirt is covered with broad stains of blood. The block for juvenile boys is, by contrast, utterly silent—empty corridor, empty cells. There is only one prisoner. He is small and black and appears to be thirteen. He says he is sixteen and that he has been alone in here for three days.

"Why are you here? What did you do?"

"I hit a jitney driver."

•

The series stands at three all. We have split the fifth and sixth games. We are scrambling for property. Around the board we fairly fly. We move so fast because we do our own banking and search our own deeds. My opponent grows tense.

•

Ventnor Avenue, a street of delicatessens and doctors' offices, is leafy with plane trees and hydrangeas, the city flower. Water Works is on the mainland. The water comes over in submarine pipes. Electric Company gets power from across the state, on the Delaware River, in Deepwater. States Avenue, now a wasteland like St. Charles, once had gardens running down the middle of the street, a horse-drawn trolley, private homes. States Avenue was as exclusive as the Brighton. Only an apartment house, a small motel, and the All Wars Memorial Building—monadnocks spaced widely apart—stand along States Avenue now. Pawnshops, convalescent homes, and the Paradise Soul Saving Station are on Virginia Avenue. The soul-saving station is pink, orange, and yellow. In the windows flanking the door of the Virginia Money Loan Office are Nikons, Polaroids, Yashicas, Sony TVs, Underwood typewriters, Singer sewing machines, and pictures of Christ. On the far side of town, beside a single track and locked up most of the time, is the new railroad station, a small hut made of glazed firebrick, all that is left of the lines that built the city. An authentic phrenologist works on New York Avenue close to Frank's Extra Dry Bar and a church where the sermon today is "Death in the Pot." The church is of pink brick, has blue and amber windows and two red doors. St. James Place, narrow and twisting, is lined with boarding houses that have wooden porches on each of three stories, suggesting a New Orleans made of salt-bleached pine. In a vacant lot on Tennessee is a white Ford station wagon stripped to the chassis. The windows are smashed. A plastic Clorox bottle sits on the driver's seat. The wind has pressed newspaper against the chain-link fence around the lot. Atlantic Avenue, the city's principal thoroughfare, could be seventeen American Main Streets placed end to end—discount vitamins and Vienna Corset shops, movie theatres, shoe stores, and funeral homes. The Boardwalk is made of yellow pine and Douglas fir, soaked in pentachlorophenol. Downbeach, it reaches far beyond the city. Signs everywhere—on windows, lampposts, trash baskets— proclaim "Bienvenue Canadiens!" The salt air is full of Canadian French. In the Claridge Hotel, on Park Place, I ask a clerk if she knows where Marvin Gardens is. She says, "Is it a floral shop?" I ask a cabdriver, parked outside. He says,

"Never heard of it." Park Place is one block long, Pacific to Boardwalk. On the roof of the Claridge is the Solarium, the highest point in town—panoramic view of the ocean, the bay, the salt-water ghetto. I look down at the rooftops of the side-avenue motels and into swimming pools. There are hundreds of people around the rooftop pools, sunbathing, reading—many more people than are on the beach. Walls, windows, and a block of sky are all that is visible from these pools—no sand, no sea. The pools are craters, and with the people around them they are countersunk into the motels.

•

The seventh, and final, game is ten minutes old and I have hotels on Oriental, Vermont, and Connecticut. I have Tennessee and St. James. I have North Carolina and Pacific. I have Boardwalk, Atlantic, Ventnor, Illinois, Indiana. My fingers are forming a "V." I have mortgaged most of these properties in order to pay for others, and I have mortgaged the others to pay for the hotels. I have seven dollars. I will pay off the mortgages and build my reserves with income from the three hotels. My cash position may be low, but I feel like a rocket in an underground silo. Meanwhile, if I could just go to jail for a time I could pause there, wait there, until my opponent, in his inescapable rounds, pays the rates of my hotels. Jail, at times, is the strategic place to be. I roll boxcars from the Reading and move the flatiron to Community Chest. "Go to Jail. Go directly to Jail."

•

The prisoners, of course, have no pens and no pencils. They take paper napkins, roll them tight as crayons, char the ends with matches, and write on the walls. The things they write are not entirely idiomatic; for example, "In God We Trust." All is in carbon. Time is required in the writing. "Only humanity could know of such pain." "God So Loved the World." "There is no greater pain than life itself." In the women's block now, there are six blacks, giggling, and a white asleep in red shoes. She is drunk. The others are pushers, prostitutes, an auto thief, a burglar caught with pistol in purse. A sixteen-year-old accused of murder was in here last week. These words are written on the wall of a now empty cell: "Laying here I see two bunks about six inches thick, not counting the one I'm laying on, which is hard as brick. No cushion for my back. No pillow for my head. Just a couple scratchy blankets which is best to use it's said. I wake up in the morning so shivery and cold, waiting and waiting till I am told the food is coming. It's on its way. It's not worth waiting for, but I eat it anyway. I know one thing when they set me free I'm gonna be good if it kills me."

•

How many years must a game be played to produce an Anthony J. Drexel Biddle and chestnut geldings on the beach? About half a century was the original answer, from the first railroad to Biddle at his peak. Biddle, at his peak, hit an Atlantic City streetcar conductor with his fist, laid him out with one punch. This increased Biddle's legend. He did not go to jail. While John Philip Sousa led his band along the Boardwalk playing "The Stars and Stripes Forever" and Jack Dempsey ran up and down in training for his fight with Gene Tunney, the city crossed the high curve of its parabola. Al Capone held conventions here—upstairs with his sleeves rolled, apportioning among his lieutenant governors the states of the Eastern seaboard. The natural history of an American resort proceeds from Indians to French Canadians via Biddles and Capones. French Canadians, whatever they may be at home, are Visigoths here. Bienvenue Visigoths!

•

My opponent plods along incredibly well. He has got his fourth railroad, and patiently, unbelievably, he has picked up my potential winners until he has blocked me everywhere but

Marvin Gardens. He has avoided, in the fifty-dollar zoning, my increasingly petty hotels. His cash flow swells. His railroads are costing me two hundred dollars a minute. He is building hotels on States, Virginia, and St. Charles. He has temporarily reversed the current. With the yellow monopolies and my blue monopolies, I could probably defeat his lavenders and his railroads. I have Atlantic and Ventnor. I need Marvin Gardens. My only hope is Marvin Gardens.

•

There is a plaque at Boardwalk and Park Place, and on it in relief is the leonine profile of a man who looks like an officer in a metropolitan bank—"Charles B. Darrow, 1889–1967, inventor of the game of Monopoly." "Darrow," I address him, aloud. "Where is Marvin Gardens?" There is, of course, no answer. Bronze, impassive, Darrow looks south down the Boardwalk. "Mr. Darrow, please, where is Marvin Gardens?" Nothing. Not a sign. He just looks south down the Boardwalk.

•

My opponent accepts the trophy with his natural ease, and I make, from notes, remarks that are even less graceful than his.

•

Marvin Gardens is the one color-block Monopoly property that is not in Atlantic City. It is a suburb within a suburb, secluded. It is a planned compound of seventy-two handsome houses set on curvilinear private streets under yews and cedars, poplars and willows. The compound was built around 1920, in Margate, New Jersey, and consists of solid buildings of stucco, brick, and wood, with slate roofs, tile roofs, multi-mullioned porches, Giraldic towers, and Spanish grilles. Marvin Gardens, the ultimate outwash of Monopoly, is a citadel and sanctuary of the middle class. "We're heavily patrolled by police here. We don't take no chances. Me? I'm living here nine years. I paid seventeen thousand dollars and

I've been offered thirty. Number one, I don't want to move. Number two, I don't need the money. I have four bedrooms, two and a half baths, front den, back den. No basement. The Atlantic is down there. Six feet down and you float. A lot of people have a hard time finding this place. People that lived in Atlantic City all their life don't know how to find it. They don't know where the hell they're going. They just know it's south, down the Boardwalk."

Pieces of
the Frame

ON THE EDGE OF INVERMORISTON FOREST, I was trying to explain raised beaches, the fifty-foot beaches of Scotland, so called because they are about that far above the sea. Waves never touch them. Tides don't come near reaching them. Shell and shingle, whitened like bones, they are aftereffects of the ice, two miles thick, that once rested on Scotland and actually shoved Scotland down into the earth. When the ice melted, the sea slowly came up, but so did the land, sluggishly recovering its buoyancy over the molten center of things. After the sea had increased as much as it was going to, the land kept rising, and beaches were lifted into the air, some as much as fifty feet.

That was how I understood the story, and I was doing what I could to say it in a way that would make it intelligible to an audience of four children (mine—all girls, and all quite young), but the distractions were so numerous that I never really had a chance. My family and I were having a lakeside lunch—milk, potato sticks, lambs' tongues, shortbread, white chocolate, Mini-Dunlop cheese—beside a stream in a grove of birches that was backed by dense reforested pines. The pines covered steep slopes toward summits two thousand feet above us. It was late spring, but there were snowfields up there nonetheless, and the water we drank had been snow in the mountains that morning.

Near us, another family, also with small children, was having what was evidently a birthday picnic. They had arrived after we were already settled, and they had chosen—I don't know why, with acre upon acre of unpeopled and essentially similar terrain to move about in—to unpack all their special effects (a glistening white cake, noisemakers, conical cardboard orange hats) only forty or fifty yards away. I tried to ignore them and go on with my ruminations on the raised beaches. There were no raised beaches in that place, at least not in the usual form, but the children had seen them and had played on them elsewhere in the Highlands, and I thought that if they could understand how such phenomena had come to be, they might in turn be able to imagine the great, long lake now before them—Loch Ness—as the sea loch, the arm of the Atlantic, that it once was, and how marine creatures in exceptional variety had once freely moved in and out of it, some inevitably remaining.

Losing interest in the birthday party, my youngest daughter said, "I want to see the monster."

This had already become another distraction. In much the way that, in the United States, NO HUNTING signs are posted on every other tree along blacktop country roads, cardboard signs of about the same size had been tacked to trees and poles along the lake. There were several in the birch grove. Printed in royal blue on a white background, they said, "Any members of the general public who genuinely believe they have seen an unusual creature or object in or on the shores of Loch Ness are requested to report the occurrence to Expedition Headquarters at Achnahannet, two miles south of Urquhart Castle. If unable to report in person, they may telephone the Expedition (No. Drumnadrochit 358). Reports will only be of interest from people willing to give their full name and address and fill in a Sighting Report Form, which will be sent on request. Thank you for your cooperation. Published by the Loch Ness Phenomena Investigation Bureau, 23 Ashley Place, London, S.W. 1, and printed at the Courier Office, Inverness."

"What makes you think the monster wants to see *you?*" I said to my youngest one. "There won't be any sightings today, anyway. There's too much wind out there."

The wind on the lake was quite strong. It was blowing from the north. There were whitecaps, and the ranks of the waves were uniform in our perspective, which was high. Watching the waves, I remembered canoe trips when I was ten or eleven years old, trying to achieve some sort of momentum against white-capping headwinds between Rogers Rock and Sabbath Day Point on Lake George. Lake George was for beginners, who could learn in its unwild basin the essentials they would need to know on longer trips in later years in wildernesses they would seek out. But now, watching the north wind go down the lake in Scotland, I could not remember headwinds anywhere as powerful and savage as they had been in that so-styled lake for beginners, and I could feel again the skin rubbed off my hands. The likeness was in more than the wind, however. It was in the appearance, the shape, and the scale—about a mile from side to side—of Loch Ness, which, like the American lake, is at least twenty times longer than it is wide, a long deep cleft, positioned like some great geophysical ax-cut between its lateral hills. I remember being told, around the fire at night, stories of the first white man who saw Lake George. He was a travelling French priest, intent on converting the Mohawks and other nations of the Iroquois. He had come from Orléans. He said that the lake was the most beautiful he had ever seen, and he named it the Lake of the Blessed Sacrament. The Indians, observing that the priest blessed them with his right hand, held him down and chewed away his fingers until the fingers were stumps and the hand was pulp. Later, when the priest did not stop his work, the Indians axed the top of his skull, and then cut off his head.

Lake George is so clear that objects far below its surface, such as white stones or hovering bass, can be seen in total definition. The water of Loch Ness is so dark with the tints of peat that on a flat-calm day it looks like black glass. Three or four feet below the surface is an obscurity so complete that experienced divers have retreated from it in frustration, and in some cases in fear. A swimmer looking up toward a bright sky from a distance of inches beneath the surface has the impression that he is afloat in very dark tea. Lake George is nearly two hundred feet deep in places, has numerous islands, and with its bays and points, is prototypal of beautiful mountain lakes of grand dimension in every part of the world. Loch Ness is like almost no other lake anywhere. Its shores are formidably and somewhat unnaturally parallel. It has no islands. Its riparian walls go straight down. Its bottom is flat, and in most places is seven hundred feet deep, a mean depth far greater than the mean depth of the North Sea. Loch Ness holds a fantastic volume of water, the entire runoff of any number of northern glens—Glen Affric, Glen Cannich, Glen Moriston, Glen Farrar, Glen Urquhart. All of these valleys, impressive in themselves, are petals to Glen More, the Great Glen. Loch Ness is the principal basin of the Great Glen, and the Great Glen is the epicenter of the Highlands. A few miles of silt, carried into the lake by the rivers, long ago dammed the seaward end, changing the original sea loch into a fresh-water lake, but so slowly that marine creatures trapped within it had a chance to adapt themselves. Meanwhile the land kept rising, and with it the new lake. The surface of Loch Ness is fifty-two feet above sea level.

My wife listened with some interest when, repeating all this, I made an expanded attempt to enrich everyone's experience, but nothing was going through to the children. "I want to see the monster," the youngest one said again, speaking for all. They didn't want to know how or why the so-called monster might have come into that particular lake. They just wanted to see it. But the wind was not slowing up out there on the lake.

All of us looked now at the family that was having the birthday picnic, for the father had stood up shouting and had flung a large piece of the birthday cake at his wife. It missed her and spattered in bits in the branches of a tree. She shouted back at him something to the effect that he was depraved and cruel, and he in turn bellowed that she was a carbon of her bloody mother and that he was fed up. She said she had had all she could ever take, and was going home—to England, apparently. With that, she ran up the hillside and soon was out of sight in the pines. At first, he did not follow, but he suddenly was on his feet and shouting serial threats as he too went out of range in the pines. Meanwhile, their children, all but one, were crying. The one that wasn't crying was the girl whose birthday it was, and she just sat without moving, under a conical orange hat, staring emptily in the direction of the lake.

We went to our car and sat in it for some time, trying not to be keeping too obvious an eye on the children in the birch grove, who eventually began to play at being the bailiffs of the birthday picnic and made such a mess that finally the girl whose birthday it was began to cry, and she was still crying when her father came out of the pines. I then drove north.

The road—the A-82—stayed close to the lake, often on ledges that had been blasted into the mountainsides. The steep forests continued, broken now and again, on one shore or the other, by fields of fern, clumps of bright-yellow whin, and isolated stands of cedar. Along the far shore were widely separated houses and farms, which to the eyes of a traveller appeared almost unbelievably luxuriant after the spare desolation of some of the higher glens. We came to the top of the rise and suddenly saw, on the right-hand side of the road, on the edge of a high meadow that sloped sharply a considerable distance to the lake, a cluster of caravans and other vehicles, arranged in the shape of a C, with an opening toward the road—much like a circle of prairie schooners, formed for protection against savage attack. All but one or two of the vehicles were painted bright lily-pad green. The compound, in its compact half acre, was surrounded by a fence, to keep out, among other things, sheep, which were grazing all over the slope in deep-green turf among buttercups, daisies, and thistles. Gulls above beat hard into the wind, then turned and planed toward the south. Gulls are inland birds in Scotland, there being so little distance from anywhere to the sea. A big fireplace had been made from rocks of the sort that were scattered all over the meadow. And on the lakeward side a platform had been built, its level eminence emphasizing the declivity of the hill, which dropped away below it. Mounted on the platform was a thirty-five-millimeter motion-picture camera with an enormous telephoto lens. From its point of view, two hundred feet above the lake and protruding like a gargoyle, the camera could take in a bedazzling panorama that covered thousands of acres of water.

This was Expedition Headquarters, the principal field sta-

tion of the Loch Ness Phenomena Investigation Bureau—
dues five pounds per annum, life membership one hundred
pounds, tax on donations recoverable under covenant. Those
who join the bureau receive newsletters and annual reports,
and are eligible to participate in the fieldwork if they so desire.
I turned into the compound and parked between two bright-
green reconditioned old London taxis. The central area had
long since been worn grassless, and was covered at this
moment with fine-grain dust. People were coming and going.
The place seemed rather public, as if it were a depot. No one
even halfway interested in the natural history of the Great
Glen would think of driving up the A-82 without stopping in
there. Since the A-82 is the principal route between Glasgow
and Inverness, it is not surprising that the apparently amphibi-
ous creature as yet unnamed, the so-called Loch Ness Monster, has been seen not only from the highway but on it.

The atmosphere around the headquarters suggested a scientific frontier and also a boom town, much as Cape Canaveral
and Cocoa Beach do. There were, as well, cirrus wisps of show
business and fine arts. Probably the one word that might have
been applied to everyone present was adventurer. There was,
at any rate, nothing emphatically laboratorial about the place,
although the prevailing mood seemed to be one not of holiday
but of matter-of-fact application and patient dedication. A
telephone call came in that day, to the caravan that served as
an office, from a woman who owned an inn south of Inverarigaig, on the other side of the lake. She said that she had seen
the creature that morning just forty yards offshore—three
humps, nothing else to report, and being very busy just now,
thank you very much, good day. This was recorded, with no
particular display of excitement, by an extremely attractive
young woman who appeared to be in her late twenties, an
artist from London who had missed but one summer at Loch
Ness in seven years. She wore sandals, dungarees, a firmly

stretched black pullover, and gold earrings. Her name was
Mary Piercy, and her toes were painted pink. The bulletin
board where she recorded the sighting resembled the kind
used in railway stations for the listing of incoming trains.

The office walls were decorated with photographs of the
monster in various postures—basking, cruising, diving, splash-
ing, looking up inquisitively. A counter was covered with some
of the essential bibliography: the bureau's annual report
(twenty-nine sightings the previous year), J. A. Carruth's
Loch Ness and Its Monster (The Abbey Press, Fort Augus-
tus), Tim Dinsdale's *Loch Ness Monster* (Routledge and
Kegan Paul, London), and a report by the Joint Air Recon-
naissance Center of the Royal Air Force on a motion picture of
the monster swimming about half a mile on the lake's surface.
These books and documents could, in turn, lead the interested
reader to less available but nonetheless highly relevant works
such as R. T. Gould's *The Loch Ness Monster and Others* and
Constance Whyte's *More Than a Legend*.

My children looked over the photographs with absorption
but not a great deal of awe, and they bought about a dozen
postcards with glossy prints of a picture of the monster—three
humps showing, much the same sight that the innkeeper had
described—that had been taken by a man named Stuart,
directly across the lake from Urquhart Castle. The three
younger girls then ran out into the meadow and began to pick
daisies and buttercups. Their mother and sister sat down in
the sun to read about the creature in the lake, and to write
postcards. We were on our way to Inverness, but with no need
to hurry. "Dear Grammy, we came to see the monster today."

From the office to the camera-observation platform to the
caravan that served as a pocket mess hall, I wandered around
among the crew, was offered and accepted tea, and squinted
with imaginary experience up and down the lake, where the

whitecaps had, if anything, increased. Among the crew at the time were two Canadians, a Swede, an Australian, three Americans, two Englishmen, a Welshman, and one Scot. Two were women. When I asked one of the crew members if he knew what some of the others did, vocationally, when they were not at Loch Ness, he said, "I'm not sure what they are. We don't go into that." This was obviously a place where now was all that mattered, and in such a milieu it is distinctly pleasant to accept that approach to things. Nonetheless, I found that I couldn't adhere completely to this principle, and I did find out that one man was a medical doctor, another a farmer, another a retired naval officer, and that several, inevitably, were students. The daily watch begins at four in the morning and goes on, as one fellow put it, "as long as we can stand up." It has been the pattern among the hundreds of sightings reported that the early-morning hours are the most promising ones. Camera stations are manned until ten at night, dawn and sunset being so close to midnight at that latitude in summer, but the sentries tend to thin out with the lengthening of the day. During the autumn, the size of the crew reduces precipitously toward one.

One man lives at the headquarters all year long. His name is Clem Lister Skelton. "I've been staring at that bloody piece of water since five o'clock," he said, while he drank tea in the mess caravan.

"Is there a technique?" I asked him.

"Just look," he said. "Look. Run your eye over the water in one quick skim. What we're looking for is not hard to see. You just sit and sort of gaze at the loch, that's all. Mutter a few incantations. That's all there is to do. In wintertime, very often, it's just myself. And of course one keeps a very much more perfunctory watch in the winter. I saw it once in a snowstorm, though, and that was the only time I've had a clear view of the head and neck. The neck is obviously very mobile.

The creature was quite big, but it wasn't as big as a seventy-foot MFV. Motor fishing vessel. I'd been closer to it, but I hadn't seen as much of it before. I've seen it eight times. The last time was in September. Only the back. Just the sort of upturned boat, which is the classic view of it."

Skelton drank some more tea, and refilled a cup he had given me. "I must know what it is," he went on. "I shall never rest peacefully until I know what it is. Some of the largest creatures in the world are out there, and we can't name them. It may take ten years, but we're going to identify the genus. Most people are not as fanatical as I, but I would like to see this through to the end, if I don't get too broke first."

Skelton is a tall, offhand man, English, with reddish hair that is disheveled in long strings from the thinning crown of his head. In outline, Skelton's life there in the caravan on the edge of the high meadow over the lake, in a place that must be uncorrectably gloomy during the wet rains of winter, seemed cagelike and hopeless to me—unacceptably lonely. The impression he gave was of a man who had drawn a circle around himself many hundreds of miles from the rest of his life. But how could I know? He was saying that he had flown Supermarine Spitfires for the R.A.F. during the Second World War. His father had been a soldier, and when Skelton was a boy, he lived, as he put it, "all over the place." As an adult, he became first an actor, later a writer and director of films. He acted in London in plays like *March Hare* and *Saraband for Dead Lovers*. One film he directed was, in his words, "a dreadful thing called *Saul and David.*" These appearances on the surface apparently did not occur so frequently that he needed to do nothing else for a livelihood. He also directed, in the course of many years, several hundred educational films. The publisher who distributed some of these films was David James, a friend of Skelton's, and at that time a Member of Parliament. James happened to be, as well, the founder of the

Loch Ness Phenomena Investigation Bureau—phenomena, because, for breeding purposes, there would have to be at least
two monsters living in the lake at any one time, probably
more, and in fact two had on occasion been sighted simul-
taneously. James asked Skelton if he would go up to the lake
and give the bureau the benefit of his technical knowledge of
movie cameras. "Anything for a laugh," Skelton had said to
James. This was in the early nineteen-sixties. "I came for a
fortnight," Skelton said now, in the caravan. "And I saw it. I
wanted to know what it was, and I've wanted to know what it
was ever since. I thought I'd have time to write up here, but I
haven't. I don't do anything now except hunt this beast."

Skelton talked on about what the monster might be—a
magnified newt, a long-necked variety of giant seal, an unex-
tinct *Elasmosaurus*. Visitors wandered by in groups outside
the caravan, and unexplained strangers kept coming in for tea.
In the air was a feeling, utterly belied by the relative perma-
nence of the place, of a country carnival on a two-night stand.
The caravans themselves, in their alignment, suggested a
section of a midway. I remembered a woman shouting to
attract people to a big caravan on a carnival midway one night
in May in New Jersey. That was some time ago. I must have
been nineteen. The woman, who was standing on a small
platform, was fifty or sixty, and she was trying to get people to
go into the caravan to see big jungle cats, I suppose, and
brown bears—"Ferocious Beasts," at any rate, according to
block lettering on the side of the caravan. A steel cage containing a small black bear had been set up on two sawhorses
outside the caravan—a fragment to imply what might be
found on a larger scale inside.

So young that it was no more than two feet from nose to tail,
the bear was engaged in desperate motion, racing along one
side of the cage from corner to corner, striking the steel bars
bluntly with its nose. Whirling then, tossing its head over its

shoulder like a racing swimmer, it turned and bolted crazily for the opposite end. Its eyes were deep red, and shining in a kind of full-sighted blindness. It had gone mad there in the cage, and its motion, rhythmic and tortured, never ceased, back and forth, back and forth, the head tossing with each jarring turn. The animal abraded its flanks on the steel bars as it ran. Hair and skin had scraped from its sides so that pink flesh showed in the downpour of the carnival arc lights. Blood drained freely through the thinned hair of its belly and dropped onto the floor of the cage. What had a paralyzing effect on me was the animal's almost perfect and now involuntary rhythm—the wild toss of the head after the crash into the corner, the turn, the scraping run, the crash again at the other end, never stopping, metronomic—the exposed interior of some brutal and organic timepiece.

Beside the cage, the plump, impervious woman, red-faced, red-nosed, kept shouting to the crowds, but she said to me, leaning down, her own eyes bloodshot, "Why don't you move on, sonny, if you ain't going to buy a ticket? Beat it. Come on, now. Move on."

"We argue about what it is," Skelton said. "I'm inclined to think it's a giant slug, but there is an amazingly impressive theory for its being a worm. You can't rule out that it's one of the big dinosaurs, but I think this is more wishful thinking than anything else." In the late nineteen-thirties, a large and exotic footprint was found along the shore of Loch Ness. It was meticulously studied by various people and was assumed, for a time, to be an impression from a foot or flipper of the monster. Eventually, the print was identified. Someone who owned the preserved foot of a hippopotamus had successfully brought off a hoax that put layers of mockery and incredibility over the creature in the lake for many years. The Second World War further diverted any serious interest that amateurs or naturalists might have taken. Sightings continued, however, in a consistent pattern, and finally, in the early nineteen-sixties, the Loch Ness Phenomena Investigation Bureau was established. "I have no plans whatever for leaving," Skelton said. "I am prepared to stay here ad infinitum. All my worldly goods are here."

A dark-haired young woman had stepped into the caravan and poured herself a cup of tea. Skelton, introducing her to me, said, "If the beast has done nothing else, it has brought me a wife. She was studying Gaelic and Scottish history at Edinburgh University, and she walked into the glen one day, and I said, 'That is the girl I am going to marry.'" He gestured toward a window of the caravan, which framed a view of the hills and the lake. "The Great Glen is one of the most beautiful places in the world," he continued. "It is peaceful here. I'd be happy here all my life, even if there were nothing in the loch. I've even committed the unforgivable sin of going to sleep in the sun during a flat calm. With enough time, we could shoot the beast with a crossbow and a line, and get a bit of skin. We could also shoot a small transmitter into its hide and learn more than we know now about its habits and characteristics."

The creature swims with remarkable speed, as much as ten or fifteen knots when it is really moving. It makes no noise other than seismic splashes, but it is apparently responsive in a highly sensitive way to sound. A shout, an approaching engine, any loud report, will send it into an immediate dive, and this shyness is in large part the cause of its inaccessibility, and therefore of its mystery. Curiously, though, reverberate sound was what apparently brought the creature widespread attention, for the first sequence of frequent sightings occurred in 1933, when the A-82 was blasted into the cliffsides of the western shore of the lake. Immense boulders kept falling into the depths, and shock waves from dynamite repeatedly ran through the water, causing the creature to lose confidence in its environment and to alter, at least temporarily, its shy and preferentially nocturnal life. In that year it was first observed on land, perhaps attempting to seek a way out forever from the detonations that had alarmed it. A couple named Spicer saw it, near Inverarigaig, and later described its long, serpentine neck, followed by an ungainly hulk of body, lurching toward the lake and disappearing into high undergrowth as they approached.

With the exception of one report recorded in the sixth century, which said that a monster (fitting the description of the contemporary creatures in the lake) had killed a man with a single bite, there have been no other examples of savagery on its part. To the contrary, its sensitivity to people seems to be acute, and it keeps a wide margin between itself and mankind. In all likelihood, it feeds on fish and particularly on eels, of which there are millions in the lake. Loch Ness is unparalleled in eel-fishing circles, and has drawn commercial eel fishermen from all over the United Kingdom. The monster has been observed with its neck bent down in the water, like a swan feeding. When the creatures die, they apparently settle into the seven-hundred-foot floor of the lake, where the temperature is always forty-two degrees Fahrenheit—so cold that the lake is known for never giving up its dead. Loch Ness never freezes, despite its high latitude, so if the creature breathes air, as has seemed apparent from the reports of observers who have watched its mouth rhythmically opening and closing, it does not lose access to the surface in winter. It clearly prefers the smooth, sunbaked waterscapes of summer, however, for it seems to love to bask in the sun, like an upturned boat, slowly rolling, plunging, squirming around with what can only be taken as pleasure. By observers' reports, the creature has two pairs of lateral flippers, and when it swims off, tail thrashing, it leaves behind it a wake as impressive as the wake of a small warship. When it dives from a still position, it inexplicably goes down without leaving a bubble. When it dives as it swims, it leaves on the surface a churning signature of foam.

Skelton leaned back against the wall of the caravan in a slouched and nonchalant posture. He was wearing a dark blue tie that was monogrammed in small block letters sewn with white thread—L.N.I. (Loch Ness Investigation). Above the monogram and embroidered also in white thread was a small depiction of the monster—humps undulant, head high, tail extending astern. Skelton gave the tie a flick with one hand. "You get this with a five-pound membership," he said.

The sea-serpent effect given by the white thread on the tie was less a stylization than an attempt toward a naturalistic sketch. As I studied it there, framed on Skelton's chest, the thought occurred to me that there was something inconvenient about the monster's actual appearance. In every sense except possibly the sense that involves cruelty, the creature in Loch Ness is indeed a monster. An average taken from many films and sightings gives its mature length at about forty feet. Its general appearance is repulsive, in the instant and radical sense in which reptiles are repulsive to many human beings, and any number of people might find difficulty in accepting a creature that looks like the one that was slain by St. George. Its neck, about six feet long, columnar, powerfully muscled, is the neck of a serpent. Its head, scarcely broader than the neck, is a serpent's head, with uncompromising, lenticular eyes. Sometimes as it swims it holds its head and neck erect. The creature's mouth is at least a foot wide. Its body undulates. Its skin glistens when wet and appears coarse, mottled, gray, and elephantine when exposed to the air long enough to become dry. The tail, long and columnar, stretches back to something of a point. It seemed to me, sitting there at Headquarters, that the classical, mythical, dragon likeness of this animate thing—

the modified dinosaur, the fantastically exaggerated newt—
was an impediment to the work of the investigation bureau,
which has no pertinent interest in what the monster resembles
or calls to mind but a great deal in what it actually is, the goal
being a final and positive identification of the genus.

"What we need is a good, lengthy, basking sighting," Skelton said. "We've had one long surfacing—twenty-five minutes.
I saw it. Opposite Urquhart Castle. We only had a twelve-inch
lens then, at four and a half miles. We have thirty-six-inch
lenses now. We need a long, clear, close-up—in color."

My children had watched, some months earlier, the killing
of a small snake on a lawn in Maryland. About eighteen inches
long, it came out from a basement-window well, through a
covering lattice of redwood, and was noticed with shouts and
shrieks by the children and a young retriever that barked at
the snake and leaped about it in a circle. We were the weekend guests of another family, and eight children in all
crowded around the snake, which had been gliding slowly
across the lawn during the moments after it had been seen,
but had now stopped and was turning its head from side to
side in apparent indecision. Our host hurried into his garage
and came running back to the lawn with a long shovel. Before
he killed the snake, his wife urged him not to. She said the
snake could not possibly be poisonous. He said, "How do you
know?" The children, mine and theirs, looked back and forth
from him to her. The dog began to bark more rapidly and at a
higher pitch.

"It has none of the markings. There is nothing triangular
about its head," she told him.

"That may very well be," he said. "But you can't be sure."

"It is *not* poisonous. Leave it alone. Look at all these
children."

"I can't help that."

"It is *not* poisonous."

"How do you know?"

"I know."

He hit the snake with the flat of the shovel, and it writhed. He hit it again. It kept moving. He hit it a third time, and it stopped. Its underside, whitish green, segmental, turned up. The children moved in for a closer look.

Josie's Well

THE LAPHROAIC DISTILLERY IS ON THE SOUTHERN SHORE OF ISLAY, one of the isles of Argyll, in the Inner Hebrides. The buildings are all white and rise among dark-green Scotch pines by the water's edge. A clear burn flows to the distillery through acres of peats, over rocks, more peats, more rocks, more peats, into the buildings, and out in barrels and bottles of the whisky, Laphroaig. The distiller's home is a part of the compound and is full of light, for its seaward walls are largely glass. His living room is upstairs and is cantilevered toward a spectacular and often misty view over the pines and the sea. Multiple white couches are covered with pillows in blazing color. The bar is quilted. There is a white grand piano. Two golden retrievers lie on the floor. The distiller, whose name is Wishart Campbell, stands beside a Sony solid-state stereo tape recorder, his hand on the bass control. He wears a sport jacket,

and he is somewhat heavyset but nonetheless athletic in
carriage, a glib man, quick, fluid, idiomatic. He refers to his
wife as "Mrs. C." His whisky is so smoky, so heavy, so redo-
lently peaty that a consumer feels he is somehow drinking a
slab of bacon. There is some Laphroaig—a few drops per
fifth—in Ballantine's, Teacher's, Dewar's, White Horse,
Johnnie Walker, Black & White, Haig & Haig, thirty-odd
Scotches in all. "If the blenders want a Hebridean malt, they
come here and get it," Campbell explains. "In a proper blend,
Laphroaig is the foundation, the real gutsy base." George
Gershwin's "Love Walked In" is pouring out of the Sony.
Campbell turns the bass control knob as far as it will go, and
the Gershwin deepens into broad profundities of sound.
Campbell says, "There you have it. That is the Laphroaig."

The Talisker distillery is also by the sea, by a long, narrow
bay on the western coast of the Isle of Skye. Talisker was a
farmer who grew barley. In 1834, he began to roast it over
burning peat, ferment it with yeast and water, distill the resulting wash, and then sell—"A wee drop of himself," as Skye
men say—the whisky that continues to carry his name. A
syndicate with headquarters in London owns Talisker's distillery now, and the syndicate has installed as general manager
Peter Hogg, a young and serious man with tie and pullover,
bright eyes, dark hair, a dangling forelock. Hogg grew up in
whisky in the way that some people are born to the stage. He
belongs to Craigellachie, a Speyside town, seat of the great
Macallan distillery. He is knowledgeable, modern, and technical. He explains that barley is the choice of grains because
barley seeds have a high content of starch and, further, are
protected by double skins, so air has less chance to get at the
starch and produce mold. He explains that germination of the
seeds promotes the enzyme diastase, which, in hot water,

helps convert the starch to the sugar that will ferment into alcohol.

Hogg opens a door at one end of a germinating floor (where barley is four inches deep and doves fly through open windows to help themselves) and he steps into the kiln. The floor of the kiln, a gridwork of thousands of thin metallic plates, is covered with several inches of germinated barley, and the smoke of peat that is burning below filters up through the grid. When the barley goes into the kiln it is known as green malt. Distillers use coke as well as peat for their fires, and the ratio they choose determines the peatiness of the ultimate whisky. Unblended, pure Highland malt whiskies are made in only a few places in Scotland—in the Hebrides, on the Mull of Kintyre, and in the riparian counties of the River Spey. They vary in taste as pronouncedly as regional wines. Talisker, on the tongue, unique among the malts, is halfway between the characteristically heavy flavors of the island whiskies and the patrician subtleties of Speyside.

By an entirely different and much cheaper process, whisky is also made in Scotland from corn. It is called grain whisky, as distinguished from malt whisky, and it is very nearly tasteless. A bottle of blended Scotch whisky consists mainly of grain whisky and is flavored by various malts. The malts are known as the top-dressing, and the grain whisky is known as the pad. In some blended whiskies there are as many as forty different malts, sitting on the pad. Twenty is average. Blended whisky, bland and facile, was developed for bland Americans, who drink most of the whisky distilled in Scotland. Highlanders, who can't tell the difference between one blend and another, roll on the floor in laughter at the thought of American sophisticates who think they can. Meanwhile, they drink their ranging malts, resonant as cognac, and so replete with flavor that a few drops are enough to perform an aromatic alchemy.

The barley has roasted for forty-eight hours and is now, in
the term of the trade, malted. Peter Hogg picks up some of the
seeds and eats them, like malted peanuts. They are delicious.
It is dram time. Twice daily, the men working in the distillery—malt men, mill men, wash men, tun-room men, still men,
some twenty-five in all—line up for their dram. At Talisker,
the whisky comes in a copper jug from the warehouse, and is
poured into something called "the horn." It is a two-inch
segment of cattle horn, fitted with a metallic bottom. Carved
on it are the words *A Wee Doch an Doris*, "a wee drink
before you leave." Everybody drinks a full measure from the
horn—everybody but Peter Hogg and the government excise
man. Each distillery has its resident excise man. This one is a
Londoner, outposted far up here on Skye, a decent enough
chap. "He turns a blind eye to the horn," says Peter Hogg.
"For myself, I taste the whisky but I never drink it. It would
take a very special occasion to get me to drink it. Working
with it, it's not policy to drink it. One might get addicted to it.
I smell it once a week to see if there's enough peat in it. When
I drink something, I like a little beer."

Wishart Campbell, of Laphroaig, generously and almost
evangelistically presses Laphroaig on friends and strangers
alike. But after booming up his hi-fi, he moves to the quilted
bar to fix his own drink, Demerara rum and Pepsi-Cola.

It is a beautiful afternoon in Banffshire. The lush, green,
rural valley of the Spey is ablaze with mustard-colored whin.
The river is fast and occasionally shivers with white water.
The sky is clear. The air is warm. The branches of birches and
pines move in a moderate wind. Distillers hate a day like this.
It's bad for germination, bad for whisky. Too many days like
this could put a distillery out of business. Whisky thrives on
gloom, fog, rain. Above the Spey in Macallan Parish, Craig-

ellachie, is the Macallan Distillery, which collects water from
the Ringorm Burn and from various springs in the local gneiss
and produces one of the three malt whiskies that are by general
consent regarded as the best distilled in Scotland. The other
two distilleries—J. & J. Grant, and George and J. G. Smith—
are only a few miles away.

The executive offices in the Macallan distillery are expen-
sively designed, darkly paneled, shining with polished wooden
desk and table surfaces and rich leather upholstery, and could
be the offices of a remarkably successful law firm in London.
The offices have emptied out at the end of the working day.
George Harbinson, managing director and chairman, is there
alone. He is a slim man, bald. At the back of his head is a thick
fringe of curly silver hair. His manner is quiet. His face is
sensitive and in its strong lines there is a suggestion, among
other things, of melancholy, but he seems to be only mildly
put out by the lovely weather. He wears a dark suit and holds
in his hand a narrow, stemmed glass that is tapered toward
the top and partly filled with Macallan Pure Highland Malt
Scotch Whisky. He adds a little water "to bring out the nose."
He inhales the aroma. He seems to like what he is doing.
"When it's free, it has a very sweet, aromatic nose to it"
Harbinson says. "It makes me immediately think of mountain
air."

The whisky in his glass was made in 1950, drawn from the
cask in 1962, and is part of Macallan's "library," or, perhaps
more appropriately, *bibliothèque,* kept for the record, to assure
the continuity of standard.

"Other single whiskies have a heavier nose," he goes on. "We
don't aim to have a heavily peated malt." He sips. "One has to
drink in moderation," he says. "Otherwise one wouldn't last
very long. Many years ago, they used to say that whisky was
old if it was cool from the stills. It went straight to the pubs.
The body gets along better with older whisky. In maturer

whisky, you've got rid of a lot of the lighter, rather objectionable alcohols."

Twelve years is the prime age, most agree, but Harbinson dissents. He thinks whisky gets better the longer it ages. Whisky is sold the day it is made, but is stored by the maker. In the vastness of the warehouses, barrels sometimes become misplaced and are found many years after they would otherwise have been delivered. Such a barrel was recently found at Macallan. The whisky in it was thirty-five years old, and Harbinson places it among the best he has ever tasted.

The greatness of Macallan whisky, Harbinson says, is "a matter of luck—the people that developed the plant happened onto the right shape of stills." Barley soup ferments in tuns and is then boiled away in wash stills. The resulting liquor—called low wine—is boiled again in spirit stills. The wash stills are tall and bulbous, often shaped like lamp glasses; the spirit stills are smaller and conical, suggesting the hats of leprechauns. All are copper, for the heat transfer is better in copper than in any other metal. Much in the way that Ph.D. candidates will fasten upon and attempt to explicate a great work of the imagination, minor and would-be distillers examine the stills of a place like Macallan. Some distilleries permit no photographs, nervously keeping to themselves the exact curve of the shoulders, the style of the ogee, the relative grace of the swan neck, the size and attitude of the lynne arm. The lynne arm extends away from the uppermost part of the still, above the neck, and carries the vaporous liquor to the condenser. Some lynne arms curve like the tops of coat hangers. Others wiggle away in right angles. Some are narrow, some wide. The lynne arms at Talisker go straight out horizontally, as if to suggest that there will be no nonsense at Talisker. The lynne arms at Macallan are extraordinarily thick—about fourteen inches in diameter—and slope downward on a gentle grade.

Harbinson seems to doubt that this could open the secret of Macallan.

"The way a plant is operated is as important as the design," he says. "You get better whisky if you run fairly slowly. Modern demand causes many distilleries to run fast. We have small, individual stills. Like anything else you are cooking, smaller boilings are better for flavor."

When the whisky runs out of the condensers it is as clear and colorless as water. Whether it is heavy or light it all looks like water, and the amount of color that is ultimately given to it is almost strictly a matter of show business. Whisky is aged in casks of new oak, or in used casks that previously held sherry. The sherry colors the whisky. If the maker wants a light-colored whisky, he uses fewer sherry casks per lot. Makers try to match the color to what they think the taste is, but color of whisky has nothing whatever to do with its true lightness. Harbinson is holding his glass up before a window in what is now fading daylight. "Sherry does, to a minor extent, affect the taste of the spirit," he says in a ruminative way. "We've tried putting it in refilled whisky casks, in brandy casks, in Madeira casks, but the whisky was a wee bit spiritous. Freshly emptied sherry casks are the best. They placate the spirit. They calm it down."

Macallan and J. & J. Grant's Glen Grant together form the baseline of the triumvirate of malt whisky. The apex above them is George & J. G. Smith's The Glenlivet, the finest whisky made in Scotland. Why do the Scots think so? What is the secret of The Glenlivet? Could it be the altitude? The distillery is the highest in Scotland, but is only nine hundred feet above sea level. Is it the Livet? The Livet is a clear, tumbling tributary of the Spey, but the distillery uses its water only as a coolant. Is it the shape of the stills? the quality of the malt? the source of the peats? Or is the nature of the whisky in the nature of the man, the owner, the chairman, who now, in his offices in the distillery, waves a brace of pistols that his great-grandfather, the founder, was the last man to fire in anger? The two greatest individual names in the history of malt whisky are Smith and Grant, and this man's name is Captain Smith Grant.

He went to Downside and Sandhurst, years ago. There could be little doubt that he would have retired from the Army as Field Marshal Smith Grant had he not gone back to the stills in his youth. He is in his sixties, tall, powerfully framed, with a large head, a heavy face, and a look that, despite its elements of weariness, suggests that life has been good in Glenlivet. Captain Smith Grant seems completely unbound, and in that sense must be the loosest man in the Highlands. He wears his Highland Brigade tie and his kilt in Hunting Grant. He waves his great-grandfather's pistols. "Venomous-looking things, are they not?" he says. "I mean, if you got hit with a bullet out of *that* . . ." His full-bodied voice fades for a moment as he thinks about his whisky and the process by which it is made. "There's nothing secret about any of it," he says. "It just happens that it comes out like that. People come here and ask if they can measure the stills. 'Measure them,' I say. 'Photograph them. Do anything you like with them so long as you leave them here.' Many people have copied them. Actually, we chucked out a still three years ago that was ninety-eight years old. We put in a new one and it didn't seem to affect anything. We buy our peats from a subcontractor in Tomintoul. We're using British barley, the same barley everyone else uses. We *have* used California barley, Danubian barley, Karachi barley—Tunisian, Australian, Danish island barley. It isn't the barley. We can't be bothered malting our own barley. We buy it from maltsters in the south of Scotland."

Captain Smith Grant takes a walk around his distillery. It is a beautifully unprepossessing compound of buildings set in high, open, hill country, looking out over a field of oats, in which stand the semi-ruins of Blairfindy Castle. The distillery—its long, low buildings covered with roughcast; its eaves, window frames, and doorways painted dark red—might be a dairy farm. Its warehouses, full of butts and hogsheads stacked over an earth floor (some think the best whisky ages closest to the dank ground), reek of malt whisky. The Glenlivet wash stills, plump and very narrow-waisted, are buxom. There are just two of them, twenty-five feet high, pure copper, and they look remarkably like a pair of tightly bodiced Victorian women, hardly promising as vessels for the gestation of a drink whose very name in Gaelic—*uisge-beatha*—means "the water of life." The lynne arms droop unimaginatively. The spirit stills, also two in number, are small replicas of the wash stills.

"It's not really the stills," says Captain Smith Grant. "I think it's ninety-nine and a half percent the water—the water, and a sort-of certain fiddle-faddle in the manufacture. The water comes from Josie's Well. Who Josie was I don't know, but the water comes from Josie's Well."

Talking all the way, Captain Smith Grant goes out the front door of his distillery, crosses the road, lifts his kilt, climbs a fence and moves through the waist-deep golden oats toward Josie's Well. He regards the hike as insanity—"to see a bloody hole in the ground"—but he is cheerfully willing to go. "The Invergordon people thought they would expand into the malt market a few years ago, and they built a distillery just up the road here, built a distillery to produce a million gallons a year," he says. "They're struggling to get about two hundred thousand gallons. They make bloody awful whisky. We think it rather heavy. They're not in the same watershed, quite. We produce seven hundred and fifty thousand gallons a year. Ninety-eight percent of it goes into blended whiskies. John

Walker uses thirty thousand gallons of The Glenlivet a year, Black or Red, we don't know. We fill large orders from Haig, and so forth. Our job is to sell to the blenders. They use The Glenlivet as a top-dressing, to cover up the multitude of sins in the vat, to give it some sort of quality. People have spread the fact that there is nothing to touch The Glenlivet, so we must eternally turn out the same whisky. We could make it more cheaply, but we don't dare try. It might change it. It is a full-bodied, slow-maturing whisky which has a great deal of quality. The Scotch whisky trade have come to rely on it as an unaltering standard."

This reminds him of the way the name of his whisky has been poached and poached again, and he fulminates. His is the one distillery in Glenlivet, but whisky-makers all over Strathspey have long made use of the name, slipping the word Glenlivet onto their labels in order to arrogate to themselves some of The Glenlivet's stature.

"In the United Kingdom, you can't have a geographical name as a trademark," he explains. "That's why they've had so much trouble over Harris tweed. A few years ago, damned near all whisky was labelled as coming from Glenlivet. Glenlivet was the longest glen in Scotland, with all the people stealing the name." He pronounces the name *glen leave it,* although nearly everyone else in Scotland says *glen live it.* "We've succeeded in shoving everybody off," he continues. "We took the case up to the House of Lords and spent God knows what, about twenty thousand quid. The people of Speyside argued that they put Livet water in their whisky, for the Livet flows into the Spey. We should have put the Provost of Grant into the box and asked him where he puts Grantown sewage. He would have had to say that that, too, goes into the Spey. All whisky distilleries use water from springs and burns, anyway, not from rivers. Rivers are too dangerous. The water is different at different times. We settled it, finally, after a fashion. These people in Speyside have to hyphenate the name Glenlivet with their own name, if they're going to use Glenlivet. And they have to print both names the same size—Glenfarclas-Glenlivet, Mortlach-Glenlivet, Longmorn-Glenlivet, Linkwood-Glenlivet, nearly all of them do it. The full name of the Macallan company is R. Kemp, Macallan-Glenlivet. But our whisky is The Glenlivet, and no one else can call their whisky simply that."

Striding on, he drops into a calmer mood. "Macallan is nice whisky. I had some two years ago. Glenfarclas is a very nice little whisky, but it has no particular stature or character. It's a well-made, above-average Highland malt. I had some seven years ago. Glen Grant is a thinner whisky than The Glenlivet. It does not have the same body. It's sweet, and useful for blending. I had some last fall. A drop or two of water brings out the nose. I know no one who does not drink whisky with water. There doesn't seem to be much future in just knocking it back. You have half a taste of it and it's gone."

In the middle of the oat field is a small, fenced enclosure, eight feet square. The fence is made of wood so old that it is dark gray and covered with lichen. Three rails are broken down. Bits of rusted wire hold the rest together. Sheep that have somehow got into the field have left wool on the barbs of the wire. On the ground, among weeds and buttercups in the middle of the enclosure, is a large flagstone five inches thick. Grant heaves away the slab. Beneath it is—just as he said—a mere hole in the ground, almost square at the surface, eighteen inches across, and fully five feet deep. At the bottom, water voluminously rushes out of the earth, out of some fateful crack in the granite of the glen, whirling, eddying, prodigiously, noisily gurgling. A three-inch pipe carries it under the oats to the distillery.

"What if Josie's Well should ever go dry?"

"It's not allowed to go dry. We couldn't do without it."

Grant's kilt is blowing in the wind. He leans on the fence. A rail cracks. He almost falls.

"Why don't you build a brick enclosure here? Why don't you make a shrine out of this place?"

"If someone mucks about with that well, it may disappear. The mason may put his foot in it. I think we can class ourselves as fairly prosperous. We want to stay that way."

Captain Smith Grant is hungry from the open air, and after returning from the oat field has his lunch. Beforehand, he pours a glass of The Glenlivet, drops just enough water into it for a perfect nose, and hands it to me. Then he mixes for himself a gin and tonic.

From Birnam Wood
to Dunsinane

IN MOST FAMILIES, a generation or two is time enough to erase even a major infamy, but centuries upon centuries have not in this respect been kind to the Macbeths, as anyone knows who knows one. I've known several Macbeths, and I particularly remember the moments in which I met them, because in most instances a faint shadow seemed to cross their faces when their surname was exposed to yet another stranger. The latest of these is R. G. Macbeth, of Scarsdale. We were introduced—as travellers, as strangers, in a small town in New England—by a motelkeeper who was serving our breakfast, and who in her friendly way seemed to think that we would have much to say to each other simply because our names were derivationally Scottish. This Macbeth was a big, broad-shouldered man with bright eyes and an engagingly unprepossessing manner. As it happened, he did have a lot to say. He had scarcely sat down before he was well into a mild harangue about the injuries that had been done to his family through poetic license and dramatic journalism—manipulations of the pen. He said that his collateral ancestor Macbeth, King of Scotland, was a good king and is buried with other Scottish kings on the island Iona in a sanctuary where only authentic and duly entitled kings are at rest; that no one who had poached the throne of Scotland would ever have been buried, or at least would have long remained buried, on Iona; that Macbeth, in 1040, killed King Duncan not in bed but in battle; that Macbeth's claim to rule the Scots was as legitimate as Duncan's, each, through his mother, being a great-grandson of King Kenneth I; and that Macbeth settled the claim, as was the custom in his time, with his sword in fair and open fight. His reign lasted seventeen years. I could be well assured that something quite different from tyranny or depravity was the atmosphere that generally emanated from his fortress on the summit of Dunsinane Hill.

I said to Mr. Macbeth, "I'm sorry you have this cross to bear."

Macbeth lifted his coffee cup, indicating that he would drink to that. He drank. Then he said, "I've never been to Scotland. In a year or two, though, I'm going to go."

I said, "Let me give you a name and address. Donald Sinclair, Balbeggie, Perthshire. I'll write it down. He's a farmer. He's the cousin of a friend of mine. I don't know Sinclair very well, but I don't think he would mind if you were to seek him out, which is what I did once. I was in Scotland with my family, and one day—just for the experience—we went by the most direct way we could find from Birnam Wood to Dunsinane. It's a ten-mile trip. Sinclair calls himself a tenant farmer. Technically, that's what he is, but his father-in-law happens to be his landlord, and the family owns a very handsome piece of Perthshire—five thousand acres. Their estate is called Dunsinnan, and more or less in the middle of it is Dunsinane Hill."

Macbeth slowly set down his plastic coffee cup on the Formica surface of the table. I told him the details of the pilgrimage as I had made it.

Birnam Wood, on the edge of the Craigvinean Forest, stands across the River Tay from a medieval town, Dunkeld, and has been replaced to some extent by Birnam, a village that developed in the late nineteenth century. Birnam Wood now is deep and thick, dark green, with an understory of gorse and bracken, and white slashes of birch angling upward among larches and pines. In all likelihood, the boughs of such trees could not have been the boughs that went to Dunsinane. Apparently the forest was once predominantly oak. The present Birnam Wood, cut who knows how many times, seems to be merely a collateral descendant of the forest that once was there, for the presence of a number of slim oaks among the pines suggests what must have been, in the virgin stand, the climax tree. The army assembled by Siward, Malcolm, and Macduff would have marched under oak leaves. By the river is one immensely impressive piece of evidence suggesting that this was so. One tree, an oak, remains from—according to local testimony—the time of Macbeth. It stands in a riparian grove of grasses, weeds, and rusting junk. Nothing much is made of it. I used up half a morning finding it. A postman on the principal street of Birnam had told me about it. "The old trees are away now, unfortunately. But there is still one left. It is propped up." We picked our way downhill—my four small daughters, my wife, and I—along dirt pathways strewn with discarded plastic bottles and fragments of broken glass. The groundscape was somewhat cleaner and more inviting closer to the river, where another path ran along parallel to the current and passed under the high canopies of trees at least a century old. These were whips, seedlings, saplings by comparison with the tree we finally found. There it was, standing without fence or fanfare, its trunk outmassing the Heidelberg tun, its roemerian canopy all but stopping the sunlight: the last tree of Birnam Wood, a living monument to the value of staying put.

My wife and children and I joined hands, and we wrapped ourselves to the tree with arms extended. The six of us reached less than halfway around. The big oak was so gnarled that it appeared to be covered with highly magnified warts. Each of ten principal limbs had the diameter of a major oak in itself, and the lower ones, jutting out almost horizontally, were supported in six places by columns set in the ground. One great limb was dead. In the base of the trunk were cavelike holes. Lichen grew on the bark as if the tree were already down and moldering. But despite all that, the tree was green throughout its canopy—leafy and alive. This big oak alone could have camouflaged an army.

We sat down on the riverbank and had lunch. The Tay was fast, clear, and shallow, and about two hundred yards downstream was a small rip, a touch of white water. The flow was southerly, in the general direction of Dunsinane, so the army would have moved for some distance along the river on its way to the hill. We ate cold roast beef, white chocolate, and Islay Mini-Dunlop cheese. I reached up and took a leaf from the great oak, and we began the journey.

First, we stopped in at the Esso Autodiesel & Petrol Agency in Birnam and had the tank of our car filled, for five shillings sixpence halfpenny the gallon. The attendant gave the children Esso tiger tails. Below Birnam the riverine countryside was lush with wheat fields, haycocks, oats, barley. Multi-colored lupines and wild foxgloves grew in meadows where herds of Aberdeen Angus were sleeping, all draped together with their necks across the necks of the cows beside them. It

was a clear day, warm but not hot. A tractor plowing a field
was followed by flights of seagulls. The gulls were eating the
worms that the tractor turned up. We moved through a grove
of seventy-foot cedars, copper beeches, and hemlocks on a
dark lane running among standing stones, through weirdly
overgrown formal gardens, and past an Italianate castle no
more than a century old, now boarded shut and falling to ruin.
We later found in a book on Dunkeld and Birnam that this
(Murthly Castle) had been the home of an exotic peer who
had once ornamented the grounds with herds of buffalo from
Wyoming. In his milieu, he may not have been eccentric. Even
today, we know someone in the same part of Perthshire who
keeps a considerable herd of pet red deer, and when he goes
off in summer to the far north—to Caithness—he takes his red
deer with him in chartered freight cars.

Murthly Hospital, for mental patients, came soon after
Murthly Castle and was about a third of the way from Birnam
Wood to Dunsinane. Like the decaying structure upriver, the
main buildings of the hospital, amorphous and ugly, must
have been about a century old, and in their setting among
woods and fields by the Tay they did not seem as forbidding
in the sunlight as they must in the gloom of rain. The place
belied itself, if it ever could, this day. Women sat on benches
in brightly colored straw hats. Men in coveralls bowled on a
lawn. Others gardened. Distress was invisible, but nonetheless
my children were unnaturally quiet. Doctors crossed the
grounds in white jackets. A big nurse, whose size was a kind of
manifesto of control, carried a fragile and extremely old
woman in her arms. Rows of stone cottages had names over
their doors like Tuke, Robertson, Bruce. Among them, a giant
and rusting television aerial was planted in the earth like a
tree. One of the men on the bowling court left the game and
ran toward us, smiling and waving his arms. I did not for a
moment know what I wanted to do. He was running hard.

Was I going to avoid him and renew, in one more way, his hurt; or was I going to become enskeined in a dialogue that could, in the end, be even less successful in the breaking? I left him behind, standing by the road, without expression, watching us go.

The country opened out again beyond the hospital, and the river made an erratic series of turns to the north, the east, the southeast, and, finally, the southwest, forming an irregular loop about two miles broad. Anybody moving overland from Birnam Wood to Dunsinane would cross this loop, and so did we, first going through the Haugh of Kercock, a low-lying meadow by the river. In a fank in the meadow, men were shearing sheep. Lambs were bleating wildly. Shorn ewes stood around looking silly and naked. One man had the head of a ewe in his arms, and was wrestling with her desperately, rolling on the ground. Moving on, we skirted a marshland called the Bloody Inches. Beautiful farm country followed toward Kinclaven, a village by the Tay, on the far side of the loop. In the fields, huge strawstacks had been constructed like houses—rectangular, with vertical walls, and tops sloping up to ridgelines. Moving along an unpaved lane, we came to a church that was black with age, and among the tombstones beside it a man was digging a grave. We stopped to ask him the way to Dunsinane. He said he had been digging graves there forty-four years and had been born and raised in Kinclaven but had no idea how to get to Dunsinane. He said, "It's not far. It's a small place, I can tell you that." His shovel struck something in the ground. He explained that when he digs graves he often encounters the foundations of churches that, one after another, had been on the site before this one. A church must have been there when Macbeth's castle stood on Dunsinane Hill. According to the Scottish historian R. L. Mackie, Macbeth was so religious that he once made a pil-

grimage to Rome. All the way to the Vatican and back, he
flung money at the poor. Since he lived less than five miles
away from Kinclaven, he and Lady Macbeth must have gone
to church here from time to time.

We crossed the river, made a right, went through a railway
embankment, made a left at Cargill Smithy, and began a long
upgrade toward Gallowhill, Wolfhill, and Dunsinnan, through
villages of strawstacks, and more wheat, oats, and barley in
dark-red earth. We found Donald Sinclair among his stead-
ings, some two miles from Dunsinane Hill.

Sinclair seemed amused that we wanted to climb his hill,
and not at all put out. I had thought that people must come in
battalions to Dunsinane, and that Sinclair probably spent a lot
of his time protecting his land. He said that was not the case.
A busload of Boy Scouts from Perth might turn up once in a
rare while, but that was about all. Few people seem to realize
that there really is a Dunsinane Hill. Shakespeare, he said,
took an "n" out of Dunsinnan and added an "e," but did not
create the hill. "The name in Gaelic means 'hill of the ants.'
Streams of little men went up and down the hill when the
castle was being built. Shall we go?"

We drove with him through fields and in woodland, made a
few turns, and all at once saw a high green hill fringed with
rowan trees and mountain ash in blossom. Dunsinane is at the
southwestern end of the serrated line of the Sidlaw Hills. The
other Sidlaws, reaching away to the northeast, were all mauve-
brown with heather, and Dunsinane stood out among them
because it was bright green. Heather apparently will not grow
where man has ever performed his constructions. Even from
the foot of Dunsinane, we could see that its summit was flat—
absolutely truncated, as if it had been sliced level with a knife.
We started up its grassy, southern slope. Sinclair's Herefords
were grazing there. "I raise beef cattle," he said. "They sum-

mer on the hill. When a busload of Boy Scouts comes, it is much to my horror, because I've got a bull amongst the cows here." Sinclair was wearing wide-wale corduroy trousers, a threadbare baggy sweater, a shirt, a wool tie. Still in his forties, a tall man, he looked weathered, as if he had always been there. He seemed to be at one with his land and his hill, and nothing about his loose-postured walk suggested that he was a graduate of Sandhurst, which he was—a career military man, born on a wheat farm in Manitoba, raised in England, an Army officer from the Second World War until the early nineteen-sixties, when he became the tenant farmer of Dunsinane Hill. We went around a shoulder of the terrain. "There he is," Sinclair said. We passed close by a congenial-looking Hereford bull. He was rust-red, almost top-heavy, the kind of animal that appears to consist of about nine tons of solid steak, and, with his white-rug face, to be as fierce as Ferdinand. "We call him Old Joe."

The slopes of the hill rose and converged with an almost volcanic symmetry, so the climb became quite steep. We passed a spring. "This is where Macbeth got his water," Sinclair said. "The sort of outer fortifications must have reached this far." We kept moving up, breathing hard and not talking for a while, until Sinclair paused for a moment, tilted his head back, looked up at the summit, and said, "It's pretty impregnable, I should think. I shouldn't like to climb up here and have people pouring boiling oil on me."

The summit was flat and oval, and Macbeth's floor plan was evident there, for the foundation protruded in lumpy ridges under the turf. The castle was no cramped little broch. It was a hundred and twenty feet wide and two hundred and twenty-five feet long—just slightly larger than the Parthenon. Hill of the ants, indeed: Macbeth apparently did not do things by halves. The view from the summit over the patchwork Scottish countryside was extraordinary. It is a virtual certainty that Shakespeare never set eyes on Dunsinane. If he had, he would have described it. In fact, his entire description of Dunsinane Hill comes in two words, "high" and "great."

> Macbeth shall never vanquished be until
> Great Birnam Wood to high Dunsinane Hill
> Shall come against him.

> Great Dunsinane he strongly fortifies:
> Some say he's mad.

Curlews and oyster catchers cried overhead. This was June, and we could see the Grampians, far in the distance, with snow still on them. We could see, three hundred and sixty degrees around us, a fifth of Scotland—to Fife, to Dundee—and out over the North Sea. It would be hard to imagine a more apt or beautiful setting for a fortress home. Sinclair said that the Picts had chosen the spot centuries before Macbeth, and that Dunsinane had been only one of a whole line of Pictish forts in the Sidlaws—"a sort of defense effort against the Vikings."

We sat down on the base of a rampart. A cool, erratic wind was blowing. Sinclair told us, offhandedly, that the supposed Stone of Scone now in Westminster Abbey is actually a worthless rock from Dunsinane Hill. He said that the real Stone of Scone had been buried in Dunsinane Hill long ago, when the substitute was chosen, and that the real one had been dug up in the nineteenth century only to be reburied after a short time, and that despite all the more recent flurries about the (fake) Stone of Scone in Westminster Abbey, the real one was still there in the hill. Sinclair pointed out Scone, over toward Perth, and added that that was the dullest direction to look in, for, with the dubious exceptions of Scone and Perth, "you can't see anything madly exciting." Closer in and on a more northerly line, he called attention to a small stone house trimmed in red, and he said, "That is where Macbeth settled his three wise women." Moving his hand, pointing, he said, "That farm down there is called Balmalcolm. The next one is Fairy Green, where they found a Pictish stone called the Spunky Dell. The trees down here on the north slope were planted by my father-in-law. He's reforesting. They are five-year-old Scotch pines and some larch."

Macbeth did not die at Dunsinane. Birnam Wood moved, and so forth, according to Holinshed's questionable *Chronicles,* but Macbeth was ignominiously driven away, a fugitive king humbled before his people, and he lived three more years before he was killed, by Malcolm Canmore (Big-Headed Malcolm), on some undramatic moor in Aberdeen. I had been reading W. C. Mackenzie's history of the Highlands only a few days before this, and there on the summit of Dunsinane I found that I could almost remember verbatim Mackenzie's summary line: "By the irony of circumstances, Macbeth, branded as long as literature lasts with the stain of blood, was the friend of the poor, the protector of the monks, and the first Scottish king whose name appears in ecclesiastical records as the benefactor of the Church." It simply was not in him to shout at an enemy here on these ramparts in the hour of his death:

> I will not yield,
> To kiss the ground before young Malcolm's feet
> And to be baited with the rabble's curse.
> Though Birnam Wood be come to Dunsinane,
> And thou oppos'd, being of no woman born,
> Yet I will try the last. Before my body
> I throw my warlike shield. Lay on, Macduff,
> And damn'd be him that first cries "Hold, enough!"

The race being what it is, we prefer him the second way, and Shakespeare knew what we wanted. I had been twirling by its stem the leaf from the Birnam oak, and I dropped it on the top of the hill. We went down to Sinclair's farmhouse for tea, and tea included, among other things, banana sandwiches and Nesquik chocolate milk shakes.

Mr. Macbeth, after a struggle over the check, paid for my breakfast. As we parted, he told me that he had once been a salesman of advertising space for a magazine, and that he had spent half his days in reception foyers waiting to get in to see various kinds of executives. On arrival, he would give his name routinely to the receptionist, then sit down, pick up a magazine, and wait. During this interval, slow, obscure, primordial stirrings would apparently go on in the receptionist's mind, for time and again—and never, he thought, with conscious intent—the receptionist would eventually say to him, "You may go in now, Mr. Macduff."

Basketball and

Beefeaters

BASKETBALL PLAYERS, years ago, used to spend hours telling about the weird places where they had played the game. They played in dance halls under ceilings they could touch with their elbows. They played on the stages of theatres where they could hip one another into the orchestra pit. They played in poorly lighted warehouses, taking shots that would disappear into upper blackness and emerge great distances away to drop without touching the rim. The game is glossy and standardized now. Courts are neat, bright rectangles in the middle of floors big enough for golf. The players are the best ever, but dull. The old stories are seldom heard.

I have one, but until recently I had never come right out with it, for fear of being taken for my grandfather. I saw my chance as I listened to a fellow I know talking about the days when he played for a grocery store in the Pacific Northwest.

He had been a steady, "set-'em-up" guard on the Melrose Market five. One night, he said, Melrose played in a dense cloud of Bull Durham in the mess hall at the Washington State Penitentiary, in Walla Walla. Here was a man I could talk to. "That's nothing," I said to him. "I once played basketball in the Tower of London."

I was lying, as a matter of fact, but the truth is so close to this particular lie that I didn't mind telling it. One season, during the middle nineteen-fifties, I was a member of the basketball team at Cambridge University. I had come there, after finishing Princeton, to read English literature, and I absorbed a fair part of it in the buses that carried us all over the Midlands to play our various matches. At first, when I arrived in Cambridge and began looking through the University handbook for some sort of team to play on, I decided against basketball without so much as looking into the matter. I thought that since basketball had been invented by an American, the Cambridge team would obviously be just a group of American students; if there were any scheduled games at all, they would be played against soldiers and airmen at American bases. I wouldn't have needed to cross the ocean for that. So, with some inconsistency, I went out for lacrosse, the game invented by American Indians. I had foreknowledge that it was played in England by Englishmen, but it turned out that they don't play lacrosse the way we do in the United States. It is a non-contact sport in England, with no pads or helmets—all ballet and stickwork. In the first scrimmage, my own stick forgot itself and all but disassembled the lower jaw of a chap from Jesus College. That was considered a poor showing. I soon decided to play basketball after all.

The building we played in was on the edge of the University cricket grounds. It served as a gymnasium, but the lettering over the entryway said "Department of Human Ecology." I walked in expecting to see thirty thousand dollars' worth of

Fulbright scholarships running around trying to keep warm. Sure enough, the first person to introduce himself was Bob Pinckert, of New York. The second was Russ Moro, also of New York. But then I met David Thomas, Scotsman; Howard Purnell, Welshman; Tudor Johnston, Canadian; Dye Thomas, Welshman; Michael Blackburn, Englishman; Dennis Cope, Englishman; Joe Romero, Filipino; and Dennis Solomon, from Trinidad. Before the season ended, we even had a man from Barbados. I was only the third American.

From Hampshire to Derbyshire, Sussex to Shropshire, we went wherever the whim of our club secretary took us. Surprisingly, potential opponents were everywhere. There is a basketball club in nearly every town in England. The game was introduced there through the Y.M.C.A. movement in 1934, the Second World War stimulated its growth, and now there is an Amateur Basketball Association and even a monthly magazine, *Basketball.* R. William Jones, secretary of the International Amateur Basketball Association, which regulates and helps standardize the game all over the world, is British. Basketball is played in all of Britain's armed services. Newspapers list basketball scores. The game, in short, is English now. And why not? It is the ideal team sport for the world's foremost indoor nation.

The first actual basketball I saw, as manufactured in England, was a disturbing sight. I suppose I was expecting at least a Voit Enduro ball out of a U.S. war-surplus store. The English ball was more like a surplus mine. Precisely, it was built much as a soccer ball is built, with the same thick leather, the same jigsaw quantity of small collected parts. Instead of going through the net with a swish, it would sometimes tear the net off. Dribbling was difficult, since the ball, to say the least, bounced unevenly. There was nothing in the English rule book requiring that a basketball be that way, so I sent back to Princeton for a contribution to Cambridge University,

which was swiftly provided: three Spalding Top-Flite basketballs, the type used by nearly all American colleges—precision
items that would bounce with obedience.

Unfortunately, there was no sending home for a new gymnasium. The Department of Human Ecology was housed in a
new building, just two years old then, but in the develop-
mental chronology of American basketball it might have been
the best new gym of 1922. Exercise bars stuck out from solid
oak walls that were just eight inches from the sidelines. The
backboards, with their attached baskets, were screwed into
end walls of yellow firebrick, so that after a driving layup a
player, unable to stop quickly enough, often collided with the
brick. Naturally, these players were almost always our visitors,
since no one on the Cambridge squad, unless carried away by
excitement, would think of driving hard toward the basket
even if he had a clear opening. We would usually stand back
and waft long shots from safe distances.

We lost only one game in our own gym during five months
of steady matches with other universities, clubs from various
towns and cities, and service teams. But for all the advantage
of the Spalding basketballs and the yellow firebrick (which
our opponents never even commented on), I nonetheless think
it remarkable that we managed to run up winning scores con-
sistently in the sixties and seventies when very few shots were
risked from distances under fifteen feet. In the first round of
the annual tournament—the somewhat inexact equivalent of
the American N.C.A.A. championships—we were hosts to a
team from Corby, in Lincolnshire, and beat them 100–32. But
the next and, for us, final round was the one game we lost at
Cambridge—to the U.S. Navy team from Grosvenor Square.

We lost a good number of games played away from Cambridge, since conditions, including the size of the court, tended
to favor the home team everywhere. While our gym was prob-

ably the newest in England, it was also in all probability the smallest. It was possible, though rarely attempted, to complete a solo fast-break from one end of the court to the other with a single high-parabola dribble. Hence, we were lost on the big courts at places like Ruislip, Loughborough, and Oxford. Had we played Oxford at Cambridge, we might have kept the score close, but I think we would have lost anyway. Whereas we were an essentially English team with strong international overtones, Oxford's basketball club was an exclusive clique of Americans. We were a sporting group. We always stopped off for a pint of mild after practice. The Oxford team was homogeneously composed of Rhodes Scholars, all of whom were dedicated to abstemiousness, exercise, and victory. They played hard, cleanly, and competently, and one got the feeling that they were representing a theological seminary.

Since Oxford had no basketball court of its own, its players used a floor at a nearby American airbase. It was in an immense hangar, heated by a jet engine that was mounted in the wall at one end. The engine drove a devastating blast of superheated air onto the court. Moving toward it—even if you were in the clear on a fast-break—you were wise to stop and take a jump shot twenty feet away. The intense heat was spent, however, long before it reached the other end of the court. You could actually see your breath in the cold end. As a team, unfortunately, we were cold in both ends. We lost miserably.

At the London School of Economics, we ran into another kind of obstacle—prejudice. It seemed to be both intranational and international: an odium for Cambridge and a manic dislike of Americans. Prejudice can be worth quite a few points in a basketball game, especially if the most actively prejudiced person is the referee. Except in tournaments and other vital events, most basketball games in England then were officiated by agents of the home team. The referee supplied by L.S.E. was, in my opinion, as prejudiced a man as has ever blown a whistle. In a normal game, the L.S.E. team could have been beaten handily, but we spent most of the evening watching L.S.E. players miss foul shots. They made enough to win, however. I was fouled out of the game in the first half. So were Dye Thomas, Pinckert, Romero, Solomon, and Moro. I drew one foul standing still with my hands on my hips, an attitude I had assumed in order to demonstrate that I was making no contact whatever with the man I was supposedly guarding. The referee would simply blow the whistle and point at you with pleasure, his eyes sparking. *I* may be prejudiced, but I'm sure he thought we were all either Americans or peers of the realm.

To the unbiassed eye, the Cambridge basketball club presented a truly curious sociological phenomenon. Almost no one played basketball according to his national characteristics. The English members of the squad, for example, were anything but reserved; they were outrageously flamboyant in their style of play, rifling flat-trajectory shots from forty feet out as if they were throwing darts, sniffing through the rule book to discover obscurities like the air dribble, even giving one another a boost in pursuit of rebounds. The Americans—Moro, Pinckert, and I—showed the least Yankee ingenuity. We were less inventive because we had seen great American players play. We slavishly imitated the controlled skills of these stars, just as most American basketball players do. The Welshmen were by far the most businesslike of the lot of us—reliable, steady, work-horse ballplayers, always cold sober (our Welsh Thomas was Dye, not Dylan). These paradoxes did not prevail throughout the squad. Our Scot did indeed have an eruptive temper, and the Caribbeans were unquestionably languid. Our Canadian, however, was fantastically out of character. On the English courts, most of which were cold, he was forever blowing on his hands, and games had sometimes gone well into the second quarter before he was fully warmed up.

During the Christmas vacation, I spent a fortnight in London, riding the high buses—once, inevitably, to the Tower. What American youth would not yearn to see the Tower of London? It was to poisoning, hanging, beheading, regicide, and torture what Yankee Stadium was to baseball. The two young sons of Edward IV were murdered in the Tower by their uncle, King Richard III. The Duke of Clarence was drowned there in a tub full of Cypriot wine. King Henry VI was hacked to death in the same turret where the crown jewels of England are now kept. Sir Thomas More was a prisoner in the Tower before he was led outside the walls onto Tower Hill and beheaded publicly. In private, Anne Boleyn knelt to the sword and Lady Jane Grey to the axe, at a beheading block within the walls.

Standing there beside that block on an overcast December morning, as one of a group of tourists, I happened to see that my feet were straddling a white line painted on the asphalt of the parade ground that adjoins Waterloo Barracks, one of the substructures within the walls. Our guide, a Yeoman Warder, or Beefeater, in medieval costume, was probably saying that the barracks were built in the middle of the nineteenth century and are the youngest of the Tower's substructures. . . . I was not listening to him. The white line made a large rectangle in the middle of the parade ground. There was a circle in the center and at each end the startling outlines of basketball foul lanes.

"Any questions?" the guide asked.

"Who plays basketball here?" I said. There must have been thirty people on the tour, and they all turned around to look at me. Some of them laughed nervously. I thought for a moment that I had imagined the court. But then the guide explained that the Tower is garrisoned by Her Majesty's Royal Fusiliers.

They stay in shape by playing basketball during non-visiting hours.

When I returned to Cambridge, I instantly got hold of the secretary of the basketball club and urged him to write to the Royal Fusiliers and set up a match. He said I was daft; but he wrote the letter. The Royal Fusiliers responded at once. They had a building in which they ordinarily played their matches, but they were delighted that Cambridge University would like to play them in their Tower.

It was the last match of our season, toward the end of the Lent term. A Beefeater led us through a gate in the Tower walls. He was excited about the game, talking animatedly as he walked, kicking ravens out of his path and praising the sharpshooting skills of the Royal Fusiliers. It was a wonderful day—the first blue sky over London in seven weeks, he said. The captain of the Fusiliers met us outside Waterloo Barracks and invited us in for tea. He said a lorry would be coming directly with the baskets and backboards, mounted on steel poles. When the lorry finally came, we were out on the parade ground dressed and ready, the Royal Fusiliers in dark uniforms, Cambridge in pale Cambridge blue. We all cheered its arrival. We were getting cold, just standing there smoking and passing basketballs around with nothing to shoot at. Pinckert set a basketball on the beheading block. Russ Moro lectured the English members of the squad on the history of the Tower, whose pinnacles soared above us in the miraculously clear air. The crowd—exclusively composed of Beefeaters and ravens—was getting bored. The Beefeaters were all but clapping their hands in unison, and the ravens were starting to leave.

The lorry backed up to the foot of one foul lane and stopped. Two soldiers got up on the tailgate. They shoved the heavy steel mounting out the back end and tilted it upward until its twin poles were secured in casings embedded in the asphalt. There at last stood the phenomenon I had been waiting to see, a basketball hoop, net, and backboard rising up in the very center of the Tower of London. In moments, we would be sending long shots arcing past the high battlements, adding a wild footnote to the history of the game. Meanwhile, the lorry driver prepared to move off to the other end of the court. After a great gnashing of gears, he started up with a violent jolt—and surged backward rather than forward, smashing into the support poles of the erected basket and snapping them off at the ground. The soldiers didn't even bother to set up the other basket. It was just jolly bad luck, that was all. There was a lot of swearing on the part of the Fusiliers, and the lorry driver had to take considerable mockery. For my part, I would have settled for an improvised half-court game there in the Tower, but that apparently did not cross the minds of our hosts, who had never completely understood why we wanted to play in the Tower in the first place.

We all climbed into the lorry and were driven to a sports hall near Tower Hill. It had a large basketball floor. Light bulbs hung from the ceiling in steel cages. The windows were sheathed with steel latticework, and some natural light was entering through filters of coal dust. "There now, chaps, this is more like it anyway, isn't it?" said the captain of the Fusiliers. We all agreed. Her Majesty's Royal Fusiliers were splendid fellows, and they were anxious that we enjoy our visit with them. We would have been uncharitable to admit our disappointment, but the ultimate score of the game was probably an indirect expression of it—Cambridge 95, Royal Fusiliers 42. It was the worst beheading in the history of the Tower, inside or outside the walls.

Centre Court

HOAD ON COURT 5, weathered and leonine, has come from Spain, where he lives on his tennis ranch in the plains of Andalusia. Technically, he is an old hero trying a comeback but, win or lose, with this crowd it is enough of a comeback that Hoad is here. There is tempestuous majesty in him, and people have congregated seven deep around his court just to feel the atmosphere there and to see him again. Hoad serves explosively, and the ball hits the fence behind his opponent without first intersecting the ground. His precision is off. The dead always rise slowly. His next serve splits the service line. Hoad is blasting some hapless Swiss into submission. As he tosses the ball up to serve again, all eyes lift above the court and the surrounding hedges, the green canvas fences, the beds of climbing roses, the ivy-covered walls—and at the top of the ball's parabola, it hangs for an instant in the sky against a background of half-timbered houses among plane trees and poplars on suburban hills. Rising from the highest hill is the steeple of St. Mary's Church, Wimbledon, where Hoad was married sixteen years ago. He swings through the ball and hits it very deep. "Fault." Hoad's wife, Jenny, and their several children are at the front of the crowd beside the court, watching with no apparent dismay as Hoad detonates his spectacularly horizontal serves.

Smith, in a remote part of the grounds, is slowly extinguishing Jaime Fillol. Tall, straightforward, All-American, Stan Smith is ranked number one in the United States. He grew up in Pasadena, where his father sold real estate. A fine basketball player, Smith gave it up for tennis. He is a big hitter who thinks with caution. Under the umpire's chair is his wallet. The locker rooms of Wimbledon are only slightly less secure than the vaults of Zurich, but Smith always takes his wallet with him to the court. Fillol, a *Chileno,* supple and blue-eyed, says "Good shot" when Smith drives one by him. Such remarks are rare at Wimbledon, where Alphonse would have a difficult time finding Gaston. The players are not, for the most part, impolite, but they go about their business silently. When they show appreciation of another player's shot, it is genuine. There is no structure to Fillol's game. Now he dominates, now he crumbles. Always he faces the big, controlled, relentless power of the all-but-unwavering Smith. Smith does not like to play on these distant courts close to the walls of the Wimbledon compound. The wind rattles the ivy and the ivy sometimes rattles Smith—but hardly enough to save Fillol.

John Alexander has brown hair that shines from washing. It hangs straight and touches the collar of his shirt in a trimmed horizontal line. The wind gusts, and the hair flows behind him. Not yet twenty, he is tall, good-looking, has bright clear eyes, and could be a Shakespearean page. In his right hand is a Dunlop. He drives a forehand deep cross-court. There is little time for him to get position before the ball comes back—fast, heavy, fizzing with topspin.

In Alexander's mind, there is no doubt that the man on the other side of the net is the best tennis player on earth. He hit with him once, in Sydney, when Laver needed someone to warm him up for a match with Newcombe. But that was all. He has never played against him before, and now, on the Number One Court, Alexander feels less the hopeless odds against him than a sense of being honored to be here at all, matched against Laver in the preeminent tournament of lawn tennis. The Number One Court is one of Wimbledon's two stadiums, and it is a separate closed world, where two players are watched in proximity by seven thousand pairs of eyes. Laver is even quicker and hits harder than Alexander had imagined, and Alexander, in his nervousness, is overhitting. He lunges, swings hard, and hits wide.

Laver is so far ahead that the match has long since become an exhibition. Nonetheless, he plays every point as if it were vital. He digs for gets. He sends up topspin lobs. He sprints and dives for Alexander's smashes. He punches volleys toward the corners and, when they miss, he winces. He is not playing against Alexander. He is playing against perfection. This year, unlike other years, he does not find himself scratching for form. He feels good in general and he feels good to be here. He would rather play at Wimbledon than anywhere else at all, because, as he explains, "It's what the atmosphere instills here. At Wimbledon things come to a pitch. The best grass. The best crowd. The royalty. You all of a sudden feel the whole thing is important. You play your best tennis."

Laver, playing Alexander in the second round, is in the process of defending the Wimbledon title. In the history of this sport, no player has built a record like Laver's. There have been only three grand slams—one by Budge, two by Laver. Wimbledon is the tournament the players most want to win. It is the annual world championship. Budge won Wimbledon twice. Perry won it three times. Tilden won it three times. Laver has won Wimbledon four times, and no one at Wimbledon this afternoon has much doubt that he is on his way to his fifth championship. There are a hundred and twenty-eight men in this tournament, and a hundred and twenty-seven of them are crowded into the shadow of this one small Australian. Winning is everything to tennis players, although more than ninety-nine per cent of them are certain losers—and they expect to lose to him. Laver, who has a narrow and delicate face, freckles, a hawk's nose, thinning red hair, and the forearm of a Dungeness crab, is known to all of them as Rocket. Alexander, who is also Australian and uses a Dunlop no doubt because Laver does, has just aced the Rocket twice and leads him forty–love. To prepare for this match, Alexander hit with Roger Taylor, who is left-handed, and practiced principally serving to Taylor's backhand. Alexander serves again, to Laver's backhand. When Laver is in trouble, fury comes into his game. He lashes out now and passes Alexander on the right. He passes Alexander on the left. He carries him backward from forty–love to advantage out. Alexander runs to the net under a big serve. A crosscourt backhand goes by him so fast that his racquet does not move. In the press section, Roy McKelvie, dean of English tennis writers, notifies all the other tennis writers that beating Laver would be a feat comparable to the running of the first four-minute mile. The match is over. "Thank you," Laver says to Alexander at the net. "I played well." A person who has won two grand slams and four Wimbledons can say that becomingly. The remark is honest and therefore graceful. Alexander took four games in three sets. "I've improved. I've learned more possibilities," he says afterward. "It should help me. The improvement won't show for a while, but it is there."

Roger Taylor leans against the guardrail on the sun-deck

roof of the Players' Tea Room. He is twenty-five feet above the ground—the Players' Tea Room is raised on concrete stilts—and from that high perspective he can see almost all the lawns of Wimbledon. There are sixteen grass courts altogether, and those that are not attended with grandstands are separated by paved walkways ten feet wide. Benches line the edges of the walkways. Wimbledon is well designed. Twenty-five thousand people can move about in its confined spaces without feeling particularly crowded. Each court stands alone and the tennis can be watched at point-blank range. The whole compound is somehow ordered within ten acres and all paths eventually lead to the high front façade of the Centre Court, the name of which, like the name Wimbledon itself, is synecdochical. "Centre Court" refers not only to the *ne plus ultra* tennis lawn but also to the entire stadium that surrounds it. A three-story dodecagon with a roof that shelters most of its seats, it resembles an Elizabethan theatre. Its exterior walls are alive with ivy and in planter boxes on a balcony above its principal doorway are rows of pink and blue hydrangeas. Hydrangeas are the hallmark of Wimbledon. They are not only displayed on high but also appear in flower beds among the outer courts. In their pastel efflorescence, the hydrangeas appear to be geraniums that have escalated socially. When the Wimbledon fortnight begins each year, London newspapers are always full of purple language about the green velvet lawns and the pink and blue hydrangeas. The lawns are tough and hard and frequently somewhat brown. Their color means nothing to the players or to the ground staff, and this is one clue to the superiority of Wimbledon courts over the more lumpy but cosmetic sods of tennis lawns elsewhere. The hydrangeas, on the other hand, are strictly show business. They are purchased for the tournament.

Taylor is watching a festival of tennis from the roof of the Tea Room. Szorenyi against Morozova, Roche against Ruffels,

Brummer against O'Hara, Drysdale against Spear—he can see fourteen matches going on at the same time, and the cork-popping sound of the tennis balls fills the air. "This is the greatest tournament in the world," he says. "It is a tremendous thrill to play in it. You try to tune yourself up for it all year." Taylor is somewhat unusual among the people milling around him on the sun deck. For the most part, of course, they are aliens, and their chatter is polyglot. Hungarians, Japanese, Finns, Colombians, Greeks—they come from forty nations, while home to Taylor is a three-room flat in Putney, just up the road from Wimbledon. Taylor is a heavyset man with dark hair and a strong, quiet manner. His father is a Sheffield steel-worker. His mother taught him his tennis. And now he is seeded sixteenth at Wimbledon. It took him five sets to get out of the first round, but that does not seem to have shaken his composure. His trouble would appear to be in front of him. In the pattern of the draw, the sixteenth seed is the nearest seeded player to the number-one seed, which is tantamount to saying that Taylor's outlook is pale.

On the promenade below, a Rolls-Royce moves slowly through the crowd. It contains Charlie Pasarell, making his appearance to compete in singles. Is Pasarell so staggeringly rich that he can afford to ride to his matches in a Rolls-Royce? Yes—as it happens—but the Rolls in this case is not his. It is Wimbledon's and it has been sent by the tennis club to fetch him. Wimbledon is uniquely considerate toward players, going to great lengths to treat them as if they were plenipotentiaries from their respective nations and not gifted gibbons, which is at times their status elsewhere. Wimbledon has a whole fleet of Rolls-Royces—and Mercedes, Humbers, and Austin Prin-cesses—that deploys to all parts of London, to wherever the players happen to be staying, to collect them for their matches. Each car flies from its bonnet a small pennon in the colors of Wimbledon—mauve and green. Throughout the afternoons, these limousines enter the gates and murmur through the crowd to deliver to the locker rooms not only the Emersons, the Ashes, the Ralstons, and the Roches but also the Dowdeswelles, the Montrenauds, the Dibleys, and the Phillips-Moores.

In the Players' Tea Room, the players sit on pale-blue wicker chairs at pale-blue wicker tables eating strawberries in Devonshire cream. The tearoom is glassed-in on three sides, overlooking the courts. Hot meals are served there, to players only—a consideration absent in all other places where they play. Wimbledon is, among other things, the business convention of the tennis industry, and the tearoom is the site of a thousand deals—minor endorsements, major endorsements, commitments to tournaments over the coming year. The Players' Tea Room is the meat market of international tennis. Like bullfight impresarios converging on Madrid from all parts of Spain at the *Feria* of San Isidro, tournament directors from all parts of the world come to the Players' Tea Room at Wimbledon to bargain for—as they put it—"the horseflesh." The Tea Room also has a first-rate bar, where, frequently enough, one may encounter a first-rate bookie. His name is Jeff Guntrip. He is a trim and modest-appearing man from Kent. His credentials go far deeper than the mere fact that he is everybody's favorite bookie. Years ago, Guntrip was a tennis player. He competed at Wimbledon.

In the Members' Enclosure, on the Members' Lawn, members and their guests are sitting under white parasols, consuming best-end-of-lamb salad and strawberries in Devonshire cream. Around them are pools of goldfish. The goldfish are rented from Harrods. The members are rented from the uppermost upper middle class. Wimbledon is the annual convention of this stratum of English society, starboard out, starboard home. The middle middle class must have its strawberries and cream, too, and—in just the way that hot dogs are sold at American sporting events—strawberries and thick

Devonshire cream are sold for five shillings the dish from stalls on the Tea Lawn and in the Court Buffet. County representatives, whoever they are, eat strawberries and cream in the County Representatives' Enclosure. In the Officials' Buttery, officials, between matches, eat strawberries and cream. An occasional strawberry even makes its way into the players' locker rooms, while almost anything else except an authentic player would be squashed en route. The doors are guarded by bobbies eight feet tall with nightsticks by Hillerich & Bradsby. The ladies' dressing room at Wimbledon is so secure that only two men have ever entered it in the history of the tournament—a Frenchman and a blind masseur. The Frenchman was the great Jean Borotra, who in 1925 effected his entry into the women's locker room and subsequently lost his Wimbledon crown.

The gentlemen's dressing room is *sui generis* in the sportive world, with five trainer-masseurs in full-time attendance. Around the periphery of the locker areas are half a dozen completely private tub rooms. When players come off the courts of Wimbledon, they take baths. Huge spigots deliver hot waterfalls into pond-size tubs, and on shelves beside the tubs are long-handled scrub brushes and sponges as big as footballs. The exhausted athletes dive in, lie on their backs, stare at the ceiling, and float with victory or marinate in defeat. The tubs are the one place in Wimbledon where they can get away from one another. When they are finally ready to arrange themselves for their return to society, they find on a shelf beneath a mirror a bottle of pomade called Extract of Honey and Flowers.

Smith comes into the locker room, slowly removes his whites, and retreats to the privacy of a tub closet, where, submerged for twenty-five minutes, he contemplates the loss of one set in the course of his match with Fillol. He concludes that his trouble was the rustling ivy. Scott comes in after a

14–12 finish in a straight-set victory over Krog. Scott opens his locker. Golf balls fall out. Scott runs four miles a day through the roughs of the golf course that is just across Church Road from the tennis club—The All-England Lawn Tennis and Croquet Club, Wimbledon. Other players—Graebner, Kalogeropoulos, Diepraam, Tiriac—are dressing for other matches. Upwards of sixty matches a day are played on the lawns of Wimbledon, from two in the afternoon until sundown. The sun in the English summer takes a long time going down. Play usually stops around 8 P.M.

Leaving the locker room dressed for action, a tennis player goes in one of two directions. To the right, a wide portal with attending bobbies leads to the outer courts. To the left is a pair of frosted-glass doors that resemble the entry to an operating amphitheatre in a teaching hospital. Players going through those doors often enough feel just as they would if they were being wheeled in on rolling tables. Beyond the frosted glass is the Centre Court—with the B.B.C., the Royal Box, and fourteen thousand live spectators in close propinquity to the hallowed patch of ground on which players have to hit their way through their nerves or fall if they cannot. There is an archway between the locker room and the glass doors, and over this arch the celebrated phrase of Kipling has been painted: "IF YOU CAN MEET WITH TRIUMPH AND DISASTER AND TREAT THOSE TWO IMPOSTORS JUST THE SAME."

Rosewall is on the Number Eight Court, anesthetizing Addison. Rosewall wears on his shirt the monogram BP. What is this for? Has he changed his name? Not precisely. Here in this most august of all the milieus of tennis, here in what was once the bastion of all that was noblest and most amateur in sport, Rosewall is representing British Petroleum. Rosewall represents the oil company so thoroughly, in fact, that on the buff blazer he wears to the grounds each day, the breast pocket is also monogrammed BP. There is nothing unusual in this

respect about Rosewall. All the tennis players are walking bill-
boards. They are extensions of the outdoor-advertising industry. Almost everything they drink, wear, and carry is an ad for
some company. Laver won his grand slams with a Dunlop. He
has used a Dunlop most of his life. His first job after he left his
family's farm in Queensland was in a Dunlop factory in
Sydney, making racquets. Recently, though, he has agreed to
use Donnay racquets in certain parts of the world, and
Chemold (gold-colored metal) racquets elsewhere, for an
aggregate of about thirty thousand dollars a year. In the
United States, he still uses his Dunlops. Donnay has him
under contract at Wimbledon; however, the word among the
players is that the Rocket is still using his Dunlops but has had
them repainted to look like Donnays. Roche and Emerson are
under contract to Chemold. They also have golden racquets.
All things together, Ashe makes about a hundred and twenty-
five thousand dollars a year through such deals. He gets fifty
thousand for using the Head Competition, the racquet that
looks like a rug beater. He gets twenty-five thousand from
Coca-Cola for personal appearances arranged by the company
and for drinking Coke in public as frequently as he can, particularly when photographers happen to be shooting him. Lutz
and Smith are under contract to consume Pepsi-Cola—in like
volume but for less pay. Ask Pasarell if he likes Adidas shoes.
"I do, in Europe," he enthuses. He is paid to wear Adidas in
Europe, but in the United States he has a different deal, the
same one Lutz, Graebner, Smith, and King have, with Uni-
royal Pro Keds.

Players endorse nets, gut, artificial court surfaces, and every
item of clothing from the jock on out. Some players lately have
begun to drink—under contract—a mysterious brown fluid
called Biostrath Elixir. Made in a Swiss laboratory, it comes in
small vials and contains honey, malt, orange juice, and the
essences of ninety kinds of medicinal herbs. Others have

signed contracts to wear copper bracelets that are said to counteract voodoo, rheumatism, and arthritis. Nearly everyone's clothing contract is with one or the other of the two giants of tennis haberdashery—Fred Perry and René Lacoste. When Pilic appears in a Perry shirt and Ashe in a Lacoste shirt, they are not so much wearing these garments as advertising them. Tennis is a closed world. Its wheeler-dealers are bygone players (Kramer, Dell). Its outstanding bookie is a former player. Even its tailors, apparently, must first qualify as Wimbledon champions—Lacoste, 1925, 1928; Perry, 1934, 1935, 1936. Rosewall has somehow escaped these two. He wears neither the alligator emblem of Lacoste nor the triumphal garland of Perry. However, he is hardly in his shirt for nothing. In addition to the BP, Rosewall's shirt displays a springing panther—symbol of Slazenger. All this heraldry makes him rich before he steps onto the court, but it doesn't seem to slow him up. He is the most graceful tennis player now playing the game, and gracefully he sutures Addison, two, four, and zero.

The Russians advance in mixed doubles. Keldie and Miss Harris have taken a set from the Russians, but that is all the Russians will yield. Keldie is a devastatingly handsome tall fellow who wears tinted wrap-around glasses and has trouble returning serve. Miss Harris has no difficulty with returns. In mixed doubles, the men hit just as hard at the women as they do at each other. Miss Harris is blond, with her part in the middle and pigtails of the type that suggests windmills and canals. She is quite pretty and her body is lissome all the way to her ankles, at which point she turns masculine in Adidas shoes with three black bands. The Russians show no expressions on their faces, which are young and attractive, dark-eyed. The Soviet Union decided to go in for tennis some years ago. A program was set up. Eight Russians are now at Wimbledon, and these—Metreveli and Miss Morozova—are

the outstanding two. Both use Dunlops. They play with bal-
letic grace—remarkable, or so it seems, in people to whose
part of the world the sport is so alien. Miss Morozova, a
severely beautiful young woman, has high cheekbones and
almond eyes that suggest remote places to the east—Novo-
sibirsk, Semipalatinsk. The Russians, like so many players
from other odd parts of the earth, are camouflaged in their
playing clothes. They are haberdashed by Fred Perry, so they
appear more to come from Tennis than from Russia. Think
how bad but how distinctive they would look if their clothes
had come from GUM. Think what the Indians would look like,
the Brazilians, the Peruvians, the Japanese, if they brought
their clothes from home. Instead, they all go to Fred Perry's
stock room on Vigo Street in London and load up for the year.
The Russians are not permitted to take cash back to Russia, so
they take clothing instead and sell it when they get home.
Perry has a line of colored garments as well as white ones, and
the Russians take all that is red. Not a red shirt remains in
stock once the Russians have been to Vigo Street. Miss
Morozova fluidly hits a backhand to Keldie's feet. He picks it
up with a half volley. Metreveli puts it away. Game, set, and
match to Metreveli and Miss Morozova. No expression.

Graebner and Tiriac, on Court 3, is a vaudeville act. The
draw has put it together. Graebner, the paper salesman from
Upper Middle Manhattan, has recently changed his image. He
has replaced his horn-rimmed glasses with contact lenses, and
he has grown his soft and naturally undulant dark-brown hair
to the point where he is no longer an exact replica of Clark
Kent but is instead a living simulacrum of Prince Valiant.
Tiriac hates Wimbledon. Tiriac, who is Rumanian, feels that he
and his doubles partner, Nastase, are the best doubles team in
the world. Wimbledon disagrees. Tiriac and Nastase are not
seeded in doubles, and Tiriac is mad as hell. He hates Wimbledon and by extension he hates Graebner. So he is killing

Graebner. He has taken a set from him, now leads him in the second, and Graebner is fighting for his life. Tiriac is of middle height. His legs are unprepossessing. He has a barrel chest. His body is encased in a rug of hair. Off court, he wears cargo-net shirts. His head is covered with medusan wires. Above his mouth is a mustache that somehow suggests that this man has been to places most people do not imagine exist. By turns, he glowers at the crowd, glares at the officials, glares at God in the sky. As he waits for Graebner to serve, he leans forward, swaying. It is the nature of Tiriac's posture that he bends forward all the time, so now he appears to be getting ready to dive into the ground. Graebner hits one of his big crunch serves, and Tiriac slams it back, down the line, so fast that Graebner cannot reach it. Graebner throws his racquet after the ball. Tiriac shrugs. All the merchants of Mesopotamia could not equal Tiriac's shrug. Graebner serves again. Tiriac returns, and stays on the base line. Graebner hits a backhand that lands on the chalk beside Tiriac. "Out!" shouts the linesman. Graebner drops his racquet, puts his hands on his hips, and examines the linesman with hatred. The linesman is seventy-two years old and has worked his way to Wimbledon through a lifetime of similar decisions in Somerset, Cornwall, and Kent. But if Graebner lives to be ninety, he will never forget that call, or that face. Tiriac watches, inscrutably. Even in his Adidas shoes and his Fred Perry shirt, Tiriac does not in any way resemble a tennis player. He appears to be a panatela ad, a triple agent from Alexandria, a used-car salesman from central Marrakesh. The set intensifies. Eleven all. Twelve all. Graebner begins to chop the turf with his racquet. Rain falls. "Nothing serious," says Mike Gibson, the referee. "Play on." Nothing is serious with Gibson until the balls float. Wimbledon sometimes has six or eight showers in an afternoon. This storm lasts one minute and twenty-two seconds. The sun comes out. Tiriac snaps a backhand past Graebner, down the line. "God damn it!" Graebner shouts at him. "You're so lucky! My God!" Tiriac has the air of a man who is about to close a deal in a back room behind a back room. But Graebner, with a Wagnerian forehand, sends him spinning. Graebner, whose power is as great as ever, has continually improved as a competitor in tight places. The forehands now come in chords. The set ends 14–12, Graebner; and Graebner is still alive at Wimbledon.

When the day is over and the Rolls-Royces move off toward central London, Graebner is not in one. Graebner and his attorney waive the privilege of the Wimbledon limousines. They have something of their own—a black Daimler, so long and impressive that it appears to stop for two traffic lights at once. Graebner's attorney is Scott, who is also his doubles partner. They have just polished Nowicki and Rybarczyk off the court, 6–3, 10–12, 6–3, 6–3, and the Daimler's chauffeur takes them the fifteen miles to the Westbury, a hotel in Mayfair that is heavy with tennis players. Emerson is there, and Ashe, Ralston, Pasarell, Smith, Lutz, van Dillen. Dell and Kramer are both there. Dell, lately captain of the American Davis Cup Team, has created a principality within the anarchy of tennis. He is the attorney-manager of Ashe, Lutz, Pasarell, Smith, Kodes, and others. Dell and Kramer sit up until 3 A.M. every night picking lint off the shoulders of chaos. Their sport has no head anymore, no effective organization, and is still in the flux of transition from devious to straightforward professionalism. Kramer, who is, among other things, the most successful impresario the game has ever known, once had all the power in his pocket. Dell, who is only thirty-two, nightly tries to pick the pocket, although he knows the power is no longer there. Every so often they shout at each other. Kramer is an almost infinitely congenial man. He seems to enjoy Dell in the way that a big mother cat might regard the most aggressive of the litter—with nostalgic amusement and, now and again, a paw in the chops.

Ashe goes off to Trader Vic's for dinner dressed in a sunburst dashiki, and he takes with him two dates. Ralston joins them, and raises an eyebrow. "There is no conflict here," Ashe says, calmly spreading his hands toward the two women. Later in the evening, Ashe will have still another date, and she will go with him to a casino, where they will shoot craps and play blackjack until around 1 A.M., when Ashe will turn into a tennis player and hurry back to the hotel to get his sleep.

In his flat in Dolphin Square, Laver spends the evening, as he does most evenings, watching Western films on television. Many players take flats while they are in England, particularly if they are married. They prefer familial cooking to the tedium of room service. Some stay in boardinghouses. John Alexander and fifteen other Australians are in a boardinghouse in Putney. Dolphin Square is a vast block of flats, made of red brick, on the Embankment overlooking the Thames. Laver sits there in the evening in front of the television set, working the grips of his racquets. He wraps and rewraps the grips, trying for just the right feel in his hand. If the movie finishes and some commentator comes on and talks tennis, Laver turns him off and rotates the selector in quest of additional hoofbeats. He unwraps a new grip for the third or fourth time and begins to shave the handle with a kitchen knife. He wraps the grip again, feels it, moves the racquet through the arc of a backhand, then unwraps the grip and shaves off a little more wood.

Gonzales sometimes drills extremely small holes in his racquets, to change the weight. Gonzales, who is not always consistent in his approach to things, sometimes puts lead tape on his racquets to increase the weight. Beppe Merlo, the Italian tennis player, strings his own racquets, and if a string breaks while he is playing, he pulls gut out of his cover and repairs the damage right there on the court. Merlo likes to string his racquets at thirty pounds of tension—each string as tight as it would be if it were tied to a rafter and had a thirty-pound weight hanging on it. Since most players like their racquets at sixty pounds minimum, Merlo is extremely eccentric. He might as well be stringing snowshoes. When someone serves to him, the ball disappears into his racquet. Eventually, it comes out, and it floats back toward his opponent like a milkweed seed. Merlo's game does not work at all well on grass. He is fantastic on clay.

Many players carry their own sets of gut with them. Professional stringers do the actual work, of course, using machines that measure the tension. Emerson likes his racquets at sixty-three pounds, very tight, and so does Smith. Since the frame weight of "medium" tennis racquets varies from thirteen to thirteen and three-quarters ounces, Smith goes to the Wilson factory whenever he can and weighs and feels racquets until he has selected a stack of them. He kills a racquet in six weeks. The thing doesn't break. It just becomes flaccid and dies. Strings go dead, too. They last anywhere from ten to twenty-eight days. Smith likes a huge grip—four and seven-eighths inches around. Some Americans wrap tape around their handles to build them up, and then they put new leather grips on. Australians generally like them smaller, four and five-eighths, four and a half. As Laver whittles away beside the television, he is progressing toward four and a half. When he is ready to go to bed, he switches off the television and, beside it, leaves a little pile of wood chips and sawdust on the floor.

Dennis Ralston carries his own pharmacy with him wherever he goes—Achromycin, Butazolidin, Oxazepam, Robaxin, Sodium Butabarbital. He is ready for anything, except sleep. The night before a match, he lies with a pillow over his head and fights total awareness. At 3 A.M., he complains bitterly about the traffic on New Bond Street, outside the Westbury. There is no traffic on New Bond Street outside the Westbury. Mayfair is tranquil in the dead of night, even if the tennis players are not. All over London, tennis players are staring open-eyed at dark ceilings. Some of them get up in the night and walk around talking to themselves—while Laver sleeps in Dolphin Square. Laver can sleep anywhere—in cars, trains, planes. He goes to bed around 1 A.M., and always sets an alarm clock or he would oversleep, even before a final.

Laver becomes quieter before a match. He and his wife, Mary, ordinarily laugh and joke and kid around a lot together, but he becomes silent as a match draws near. "The faster the pace, the more demands there are upon him, the better," she says. So Laver goes out in the morning and does the shopping. He drops off the laundry. Sometimes he washes clothes in the bathtub. He goes to his favorite butcher and buys a steak. He also buys eggs and greens. Back in the flat, two and a half hours before the match, he cooks his training meal. It is always the same—steak, eggs, and greens. He likes to cook, and prefers to do it himself. It keeps him busy. Then he gets into his car—a hired English Ford—and drives to Wimbledon. He ignores the club limousines. He wants to drive. "If he weren't a tennis player, he'd be a road racer," Mary says. "He has a quick, alert mind. He's fast. He's fast of body, and his mind works that way as well. The faster the pace of things, the faster he moves." He particularly likes driving on the left-hand side of the road. It reminds him of Australia, of which he sees very little anymore. His home is in California. Each day, he plots a different route through Greater South London to Wimbledon. This is his private rally. It is a rule of the tournament that if a player is so much as ten minutes late his opponent wins by a walkover. Laver knows his labyrinth— every route alternative, every mews and byway, between the Embankment and the tennis club, and all the traffic of London has yet to stop him. He turns off Church Road into the parking lot. His mind for many hours has been preoccupied with things other than tennis, with cowboys and sleep and shopping lists and cooking and driving. He never ponders a draw or thinks about an opponent. But now he is ready to concentrate his interest on the game—for example, on Wimbledon's opening day, when the defending champion starts the tournament with a match in the Centre Court.

Laver walks under the Kipling line and through the glass doors, and fourteen thousand people stand up and applaud him, for he is the most emphatic and enduring champion who has ever played on this court. He stacks his extra racquets against the umpire's chair, where the tournament staff has placed bottles of orange squash and of Robinson's Lemon Barley Water should he or his opponent require them during change-overs. There is plain water as well, in a jug called the Bartlett Multipot. Behind the umpire's chair is a green refrigerator, where tennis balls are kept until they are put into play. A ball boy hands him two and Laver takes the court. He swings easily through the knockup. The umpire says, "Play." Laver lifts his right hand, sending the first ball up into the air, and the tournament is under way. He swings, hits. His opponent can barely touch the ball with his racquet. It is a near ace, an unplayable serve, fifteen–love. Laver's next serve scythes into the backhand court. It is also unplayable. Thirty-love.

The man across the net is extremely nervous. His name is George Seewagen. He comes from Bayside, New York. This is his first Wimbledon and his friends have told him that if you don't get a game in the first round, you never get invited back. Seewagen would like to get two games. At Forest Hills thirty-four years ago, Seewagen's father played J. Donald Budge in the opening round. The score was 6–0, 6–1, 6–0. When Seewagen, Jr., arrived in London, he was, like nearly everyone else, tense about the luck of the coming draw, and before it was published he told his doubles partner, "Watch me. I'll have to play Laver in the Centre Court in the first round." The

odds were 111 to 1 that this would not happen, but Seewagen
had read the right tea leaf, as he soon learned.

"It was hard to believe. I sort of felt a little bit upset.
Moneywise, London's pretty expensive. First-round losers get
a hundred pounds and that's not much. I figured I needed to
win at least one match in order to meet my expenses, but now
I'd had it. Then I thought of the instant recognition. People
would say, 'There's the guy that's opening up Wimbledon with
Laver.' At least my name would become known. But then, on
the other hand, I thought, What if I don't get a game? Think
of it. What if I don't win even one game?'"

Seewagen is an extremely slender—in fact, thin—young
man with freckles, a toothy grin, tousled short hair. He could
be Huckleberry Finn. He looks nineteen and is actually twenty-
three. His credentials are that he played for Rice University,
that he beat someone named Zan Guerry in the final of an
amateur championship in Rochester, and that he is the varsity
tennis coach at Columbia University. There were, in other
words, grounds for his gnawing fears. By the eve of Wimbledon, Seewagen's appearance was gaunt.

Everyone goes to Hurlingham on that ultimate Sunday
afternoon. All through the previous fortnight, the tennis
players of the world have gradually come to London, and by
tradition they first convene at Hurlingham. Hurlingham is a
Victorian sporting club with floor-to-ceiling windows, sixteen
chimney pots, and wide surrounding lawns—bowling lawns,
tennis lawns, croquet lawns, putting lawns—under giant
copper beeches, beside the Thames. Some players play informal sets of doubles. Others merely sit on the lawns, sip
Pimm's Cups under the sun, and watch women in pastel
dresses walking by on maroon pathways. In the background
are people in their seventies, dressed in pure white, tapping
croquet balls with deadly skill across textured grasses smooth

as broadloom. A uniformed band, with folding chairs and music stands, plays "Bow, Bow, Ye Lower Middle Classes" while tea is served beneath the trees—a strawberry tart, sandwiches, petits fours, fruitcake, and a not-so-bitter macaroon. Arthur Ashe, eating his tea, drinking the atmosphere, says, "This is my idea of England." On a slope a short distance away, Graham Stillwell, Ashe's first-round opponent, sits with his wife and his five-year-old daughter, Tiffany. This is the second straight year that Ashe has drawn Stillwell in the first round at Wimbledon, and last year Stillwell had Ashe down and almost out—twice Stillwell was serving for the match—before Ashe won the fifth set, 12–10. Reporters from the *Daily Mirror* and the *Daily Sketch* now come up to Ashe and ask him if he has been contacted by certain people who plan to demonstrate against the South African players at Wimbledon. "Why should they contact me?" Ashe says. "I'm not a South African." Mrs. Stillwell rises from the sloping lawn and stretches her arms. "My God! She's pregnant again," Ashe observes. Jean Borotra, now seventy-two, is hitting beautiful ground strokes with Gardnar Mulloy. Borotra wears long white trousers. Two basset hounds walk by, leashed to a man in a shirt of broad pink and white stripes. The band is playing the music of Albéniz. The lady tennis players drift about, dressed, for some reason, in multicolored Victorian gowns. Laver, in dark slacks and a sport shirt of motley dark colors, stands near the clubhouse, watching it all with his arms folded. He seems uncomfortable. He looks incongruous— small, undynamic, unprepossessing, vulnerable—but every eye at Hurlingham, sooner or later in the afternoon, watches him in contemplation. He stands out no more than a single blade of grass, but no one fails to see him, least of all Seewagen, who stands at the edge of the party like a figure emerging from a haunted forest. He wears an old worn-out pair of lightweight sneakers, of the type that tennis players do not use and sailors do, and a baggy gray sweater with the sleeves shoved far up his thin brown arms. Veins stand out on the backs of his hands and across his forearms. He grins a little, but his eyes are sober. His look is profoundly philosophical. Gene Scott informs him that players scheduled for the Centre Court are entitled to a special fifteen minutes of practice on an outside court beforehand. "Good, I'll take McManus," Seewagen says. McManus, from Berkeley and ranked tenth in the United States, is left-handed. He is also short and redheaded. He has the same build Laver has, much the same nose and similar freckles as well. Players practicing with McManus easily fantasize that they are hitting with the Rocket himself, and thus they inflate their confidence. McManus is the favorite dummy of everyone who has to play against Laver. Ashe speaks quietly to Seewagen and tells him not to worry. "You'll never play better," Ashe says. "You'll get in there, in the Centre Court, and you'll get inspired, and then when the crowd roars for your first great shot, you'll want to run into the locker room and call it a day."

"I hope it isn't a wood shot," says Seewagen, looking straight ahead.

Game to Laver. He leads, one game to love, first set. Laver and Seewagen change ends of the court. Laver went out to the Pontevecchio last night, on the Old Brompton Road. He ate lasagna and a steak *filet* with tomato sauce. He drank Australian beer. Then he went home and whittled a bit before retiring. At Chesham House, in Victoria, Seewagen fell asleep in his bed reading *Psycho Cybernetics*, by Maxwell Maltz. After one game, Seewagen has decided that Laver is even better than he thought he was. Laver is, for one thing, the fastest of all tennis players. He moves through more square yards per second than anyone else, covering ground like a sonic boom. In his tennis clothes, he is not unprepossessing. His legs are powerfully muscled. His left forearm looks as if it could bring down a tree. He is a great shotmaker, in part because he moves so well. He has every shot from everywhere. He can hurt his opponent from any position. He has extraordinary racquet-handling ability because his wrist is both strong and flexible. He can come over his backhand or slice it. He hits big shots, flick shots, spin shots, and rifle shots on the dead run. He lobs well. He serves well. His forehand is the best in tennis. He has one weakness. According to Gonzales, that is, Laver has one weakness—his bouncing overhead. The bouncing overhead is the shot a tennis player hits when a bad lob bounces at his feet and he cannon-balls his helpless opponent. Gonzales is saying that Laver has no weaknesses at all. Seewagen walks to the base line, visibly nervous, and prepares to serve. He is not pathetic. There is something tingling about a seven-hundred-to-one shot who merely shows up at the gate. In the end, at the net, Laver, shaking hands, will say to him gently, "You looked nervous. It's very difficult playing in here the first time over." Seewagen begins with a double fault. Love–fifteen. Now, however, a deep atavistic athleticism rises in him and defeats his nerves. He serves, rushes, and punches two volleys past Laver, following them with an unplayable serve. Forty–fifteen. Serve, rush, volley—game to Mr. Seewagen. Games are one all, first set.

"His topspin is disguised," Seewagen notes, and he prepares, with a touch of unexpected confidence, for Laver's next service assault. Game to Mr. Laver. He leads, two games to one, first set. Seewagen now rises again, all the way to forty–fifteen, from which level he is shoved back to deuce. Tossing up the ball, he cracks a serve past Laver that Laver can barely touch, let alone return. Advantage Seewagen. The source of all this power is not apparent, but it is coming from somewhere. He lifts the ball. He blasts. Service ace. Right through the corner. The crowd roars. It is Seewagen's first great shot. He looks at the scoreboard—two all—and it gives him what he will describe later as a charge. ("At that moment, I should have walked off.") 6–2, 6–0, 6–2.

Hewitt, in anger, hits one into the grandstand and it goes straight toward an elderly lady. She makes a stabbing catch with one hand and flips the ball to a ball boy. There is nothing lightweight about this English crowd. Ted Heath, Margaret, Anne, Charles, Lady Churchill, and the odd duke or baron might turn up—diverting attention to the Royal Box—but withal one gets the impression that there is a high percentage of people here who particularly know where they are and what they are looking at. They queue for hours for standing room in the Centre Court. They miss nothing and they are polite. The crowd at Forest Hills likes dramaturgy and emotion—players thanking God after chalk-line shots or falling to their knees in total despair—and the crowd in the Foro Italico throws cushions. But the British do not actually approve of that sort of thing, and when one of the rogue tennis players exhibits conduct they do not like, they cry, "Shame!"

"You bloody fools!" Hewitt shouts at them.

Hewitt has the temper of a grenade. He hits another ball in anger. This time it goes over the roof and out of sight. "Shame, Hewitt, shame!"

Rain falls. Umbrellas bloom. Mike Gibson's mustache is drooping from the wet, but he says, "Play on. It's not much." All matches continue. The umbrellas are black, red, green, yellow, orange, pink, paisley, and transparent. It is cold at Wimbledon. It often is—shirt sleeves one day, two pullovers and a mack the next. Now the players are leaving water tracks on the courts, and Gibson at last suspends play. Groundsmen take down the nets and cover the lawns with canvas. The standees do not give up their places, in the cold rain. The groundsmen go in under the grandstand to the Groundsmen's Bar, where they drink lager and offer one another cigarettes. "Will you have a smoke, Jack, or would you rather have the money?" The sun comes out for exactly three minutes. Then more rain falls. Half an hour later, play resumes.

Dell is supposed to be on Court 14, playing mixed doubles, but he is still in a phone booth talking to the office of Guntrip the bookie. Dell bets heavily on his own players—a hundred pounds here, two hundred there—and even more heavily against Laver. Dell is a talented gambler and he views the odds as attractive. Besides, Dell and Laver are the same age, and Dell can remember beating Laver when they were boys. Shrewd and realistic, Dell reasons that anyone who ever lost to Donald Dell cannot be invincible. In the end, he repeats his name to the clerk at Guntrip's, to be sure the clerk has it right. "Dell," he says. "D as in David, E as in Edward, L as in loser, L as in loser."

The field of women players is so thin that even some of the women themselves are complaining. Chubby little girls with orange ribbons in their hair hit parabolic ground strokes back and forth and seem incongruous on courts adjacent to an Emerson, a Lutz, or a Pasarell, whose ground strokes sound like gunfire. Billie Jean King slaps a serve into the net and cries out, "That stinks!" Billie Jean is trimmer, lighter, more feminine than she was in earlier years, and somehow less convincing as a challenger to Margaret Court. Yet everyone else seems far below these two. Miss Goolagong is still a few years away. "Have you seen the abo, Jack?" says Robert Twynam, head groundsman, to his assistant, John Yardley. The interesting new players are the ones the groundsmen find interesting. They go to watch Miss Goolagong and they notice that her forehand has a tendency to go up and then keep going up. When it starts coming down, they predict, she will be ready for anybody, for her general game is smooth and quite strong and unflinchingly Australian. Australians never give up, and this one is an aborigine, a striking figure with orange-brown hair and orange-brown skin, in a Teddy Tinling dress and

Adidas shoes, with a Dunlop in her hand. Margaret Court is breaking everything but the cool reserve of Helga Niessen, the Berlin model. Between points, Miss Niessen stands with her feet crossed at the ankles. The ankles are observed by a Chinese medical student who is working the tournament with the ground staff. "Look at those ankles. Look at those legs," he says. "She is a woman." He diverts his attention to Margaret Court, who is five feet eight, has big strong hands, and, most notably, the ripple-muscled legs of a runner. "Look at those legs," says the Chinese medical student. "The lady is a man."

Hoad, in the Centre Court, is moving so slowly that a serve bounces toward him and hits him in the chest. The server is El Shafei, the chocolate-eyed Egyptian. Hoad is in here because all Britain wants to see him on television. Stiffened by time and injury, he loses two sets before his cartilage begins to bend. In the third set, his power comes, and he breaks the Egyptian. The Egyptian is a heavy-framed man, like Hoad, and in the fourth set, they pound each other, drive for drive—wild bulls of the tennis court. Hoad thinks he is getting bad calls and enormous anger is rising within him. The score is three all. Shafei is serving, at deuce. He lifts the ball and blows one past Hoad for a service ace. Hoad looks toward the net-cord judge with expanding disbelief. He looks toward Shafei, who has not moved from the position from which he hit the serve—indicating to Hoad that Shafei expected to hit a second one. Slowly, Hoad walks forward, toward the officials, toward Shafei, toward the center of the court. The crowd is silent. Hoad speaks. A microphone in Scotland could pick up what he says. "That god-damned ball was a let!" The net-cord judge is impassive. The umpire says, "May I remind you that play is continuous." Hoad replies, repeats, "That god-damned ball was a let!" He turns to the Egyptian. Unstirring silence is still the response of the crowd, for one does not throw hammers back at Thor. "The serve was a let. You know that. Did you hear it hit the tape?" Hoad asks, and Shafei says, "No." Hoad lifts his right arm, extends it full length, and points steadily at the Egyptian's eyes. "You lie!" he says slowly, delivering each syllable to the roof. A gulf of quiet follows, and Hoad does not lower his arm. He draws a breath slowly, then says again, even more slowly, "You lie." Only Garrick could have played that one. It must have stirred bones in the Abbey, and deep in the churchyards of Wimbledon, for duels of great moment here have reached levels more serious than sport. This is where Canning fought Castlereagh, where Pitt fought Tierney, where Lord Winchelsea fought the Duke of Wellington. Ceawlin of the West Saxons fought Ethelbert of Kent here, when the terrain was known as Wibbas dune— home of the Saxon, Wibba (Wibbas dune, Wipandune, Wilbaldowne, Wymblyton). Hoad returns to the base line, and when the Egyptian serves again, Hoad breaks him into pieces. Game and fourth set to Hoad. Sets are two all. In his effort, though, Hoad has given up the last of his power. Time has defeated him. Twice the champion, he has failed his comeback. His energy drains away in the fifth set—his last, in all likelihood, at Wimbledon.

Ralston, at the umpire's chair, pries the cap off a vial of Biostrath and sucks out the essences of the ninety medicinal herbs. Dennis has no contract with Biostrath. He is not drinking the stuff for money. He is drinking it for his life. Beside him stands his opponent, John Newcombe, the secondbest forehand, the second-best volley, the second-best tennis player in the world. Dennis follows the elixir with a PepsiCola, also without benefit of a contract. The score is 4–5, first set. Ralston and Newcombe return to the base lines, and Ralston tosses up a ball to serve. The crowd is chattering, gurgling like a mountain stream. Prince Charles has just come in and is settling into his seat. "Quiet, please," says the umpire, and the stream subsides. Ralston serves, wins—six all. Seven

all. Eight all. Nine all. Ten all. There is a lot of grinning back
and forth across the net. Newcombe drives a backhand down
the line. Ralston leaps, intercepts it, and drops the ball into
Newcombe's court for a winner. Newcombe looks at Ralston.
Ralston grins. Newcombe smiles back. It is an attractive
match, between two complete professionals. Newcombe passes
Ralston with a forehand down the line. "Yep," says Ralston.
Ralston finds a winner in a drop shot overhead. "Good shot,"
calls Newcombe. Eleven all. When they shout, it is at themselves. Newcombe moves to the net behind a fragile approach
shot, runs back under a humiliatingly good lob, and drives an
off-balance forehand into the net. "John!" he calls out. "Idi-
otic!" Ralston tosses a ball up to serve, but catches it instead of
hitting it. He is having a problem with the sun, and he pauses
to apologize to Newcombe for the inconvenience the delay
might be causing him. Small wonder they can't beat each
other. Grace of this kind has not always been a characteristic
of Ralston—of Newcombe, yes, but Ralston grew up tightly
strung in California, and in his youth his tantrums were a
matter of national report. He is twenty-seven now and has
changed. Quiet, serious, introspective, coach of the U.S. Davis
Cup Team, he has become a professional beyond the imagination of most people who only knew him long ago. He plans his
matches almost on a drawing board. Last night, he spent
hours studying a chart he has made of every shot Newcombe
has hit in this tournament. 13–12. Dennis opens another
Biostrath and another Pepsi-Cola. He knows what the odds
have become. The winner of this set, since it has gone so far,
will in all likelihood be the winner of the match. Ralston has
been a finalist at Wimbledon. But he has never won a major
international tournament. In such tournaments, curiously
enough, he has played Newcombe ten times and has won
seven, but never for the biggest prize. Newcombe has a faculty
for going all the way. Ralston, meanwhile, has pointed his life

toward doing so at least once, and, who knows, he tells himself, this could be the time. He toes the line and tosses up the ball. He catches it, and tosses it up again. The serve is bad. The return is a winner. Love–fifteen. He has more trouble with the sun. Love–thirty. Catastrophe is falling from nowhere. Love–forty. Serve, return, volley. Fifteen–forty. He serves. Fault. He serves again. Double fault. Game and first set to Newcombe, 14–12. Ralston looks up, over the trigger of a thousand old explosions, and he forces a smile. 14–12, 9–7, 6–2. When it is over, the ball boys carry out seven empty bottles of Pepsi-Cola and four empty vials of the ninety medicinal herbs.

Kramer is in a glassed-in booth at one corner of the court, commenting on the action for the BBC. For an American to be engaged to broadcast to the English, extraordinary credentials, of one kind or another, are required. Just after the Second World War, Kramer first displayed his. Upwards of fifty American players now come to Wimbledon annually, but Kramer, in 1946, was one of three to cross the ocean. "Now it's a sort of funsy, 'insy' thing to do," he has said. "But in my time, if you didn't think you had a top-notch chance, you didn't come over. To make big money out of tennis, you had to have the Wimbledon title as part of your credits. I sold my car, a 1941 Chevrolet, so I could afford to bring my wife, Gloria, with me." That was long before the era of the Perry-Lacoste-Adidas bazaar, and Kramer, at Wimbledon, wore his own clothes—shorts that he bought at Simpson's and T-shirts that had been issued to him during the war, when he was a sailor in the United States Coast Guard. Now, as he watches the players before him and predicts in his expert way how one or the other will come slowly unstuck, he looks past them across the court and up behind the Royal Box into an entire segment of the stadium that was gone when he first played here. At some point between 1939 and 1945, a bomb hit the All-

England tennis club, and with just a little more wind drift it would have landed in the center of the Centre Court. Instead, it hit the roof over the North East Entrance Hall. Kramer remembers looking up from the base line, ready to serve, into a background of avalanched rubble and twisted girders against the sky. He slept in the Rembrandt, which he remembers as "an old hotel in South Kensington," and he ate steak that he had brought with him from the United States, thirty pounds or so of whole tenderloins. Needless to say, there was no Rolls-Royce flying Wimbledon colors to pick him up at the Rembrandt. Kramer went to Wimbledon, with nearly everyone else, on the underground—Gloucester Road, Earl's Court, Fulham Broadway, Parsons Green, Putney Bridge, East Putney, Southfields, Wimbledon. He lost the first time over. A year later, he returned with his friend Tom Brown, and together they hit their way down opposite sides of the draw and into the Wimbledon final. A few hours before the match, Kramer took what remained of his current supply of *filet mignon*, cut it in half, and shared it with Tom Brown. Kramer was twenty-five and his game had come to full size—the Big Game, as it was called, the serve, the rush, the jugular volley. When Kramer proved what he could do, at Wimbledon, he changed for all foreseeable time the patterns of the game. He destroyed Brown in forty-seven minutes, still the fastest final in Wimbledon's history, and then—slender, crewcut, big in the ears—he was led to the Royal Box for a word or two with the King and Queen. The Queen said to him, "Whatever happened to that redheaded young man?" And Kramer told her that Donald Budge was alive and doing O.K. The King handed Kramer the Wimbledon trophy. "Did the court play well?" the King asked him. "Yes, it did, sir," Kramer answered. It was a tennis player's question. In 1926, the King himself had competed in this same tournament and had played in the Centre Court. A faraway smile rests on Kramer's face as he remembers all this. "Me in my T-shirt," he says, with a slight shake of his head.

Frew McMillan, on Court 2, wears a golfer's billowing white visored cap, and he looks very much like a golfer in his style of play, for he swings with both hands and when he completes a stroke, his arms follow the racquet across one shoulder and his eyes seem to be squinting down a fairway. Court 2 has grandstands on either side and they are packed with people. McMillan is a low-handicap tennis player who can dig some incredible ground strokes out of the rough. A ball comes up on his right side and he drives it whistling down the line, with a fading hook on the end. The ball comes back on his left side, and, still with both hands, overlapping grip, he hits a cross-court controlled-slice return for a winner. The gallery applauds voluminously. McMillan volleys with two hands. The only strokes he hits with one hand are the serve and the overhead. He has an excellent chip shot and a lofty topspin wedge. He putts well. He is a lithe, dark, attractive, quiet South African. In the South African Open, he played Laver in the final. Before Laver had quite figured out what sort of a match it was, McMillan had him down one set to nought. Then Laver got out his mashie and that was the end of McMillan in the South African Open. When McMillan arrived in London and saw the Wimbledon draw, he felt, in his words, a cruel blow, because his name and Laver's were in the same pocket of the draw, and almost inevitably they would play in the third round. "But maybe I have a better chance against him earlier than later," he finally decided. "You feel you have a chance. You have to—even if it is a hundred to one." Now the grandstands are jammed in Court 2, and, high above, the railing is crowded on the Tea Room roof, for McMillan, after losing the first set, has broken Laver and leads him 5–3 in the second.

"I got the feeling during the match that I had more of a chance beating him on the court than thinking about it beforehand. You realize the chap isn't infallible. It's almost as if I detected a chip in his armor."

Laver has netted many shots and has hit countless others wide or deep. He cannot find the lines. He is preoccupied with his serves, which are not under control. He spins one in too close to the center of the service box. McMillan blasts it back. Advantage McMillan. Laver lifts the ball to serve again. Fault. He serves again. Double fault. Game and set to McMillan, 6–3.

When this sort of thing happens, Laver's opponent seldom lives to tell the tale. One consistent pattern in all the compiled scores in his long record is that when someone takes a set from him, the score of the next set is 6–0, Laver, or something very near it. Affronted, he strikes twice as hard. "He has the physical strength to hit his way through nervousness," McMillan says. "That's why I believe he's a great player."

Laver breaks McMillan in the opening game of the third set. He breaks him again in the third game. His volleys hit the corners. His drives hit the lines. McMillan's most powerful blasts come back at him faster than they left his racquet. McMillan hits a perfect drop shot. Laver is on it like the light. He snaps it unreachably down the line. Advantage Laver. McMillan hits one deep to Laver's backhand corner, and Laver, diving as he hits it, falls. McMillan sends the ball to the opposite corner. Laver gets up and sprints down the base line. He not only gets to the ball—with a running forehand rifle shot, he puts it away. It is not long before he is shaking McMillan's hand at the net. "Well played," McMillan says to him (6–2, 3–6, 6–0, 6–2). "Yes, I thought I played pretty well," Laver tells him. And they make their way together through the milling crowd. McMillan will frequently say what a gentle and modest man he finds Laver to be. "It may be why he is what he is," McMillan suggests. "You can see it in his eyes."

B. M. L. de Roy van Zuydewijn is a loser in the Veterans'

Event—gentlemen's doubles. So is the seventy-two-year-old Borotra. Riggs and Drobny, on Court 5, persevere. Over the years, Riggs and Drobny have eaten well. Each is twice the shadow of his former self. The Hungarians Bujtor and Stolpa are concentrating on Riggs as the weaker of the two.

Game to Seewagen and Miss Overton, the honey-blond Miss Overton. They lead Dell and Miss Johnson five games to four, second set. Dell is not exactly crumbling under the strain. These peripheral matches are fairly informal. Players talk to one another or to their friends on the side lines, catching up on the news. Seewagen and Miss Overton appear to be playing more than tennis. Dell is tired—up half the night making deals and arguing with Kramer, up early in the morning to do business over breakfast with bewildered Europeans, who find him in his hotel room in a Turkish-towel robe, stringy-haired and wan, a deceptive glaze in his eyes, offering them contracts written on flypaper.

The Russians enter the Centre Court to play mixed doubles. Princess Anne is in the Royal Box. The Russians hesitate, and look at each other in their ceramic way, and then they grin, they shrug, and they turn toward the Royal Box and bend their heads. The people applaud.

Nastase is Nijinsky—leaping, flying, hitting jump-shot overheads, sweeping forehands down the line. Tiriac is in deep disgrace. Together they have proved their point. They have outlasted most of the seeded pairs in the gentlemen's doubles. But now they are faltering against Rosewall and Stolle, largely because Tiriac is playing badly. Stolle hits an overhead. Tiriac tries to intercept it near the ground. He smothers it into the court. Nastase, behind him, could have put the ball away after it had bounced. Tiriac covers his face with one hand and rubs his eyes. He slinks back to the base line like someone caught red-handed. But now he redeems himself. The four players close in for a twelve-shot volley, while the ball never touches the ground. It is Tiriac who hits number twelve, picking it off at the hip and firing it back through Stolle.

Lutz crashes, and the injury appears to be serious. Playing doubles in the Centre Court with his partner, Smith, he chases an angled overhead, and he crashes into the low wall at the front of the grandstand. He makes no effort to get up. He quivers. He is unconscious. "Get a doctor, please," says the umpire. A nurse, in a white cap and a gray uniform that nearly reaches her ankles, hurries across the lawn. The crowd roars with laughter. There is something wondrous in the English sense of humor that surfaces in the presence of accidents, particularly if they appear to be fatal. The laughter revives Lutz. He comes to, gets up, returns to the court, shakes his head a few times, resumes play, and drives a put-away into the corner after an eight-shot ricochet volley. Lutz is tough. He was a high school football player in California and he once promised himself that he would quit tennis and concentrate on football unless he should happen to win the national junior championship. He won, and gave up football. Additional medical aid comes from outside the stadium. Another nurse has appeared. She hovers on the edge of play. When she sees an opportunity, she hurries up to Smith and gives him an aspirin.

If Lutz had broken three ribs, he would not have mentioned it as long as he continued to play, and in this respect he is like the Australians. There is an Australian code on the matter of injuries, and it is one of the things that gives the Australians a stature that is not widely shared by the hypochondriac Americans and the broken-wing set from mainland Europe. The Australian code is that you do not talk about injuries, you hide them. If you are injured, you stay out, and if you play, you are not injured. The Australians feel contempt for players who put their best injury forward. An Australian will say of such a man, "I have never beaten him when he was healthy." Laver developed a bad wrist a year or so ago, at Wimbledon, and he and his wife got into a telephone kiosk so that she could tape the wrist in secrecy. If he had taped it himself, no one would ever have known the story. His wife would rather praise him than waltz with the Australian code. His wife is an American.

"Bad luck, Roger." This is what Roger Taylor's friends are saying to him, because he has to play Laver, in the fourth round, in the Centre Court tomorrow. The champion always plays in one of the two stadiums or on the Number Two Court, the only places that can take in all the people who want to see him. "Don't worry, though, Roger. It's no disgrace if Rocket is the man who puts you out. You've got nothing to lose."

"I've got everything to lose," Taylor tells them. "To lose at Wimbledon is to lose. This is what competition is all about. You've got to think you have a chance. You might hope for twenty-five let cords or something, but you always think there's a chance you'll get through."

"Bad luck, Roger."

Roger takes a deep hot bath, goes home to his two-bedroom flat on Putney Hill, and continues to work himself up, talking to his mother, his father, and his wife, over a glass of beer.

"That's enough beer, Roger."

"I don't live like a monk. I want to loosen up." He eats a slice of fried liver and opens another beer. "All my chances will hinge on how well I serve. I'll have to serve well to him, to keep him a little off balance on his returns. If I can't do that, I'll be in dire trouble. If you hit the ball a million miles an hour, he hits it back harder. You can't beat a player like that with sheer speed—unless he's looking the other way. I plan to float back as many service returns as I can. The idea is not to let it get on top of you that you're going to play these people. There's a tendency to sort of lie down and roll over."

Games are three all, first set. Taylor feels weak from tension.

Laver is at ease. "We'd played often enough," Laver will say later. "I knew his game—left-handed, slice serve, better forehand than backhand, a good lob. He's very strong. He moves well for a big man. There was no special excitement. My heart wasn't pounding quite as hard as it sometimes does."

Taylor floats back a service return, according to plan. Laver reaches high, hits a semi-overhead volley, and the ball lands in the exact corner of the court. It bounces into the stadium wall. The crowd roars for him, but he is also hitting bad shots. There is a lack of finish on his game. He wins the first set, 6–4.

"My concentration lapsed continually. I was aware of too many things—the troublesome wind, the court being dry and powdery. I magnified the conditions. I played scratchy in the first set. I felt I'd get better in the next set."

A break point rises against Laver in the first game of the second set. He lifts the ball to serve. He hits it into the net. "Fault." He spins the next one—into the net. "Double fault." "Oh, just throw it up and hit it," he says aloud to himself, thumping his fist into the strings of his racquet.

"When you lose your rhythm, serving, it's because of lack of concentration. I found myself thinking too much where the ball should be going. You don't think about your serve, you think about your first volley. If you think about getting your serve in, you make errors. I didn't know where my volleys were going. I missed easy smashes."

Taylor is floating back his returns. He is keeping Laver off balance. With his ground strokes, he is hitting through the wind. There is an explosion of applause for him when he wins the second set, 6–4. No one imagines that he will do more, but it is enough that Taylor, like McMillan, has won a set from Laver—and more than enough that he is English.

"Roger was playing some good tennis. When I played fairly well, he played better."

First game, third set—love–forty—Laver serving. There is chatter in the crowd, the sound of the mountain stream. "Quiet, please!" Laver hits his way back to thirty–forty. He serves, rushes, and punches a volley down the line—out. Game and another service break to Taylor. Five times, Laver has hit his running rifle-shot forehand into the net. He has repeatedly double-faulted. His dinks fall short. His volleys jump the base line. Taylor, meanwhile, is hitting with touch and power. He is digging for everything. Laver is not covering the court. Both feet off the ground, Laver tries a desperation shot from the hip, and he nets it. Advantage Taylor. Taylor serves—a near ace, unplayable. Game and third set to Taylor, 6–2. He leads two sets to one. Unbelievable. Now the time has certainly come for Laver to react, as he so often does, with vengeance.

"When your confidence is drained, you tend to do desperation shots. My desperation shots, a lot of times, turn matches. I felt something was gone. I didn't have strength to get to the net quickly. I can't explain what it was. If you're not confident, you have no weight on the ball. You chase the ball. You look like a cat on a hot tin roof."

Laver serves, moves up, and flips the volley over the base line. "Get it down!" he shouts to himself. His next volley goes over the base line. Now he double-faults. Now he moves under a high, soft return. He punches it into a corner. Taylor moves to the ball and sends it back, crosscourt. Laver, running, hits a rolling top-spin backhand—over the base line. Advantage Taylor. Break point. The whispering of the crowd has become the buzz of scandal.

His red hair blowing in the wind, Laver lifts the ball to serve against the break. Suddenly, he looks as fragile as he did at Hurlingham and the incongruity is gone. The spectators on whom this moment is making the deepest impression are the other tennis players—forty or so in the grandstands, dozens more by the television in the Players' Tea Room. Something in them is coming free. The man is believable. He is vulnerable. He has never looked more human. He is not invincible.

"The serve is so much of the game. If you serve well, you play well. If not, you are vulnerable. If you play against someone who is capable of hitting the ball as hard as Roger can, you are looking up the barrel."

Laver serves. "Fault." He serves again. "Double fault." Game and service break to Taylor, fourth set. Laver, without apparent emotion, moves into the corner—and the shadow that until moments ago seemed to reach in a hundred directions now follows him alone. The standard he has set may be all but induplicable, but he himself has returned to earth. He will remain the best, and he will go on beating the others. The epic difference will be that, from now on, they will think that they can beat him.

Taylor lobs. Laver runs back, gets under the bouncing ball, kneels, and drives it into the net. He is now down 1-5. He is serving. He wins three points, but then he volleys into the net, again he volleys into the net, and again he volleys into the net —deuce. He serves. He moves forward. He volleys into the net. Advantage Taylor—match point. The sound of the crowd is cruel. "Quiet, please!" the umpire says. Laver serves, into the net. He appears to be trembling. He serves again. The ball does not touch the ground until it is out of the court beyond the base line.

Photographers swarm around him and around Taylor. "Well done, Roger. Nice," Laver says, shaking Taylor's hand. His eyes are dry. He walks patiently through the photographers, toward the glass doors. In the locker room, he draws a cover over his racquet and gently sets it down. On the cover are the words ROD LAVER—GRAND SLAM.

"I feel a little sad at having lost. I played well early in the tournament. I felt good, but I guess deep down something wasn't driving me hard enough. When I had somewhere to aim my hope, I always played better. Deep down in, you wonder, 'How many times do you have to win it?' "

Firewood

FIREWOOD HAS BEEN SELLING, OF LATE IN NEW YORK CITY, for one dollar a stick. Piles of it. Right off the sidewalk. Split from small logs of oak or ash or maple. Split. Split again. Four pieces, four dollars. The bulk rate is around a hundred dollars a cord in the suburbs and a hundred and fifty dollars a cord in the city. From such prices, understandably, the less fortunate have turned aside. The Harvard Club is burning artificial logs made of wax and compressed sawdust. There are people enough, however, who seem prepared to pay for real wood—people, in fact, who are removing the boards and bricks from fireplaces long in disuse. With the destruction of old buildings and the erection of new ones, which tend to have fireplaces only in penthouses, fireplaces had steadily been disappearing from the city, an atrophy that has now abruptly ceased. As petroleum reserves ran low early this winter, a row of apartment buildings on Park Avenue exhausted its allocation of heating oil and the buildings went cold, bringing on a micro-crisis that was overcome by heavy deliveries of firewood handsomely packaged in burlap.

At roughly the same time, a memorandum went out from Albany, from the director of the Division of Lands and Forests to all regional foresters in the state, instructing them that it was now "the policy of this Department, as an energy conser-vation measure, to encourage the cutting of firewood for fuel on state land." For five dollars a cord, plus a dollar seventy-two for liability insurance, plus twenty cents tax, a private woodcutter could be assigned to a segment of the state's forests and permitted to remove sugar maple, red maple, ash, birch, hickory—the cutter's choice. "The major value of this new effort," the memorandum went on to say, "may be to help alleviate the energy shortage."

Interested citizens in the southeastern part of the state were to call 914-677-8268, where foresters were waiting to answer questions and to explain the terms of the state's printed con-tracts. The phone was in Millbrook, northeast of Poughkeep-sie, but there was designated forest land near Carmel, closer to the centers of population, and foresters would meet people at the site in order to complete contracts and consummate sales. After the phone number appeared in newspapers, cus-tomers began to fan in to the Carmel woods from all over the metropolitan area. Ralph Fisher, for example, a retired I.B.M. branch manager, drove up from Larchmont with his son in his son's Toyota. They took an axe and wedges, a large mallet, and a manual saw. They cut wood from trees that were down and dead, because "due to this energy problem" they wanted "a lot of heat" on short notice from wood that was ready to burn. They went home with a modest load of maple, oak, and ash. The state would allow them two months to make return trips, whenever they liked, to cut the rest of their purchased cord. William Nalepa, a Nassau County detective, drove up to Carmel just to study the situation. With the energy shortage, firewood on Long Island had all but disappeared. He bought a cord but postponed, for the time being, the work involved. "What looked good to me there was a lot of the ash," he told his family. "They're simple to split." Ed Talbert also went up from Long Island—from East Patchogue, a hundred and forty miles from Carmel. He drove a truck that carried an old farm tractor, and he took with him two chain saws and three sons. Talbert knew what he was doing. He had lived around Herkimer once, where he had been a logger. His home in Patchogue is heated by a wood-and-coal space heater. He signed a contract for five cords, paid twenty-seven dollars and seventy-two cents, and began felling trees. He hauled big logs out of the woods with the tractor. He took two and a half cords on his first trip—about fifty trees. He did not work so hard that he failed to notice other cutters in the forest. "I've seen some of them," he said later on. "They don't know what they're doing."

One woman called the foresters and asked if a cord of wood would fit into her Pinto. A cord of wood and a Pinto are about the same size. The cargo capacity of a Pinto Wagon is sixty cubic feet. A cord (four by four by eight) is a hundred and twenty-eight cubic feet. If it is hardwood, it weighs something over two tons. (A cord as commercially sold is often a "face cord"—four feet high and eight feet long but only as deep as the length of firewood. What the state is selling for five dollars is, of course, a standard cord.) Some callers seemed disappointed when told that the state's wood was not already cut, split, and stacked by the road. Others expected that the foresters would load the wood for them. One man said he had an electric chain saw and he wondered if there were electrical outlets in the forest. Another asked if there were toilet facilities close to the trees. In Albany, a man walked into the forestry office with a hacksaw and said he wanted to sign up for a cord and go cut it.

Foresters, in the main, welcomed the state's new policy, because it would publicize forestry and the forests, but they worried also about the inherent risks. A glimpse of a city person working the woods with a chain saw was enough to make a forester avert his eyes. It would be the forester's job, after all, to sort out felled limbs, seeing which had twigs and which had fingers. Felling and cutting trees was dangerous work for professionals, let alone amateurs. Workmen's-compensation rates for the logging industry were as high as for any industry in the country, and the timberlands were full of thumbless pros who seemed to be suffering from permanent concussions. Minimally, any woodcutter coming to the state woods needed a hard hat, hard shoes, and a knowledge of felling techniques. But they came instead in suède and sneakers, untutored, bareheaded. Most apparently were unaware, too, that the preponderance of trees that the foresters had marked for cutting were alive and standing—good green timber, which would be ready to blaze across the hearth and ease the energy crisis by the Fourth of July. Green wood will burn, after a fashion, but it deposits droplets of creosote inside the chimney, and the deposits build up until they themselves catch fire. Then flames lick the roof and start back down through the building toward the fireplace.

"It sounds real good on the surface. Cut a cord of wood. Take it home and burn it. But it's not that simple," one forester said.

"I've cut a lot of trees," another said. "No matter how many you've cut, it's still dangerous."

"A fireplace is an inefficient wood-burning facility anyway. It's a romantic way to suck cold air into a room, heat the air, and send it up the chimney."

"Yes, but for all that, this program is bringing foresters

closer to people. It's doing the woods a lot of good, through selective thinning. And it's a way, at last, to show people that it's not evil to cut a tree. Trees do grow again. Trees are a renewable resource. We can now explain on a one-to-one basis the renewability of the forest. We never reached the happy homeowners before."

Eric Meola, one freezing day, left his apartment at nine in the morning and drove in a small rented van to Carmel. His apartment was a floor-through loft on lower Fifth Avenue, and it was cold after ten in the evening, cold all day Sunday, and drafty in the lightest wind. He had read in the newspaper of the state's new program and had decided to add heat to his home with wood. He began with almost nothing. He had no axe, no saw, no maul, no wedge. In fact, he had no fireplace. So for three hundred and ten dollars he had bought a great inverted funnel, a hood, of red enamelled steel, whose connecting stovepipe would rise through a skylight. He was twenty-seven years old, skillful with his hands, and he did the installation himself. He was pleased with it—a handsome fireplace, freestanding. The firebed below the hood rested on, among other things, white marble chips.

Carmel was a little over sixty miles from the center of the city—far enough away to be a small and integral town, not in any apparent sense suburban. As Meola rolled in there, he passed under a railroad bridge whose most prominent graffito was "We're us." He had learned by phone where he could rent a chain saw, and now, inexactly following directions, he passed the Putnam County Courthouse (tall-columned and gleaming white), looped around, made a left by a half-frozen lake, and stopped by a sign that said "Paden Rental." Meola had two friends with him, one of whom was experienced with chain saws, having worked parts of his college summers cutting wood at a resort in Maine. His name was

Randy Phillips and he had a vested interest in the day's results, for he was cold, too. Like Meola, Phillips was a photographer, and both used Meola's apartment as a studio. The other friend, Myrna Wollitzer, was an anthropologist, whose interest was in man, not firewood. She had no idea what a chain saw was, and seemed in no hurry to find out. She had cool gray eyes and a lingeringly contemplative stare. Everybody went into Paden Rental.

Paden, if that was his name, looked from one customer to another with an expression that seemed to suggest that this energy crisis had started some extremely novel trends. The woman, in leather boots and dungarees, was wearing a thin red Chinese jacket covered with lotus blossoms, and the wind outside was bitterly cold. Meola, the leader, was a tall man in a leather jacket, leather boots, corduroy trousers—handsome, with a calm and soft voice, and such a wealth of beard and curly dark hair that he could well have played the lead in *Jesus Christ Superstar*. (He had, in fact, done the photograph of the *Superstar* cast that appeared on the cover of *Time*.) The other man, Phillips, wore hard, heavy, sensible rubber boots. He had stringy light-brown hair and a ten-day beard. The lenses of his eyeglasses were small perfect circles rimmed in metal, and he wore a knitted cap and a long overcoat, which in the woods would give him the appearance of a Byelorussian refugee painted against the snow. To Paden's apparent relief, Phillips was asking knowledgeable questions about the chain saw—a bright-yellow Partner 16, which Paden had presented for inspection. Meola paid the rent: twenty dollars and eighty cents for one day's use. Then he went across the street and into the Carmel Farm Supply Company, where he paid eight dollars and twenty-eight cents for a pair of leather work gloves and ten dollars and thirty-nine cents for a Plumb axe—the last axe in stock. The energy shortage had

touched off an axe boom. "Use it in good health," said the man
who sold it. "And don't chop your leg off."

Several miles north of town, a thin black road framed in old
stone walls led in to the state woods. The tract was about nine
hundred acres of rising ground topped by a fire tower on a hill
called Ninham Mountain. These woods were not part of the
vast acreages that the New York State constitution insists
"shall be forever kept as wild forest land." These, to the contrary, were woodlands always intended for "multiple use"—
lumbering, hunting, recreation—and now, along the south side
of the road and going back some distance, a selected and high
proportion of the trees had been daubed with large dots of
orange paint. There were many fresh stumps. Strewn over the
ground was a great deal of slash. Across the road and up a
short drive was a large equipment shed—"Ninham Mountain
Field Headquarters, Division of Lands and Forests."

The forester inside was a pale-complexioned man of middle
height with a plain and straightforward manner. His name
was Jerry Gotsch. He did not wear a uniform. He had on an
old blue quilted jacket, twill trousers, thong-laced leather
boots. He began to fill in a contract—on legal-size paper—that
contained at least four thousand words in six-point type. He
said not to worry. This was the same standard form the state
used when selling to a pulp or lumber company a hundred
thousand board feet of timber. He spoke gently, in a high
nasal voice, without a trace of rustic condescension, explaining
simple facts about the program. He had a look at the rented
van, at the request of Meola, who wanted to know how much
wood it could carry. The vehicle was a Ford Econoline (bright
yellow, bearing the Technicolor heraldry of the house of
Hertz). Wood weighing what it does, anything more than a
quarter load in the cargo space of the van would probably
destroy it, the forester said. The thing might not survive as

much as half a cord of green wood. Another time, it might be well to rent a pickup.

Myrna Wollitzer asked, "Is that the kind that's open in the back?"

"Yes, that kind."

After Meola had paid his six dollars and ninety-two cents and had signed the contract, Gotsch said, "The trees here are sugar maple, red maple, ash. Elm, too—which is harder than the devil to split. There's also some black cherry, red oak, gray birch, black birch, black locust, sassafras, wild apple, quaking aspen. Take what you want. It's your choice. But please cut the stumps low and utilize the tops up to four inches. Anything you leave on the ground should have a diameter smaller than that. You have two months in which to take your cord. To get a cord out of these woods, you may need to cut twenty trees. It's up to your honesty that you take only as much as you buy. There's an old saying about cutting wood—'It warms you twice.' It warms you when you cut it, and it warms you when you burn it. The heat value of a cord of wood equals the heat value of two hundred gallons of fuel oil."

The door opened and more customers entered the shed. Gotsch said to be careful and he would stop by in the woods later on to see how the cutting was going.

Even the light was cold outside, coming down from a pale, fluorescent sun. Snow mists were collecting around it. The sky was otherwise blue. The wind was fresh and freezing. Myrna Wollitzer shivered, and said, "So how long does it take to chop this wood?" Her friends shrugged. She waited in the van.

Meola and Phillips walked among the trees, looking for dead ones. They wanted their fires this winter. The place was beautiful, they remarked—woods on a slope down to a fast-moving and ice-rimmed stream. Just being there was worth the trip. Phillips stopped by a fourteen-inch trunk daubed

with orange paint—a big tree compared to the others there—
and looked up into the high branches.

"O.K. Let's take this one," he said.

"What is it?"

"It's dead."

"A dead what? What kind?"

"Tree," Phillips said. There was an antic professorial look
about him as he leaned down over the chain saw and inspected it through the narrow diameters of his steel-rimmed
spectacles. His long overcoat, touching the ground, formed a
drapefold curve, like the base of a tree. The saw started on the
nineteenth pull. Its din shot up the air. Deciding to drop the tree
more or less due north, Phillips made a large notch in the
north side. Then he moved around to the other side to make
the back cut. In theory, as the saw moved toward the notch,
the tree should slowly, majestically bend across the hinge
created in its heartwood and drop like a mighty arrow, pointing precisely in the direction intended by the sawyer. Deafen-
ing, staccato, the Partner 16 bit into the wood and moved
toward the notch. Suddenly, Phillips leaped out of the way.
He scrambled for his life. A ton of American elm thundered
onto the forest floor, pointing due south.

One could always pick up a telephone and call Clark &
Wilkins, on East 128th Street, and order a bag of regular. A
bag of regular, also known as a bag of standard mixture, contains, say, fifteen pieces of split oak, ash, beech, maple,
seasoned at least a year and neatly trimmed by a table saw to
an exact length. This is the firewood of the high world. A bag
costs from five dollars and fifty cents to six dollars and a
quarter, depending on how many bags are ordered and how
tough the delivery is. Three logs, split, can fill a bag. The
company stocks different lengths, but the bag price is uniform.

The shorter the length, the more pieces in the bag. In Greenwich Village, fireplaces are small, and Clark & Wilkins generally delivers twelve-inch wood there. The fireplaces in midtown apartments take sixteen-inch or eighteen-inch wood. Certain town houses require twenty-four-inch wood. These long pieces are bundled, not bagged (eight or nine are bound tightly together with plastic bands). There is a class of people who cannot enjoy a bottle of wine unless its subtle pigments are asparkle in the light of a Clark & Wilkins fire. Such people have accounts with the company. They say that getting a delivery from Clark & Wilkins is rather like getting a delivery from Tiffany. The burlap is immaculate. The company's name is boldly stencilled across it. If one pays no more for one's wine than for one's wood, and only occasionally indulges in a bag of special (cherry, birch, hickory, at seven dollars and fifty cents a bag), twenty-five hundred dollars will nicely cover the combined cost, for two, of a winter's wines and fires. Imperial and Cadillac limousines often pull up at Clark & Wilkins, which is below the Penn Central Railroad's elevated tracks. There, in the heart of Harlem, a uniformed chauffeur or a woman in fur will step out and pick up a bag of regular. They get a dollar off if they pick it up themselves.

Bagged wood is piled high in a storeroom at Clark & Wilkins over wood-splitting machines that approach a century in age. The company has been selling wood since 1870, and once had lots in various parts of town where stacked firewood filled as much as two entire blocks to a height of thirty feet—many hundreds of thousands of pieces of wood. It came down the Hudson in barges, and it came up from Virginia in the holds of merchant schooners. It was delivered by men in topcoats and bowler hats. Many pictures hang in the company office. One or two show the men in the bowler hats, but mainly the pictures are of stacked wood—of hills and mountains of stacked wood. Even the corporate records smell of smoke. An accidental fire some twenty years ago lasted more than a week and went through the total inventory of firewood. The flames got to the company's old ledger books and charred their corners.

Most of the Clark & Wilkins facility is unheated, and the office, a brick-walled room, twenty by twenty, is heated only by wood fires. The coals of hardwood ends (the bits left over when logs are trimmed to exact lengths) give off red heat from an open fireplace. Oak smoke mixes with smoke from the cigars of the boss (the semi-wild acridity of blended wood smoke and tobacco smoke is one of the great moments in the history of the nose). The manager's name is Jack Roth, and he is trim, friendly, about forty. He says Clark & Wilkins has to keep up very high standards, because of the firewood sophistication of its clientele. "It's a question of education," he explains. "There is a difference between the New York market and the suburban market. The New York market is knowledgeable. The suburban market is the uneducated firewood market. People in the suburbs know nothing. They'll burn anything. A suburb is a green-wood market. Do you know what green wood is? Green wood is wood that is *not* cut in the winter. There is green wood and winter-cut wood. If you cut in winter, the sap is out of the tree, and you get real seasoned wood. If wood is not cut in the winter, no matter how long it seasons it will never be anything but green wood. People who buy from us want wood that doesn't make much noise. It burns quietly. It throws few sparks out. It mustn't ooze. It has to be clean. It has to be free of bugs. In a New York penthouse, you can't have little things running out from under the bark. So far as I know, no one else in the country goes to the trouble to turn out a bag of wood like this."

The country seems to agree. Clark & Wilkins recently shipped a bag of firewood to a customer in Maine. Florida, too. Michigan. Indiana. Massachusetts. Brooklyn. Clark &

Wilkins sells a considerable amount of what it calls "rabbi wood" to the Chassidic bakeries of Brooklyn, some of which prefer to bake matzos on wood fires. Wherever the wood goes, it all comes from Ulster County. The company has a man there who goes around making deals with farmers. He is what is left of the barges and the schooners. The manager taps the ash from a cigar. "This is an expensive hobby, you know—to burn firewood. Most people in New York have been using it for effect. We haven't been getting the cordage in recent years. Now, though, they're beginning to buy it again for heat."

There was a time when New England farmers preferred to cut firewood under the influence of a waning moon. Something to do with the tides. Firewood, in essence, is mysterious. For example, when it is kindled and burned it almost completely disappears. The nature of firewood seems to be in the mind of the believer. Some people believe that black cherry, burning, sends out clouds of befouling soot. It no doubt does, in their houses. Others smell cherries when black cherry burns, smell apples in smoldering apple. Some people say that wood splits more easily when it is freshly cut; others say to wait until it has seasoned and checked. Still others say that it depends on the wood: you can't split fresh apple with a pile driver, but at the tap of an axe fresh oak will fall apart in boards. Most people have thought that green wood is wood that has been recently cut from a living tree, no matter at what time of year, and that seasoned wood is wood that has been drying for at least six months. This has been the impression of silviculturists, dendrologists, and foresters, for example, who go to universities and are taught that trees are full of water in the winter as in summer. Science was once certain that firewood was full of something called phlogiston, a mysterious inhabitant that emerged after kindling and danced around in the form of light and heat and crackling sound—phlogiston, the substance of fire. Science, toward the end of the eighteenth century, erased that beautiful theory, replacing it with certain still current beliefs, which are related to the evident fact that green wood is half water. Seasoning, it dries down until, typically, the water content is twenty per cent. Most hardwoods—oak, maple, cherry, hickory—will season in six months. Ash, the firewood of kings, will season in half the time. When firewood burns, it makes vapor of the water. The rest of the log is (almost wholly) carbon, hydrogen, and oxygen—the three components of cellulose, also of starch and sugar. When a log is thrown on the fire, the molecules on the surface become agitated and begin to move vigorously. Some vibrate. Some rotate. Some travel swiftly from one place to another. The cellulose molecule is long, complicated, convoluted—thousands of atoms like many balls on a few long strings. The strings have a breaking point. The molecule, tumbling, whipping, vibrating, breaks apart. Hydrogen atoms, stripping away, snap onto oxygen atoms that are passing by in the uprushing stream of air, forming even more water, which goes up the chimney as vapor. Incandescent carbon particles, by the tens of millions, leap free of the log and wave like banners, as flame. Several hundred significantly different chemical reactions are now going on. For example, a carbon atom and four hydrogen atoms, coming out of the breaking cellulose, may lock together and form methane, natural gas. The methane, burning (combining with oxygen), turns into carbon dioxide and water, which also go up the flue. If two carbon atoms happen to come out of the wood with six hydrogen atoms, they are, agglomerately, ethane, which burns to become, also, carbon dioxide and water. Three carbons and eight hydrogens form propane, and propane is there, too, in the fire. Four carbons and ten hydrogens—butane. Five carbons . . . pentane. Six . . . hexane.

Seven . . . heptane. Eight carbons and eighteen hydrogens—octane. All these compounds come away in the breaking of the cellulose molecule, and burn, and go up the chimney as carbon dioxide and water. Pentane, hexane, heptane, and octane have a collective name. Logs burning in a fireplace are making and burning gasoline.

From a small can Randy Phillips refuelled the chain saw while Eric Meola split with the axe the logs Phillips had already cut. Phillips moved on through the woods in search of a third dead tree. His second tree, like the first one, had made a hundred-and-eighty-degree error in its fall, and now Phillips seemed to be advancing somewhat stealthily through the glade, as if the next tree, even before it felt the saw, might come down and hit him. He chose one that was obviously leaning enough so that it could fall only in one direction. It had a seven-inch diameter. He did not notch it but cut it straight through. It fell uneventfully, and in a few minutes Phillips had it cut into fireplace lengths—about fifty dollars' worth of wood, had it been bought from Clark & Wilkins.

Jerry Gotsch, the forester, came into the woods and watched for a while. He said there was an ash or two nearby that would go nicely with the two elms and the maple that Phillips had already cut. He pointed out the trees he meant. "Ash is a good species," he said, "and these are good specimens, but they are already overtopped by that big sugar maple, and so they will die. When that's the case, you take them while you can." Gotsch had spent his professional life in forests. As he looked through this one, he seemed to be reading it—its history, its characteristics. He explained why he had chosen the trees he had marked for destruction. Unmarked—and the tallest and heaviest by far—were the liriodendrons, the tulip trees. They could grow to be almost two hundred feet high and twelve feet d.b.h. (diameter breast high), and they could live for three hundred years. As a species, they were the biggest trees in eastern North America, and, after the white pine, the tallest. The tulip trees that were spaced through the woods here were not even mature yet, but they so outreached and outgirthed everything else that they had clearly got here first, and by a considerable margin of years. They virtually dwarfed the sixty-foot maples and cherries and birches around them. The tulip trees appeared to have been open grown. Those old stone walls along the road, also running through the woods, implied open fields here, in the nineteenth and perhaps in the eighteenth century, and the big trees must have stood in the fields once, competing with nothing—not even each other. Look at the breadth of those crowns. Maybe they had been allowed to grow for shade, or possibly just because they would have been considered so beautiful—tall, straight as plumb lines, with a deeply cooling canopy of broad, orbicular leaves, and yellow-green flowers in May and June that very much resembled tulips. Liriodendron. People called them yellow poplars. They were not poplars. They were, familially, magnolias. Needless to say, none in these woods were going to be marked with orange paint. They were, anyway, poor for firewood and good for lumber.

For the rest, it was a woods full of pioneer species and transition trees, evolving, across a century, maybe two centuries, toward the climax forest, which would be a grove of giant oak and hickory, with everything else pensioned off to other old fields and other new beginnings. The long-run product was timber, the forester said, and it was as timber that you judged a tree, but that did not necessarily mean that the trees would ever actually be used for lumber—just that the best timber tree is also the healthiest tree. Hence the orange mark on that nine-inch red maple. It had few knots and no cankers (lesions of the bark) and twice the d.b.h. of the sugar maple standing beside it, but the sugar maple would one day be the more valuable tree, so you fell the red maple and let the sugar maple have the light.

He moved on, into a small grove of young sugar maples. Elms had stood there but had been killed by disease, opening this small area to pioneer growth. Sugar maples were ordinarily transition trees in the development of forest, but they could be pioneers, too, if there was a good seed source nearby—and those big sugar maples along the road, which must have been around as long as the tulip trees, would have helped fill in the field. These new ones now were saplings— less than four inches d.b.h. At four inches, a sapling became a "pole." At one foot d.b.h. and less than two, a tree was a "standard." When its d.b.h. reached two feet, it was called a "veteran." Those tulip trees were veterans, but, for all their local seniority, they would not be "mature" until they were two hundred years old.

Gotsch as a boy had lived in the country, he said, near Millbrook, grew up hunting, fishing, trapping. He had gone to the New York State Ranger School, at Wanakena, in the Adirondacks. "It seemed like a natural type thing to do." His father was a prison guard, and his father had emphatically told him that being a prison guard was not a natural type thing to do. After ranger school, he went on to Syracuse and its renowned school of forestry. He had finished in 1960. The tulips, the sugar maples, and the white ash were the best trees here, he said. There was some hickory on the side of Ninham Mountain, but the ground was not dry enough for hickory down near the road. Why had he marked that twelve-inch black cherry? In part, because it was near the edge of its range. It was strong and healthy, but up north here it would never amount to much, as cherry goes, and six feet away from it was a big ash, prospering, fourteen inches in diameter. Confronted with such a choice, you just had to say to yourself,

"Which is the better tree?" The decision had been easy, and the paint was on the cherry.

He came to a black birch and a sugar maple, side by side, each a terrific-looking tree, each straight and unblemished (no holes, few knots), each a mighty pole on the verge of standard. The bark of the birch in texture was much like the bark of a paper birch, but its color was dark, glossy pewter. The tree looked good now, but at fourteen to sixteen inches it would develop cankers—that sort of thing. It might have been spared had it not been growing so very close to that sugar maple, which was altogether the superior tree, for the sugar maple would live two or three centuries and be useful at any time for cabinets, chairs, bowling alleys, dance floors, shoe lasts, saddletrees, and boat keels, not to mention sugar. At breast height, the black birch bore an orange daub. To maple, birch was inferior even as firewood, but in someone's living room this gray-metal form of it was going to look better, probably, than the pictures on the walls.

Gotsch moved on into the area that had been worked over by Ed Talbert, of Patchogue. It was an example of what a stand of trees ought to look like when a cutter had worked with regard for the woods. He had worked in the one place. He had not run around like a child in a chocolate shop, grabbing what most caught his eye. It was odd what people grabbed for sometimes. They would charge into the woods like sooners into Oklahoma, heading for white birch because it was so pretty, although as fuel it would rank toward the bottom of the local list. People would run for an aspen and ignore an oak. Aspen has lovely bark. Aspen cuts easily, burns rapidly, gives little heat, rots quickly, and is hard to split. Somehow, you could see people's characters in the trees they cut, in the height of the stumps they left, and in the disposition of the slash. The best of them would choose an area, and not a set of random individual stems. Then they would cut everything marked in the area. That was what Ed Talbert had done, taking five cords out of an acre or two and leaving behind him a well-thinned stand. He had taken out the defective trees and the poor species—all the marked trees. His stumps were as low as manhole covers, and his slash was neatly piled. A fair number of red maples had been there, marked, and a big, sprawling cherry, a mazzard. If cherry bark (on an old tree) is rough and scaly, the tree is black cherry and is thoroughly wild; but if the bark retains its lenticels, its young surface of broken horizontal rings, the tree is a sweet cherry, something ancestrally tame gone wild in the forest—a feral tree—and the name for it is mazzard. Talbert's cherry had been a mazzard. Elms had been there as well, and had taken care of themselves by dying out. Talbert had cut some of the dead ones, and he had taken sugar maples that had been marked because they were competing with other sugar maples. His five cords were gone now, and what remained was a grove of sugar maples, spaced, selected, a really lyrical part of the forest. That was why Gotsch was showing it off. "People are doing the woods good. The one problem is haphazardness—high stumps, and so forth. If every area looked like this, I'd be happy."

Randy Phillips felled and segmented six trees that day, as much as the van could safely hold, and Eric Meola split all the larger pieces to appropriate size, while Myrna Wollitzer remained in the van, cold and patient. At one point while it was being loaded, she revealed that she was the president of Pure Planet, a conservation organization so much above the fruited plain that it did no conservation work on its own but existed solely to encourage other conservation organizations. Pure Planet was living up to its charter, for the president's two friends had done all the cutting and all the splitting and were now doing all the stacking. They did so with the care they might have shown in preparing a studio still-life. Meola had won awards for his work—for example, for a picture of half a dozen hand calculators spread through a forest of standing yellow pencils. His work had appeared in *Elle, Stern, Life.* Phillips, who was also twenty-seven, was ready to follow in the same general pattern but had not yet caught hold of the trapeze. The six trees had become roughly three hundred and fifty pieces of firewood—about a third of a cord. Next time, they said, they would rent a pickup, or borrow an even bigger vehicle. They would bring a wheelbarrow. They would bring sleeping bags and stay two days. Moreover, they would come in May, when the weather was warm, and cut a load of green wood against the end of the autumn.

The van had been backed a short distance into the woods, and when it tried to move out, its rear wheels spun through a frozen crust and sank down into cold mud. Gotsch, saying he thought it would make sense if the state were to push the program in May, put his shoulder behind the van. The wheels spun on—at eleven cents a mile. The forester then carried big rocks to the ruts and built a two-track drive right under the vehicle, and it lurched back out to the road.

An hour later, on the Saw Mill River Parkway, a police car overtook the van and Meola was nabbed. Although in size and shape the van was like a Volkswagen bus, it had commercial license plates. The officer listened with stoic grandeur to the tale of a day in the woods. "I believe what you're saying. I believe your alibi," he said. "But you can read the signs, and they say 'Passenger Cars Only.' Here is your ticket. If you wish to appear in court, you come back in two weeks. Court time is at 7:30 P.M. That's in the evening."

Without further event, the wood made its way through the back roads of Westchester, and on down the Major Deegan and the F.D.R. Drive to a Nineteenth Street alley behind Meola's building. In a freight elevator, it was lifted to the loft.

Saw rental	$ 20.80
Axe	10.39
Gloves	8.28
One-cord contract	5.20
Insurance	1.72
Traffic ticket	10.00
Tolls	.50
Van rental	46.77
Total	$103.66

Time, finally, to sit back and stare into the fire. Kick it. Make the sparks shoot. Change it there in its frame. Push the logs together, push up the flame. Why is the flame yellow? From sodium in the wood. Green? Copper. Violet? Potassium.

The material that goes up the chimney and out to the world weighs twice as much as the log it came from. Since almost all of it is distilled water and carbon dioxide, it is more than enough—if it could get back down—to put out the fire.

Gases, confined in pockets in the wood, will explode. So will steam. When the explosions are small, the fire crackles. When larger, it pops and throws debris out onto the rug.

Wood smoke? Unburned carbon and airborne ash. Like gun smoke. Like grass smoke.

Ash? The minerals in the wood. Sodium, boron, magnesium, silicon, copper, phosphorus, sulphur, potassium . . . Most trees are less than one per cent ash. White birch is a quarter of one per cent ash, and Douglas fir, among North American trees, has the least ash of all (eight one-hundredths of one per cent). In a fire, it all but disappears.

> Birch and fir logs burn too fast,
> Blaze up bright and do not last.
> —ANON.

Black ironwood is eight and a third per cent ash, a blizzard. Black ironwood, though, has the highest fuel value of any wood that grows in the United States. More British thermal units per cubic inch. The tree is short and strong, seldom more than a foot thick or thirty-five feet high. It grows from Cape Canaveral south. The wood is a beautiful rich orange-brown, close-grained and brittle. Drop it in water and it will sink like a stone, for it is a third again as dense as the water.

Mountain mahogany also sinks in water. So does wild dilly. So does lignum vitae. So do torchwood, poisonwood, purple haw, seven-year apple, darling plum, stopper, mastic, and mangrove. All these trees grow in the United States, and the weight of a cubic foot of each of them exceeds sixty-two and a half pounds, the weight of a cubic foot of water. Firewood connoisseurs in Manhattan go to expensive lengths to obtain some of these heavy woods, notably lignum vitae, as focal points for recherché dinner parties, along with the buffalo marrow, the yak sweetbreads, the piranha mousse.

Mangrove is the second-best firewood that grows in the United States. Lignum vitae, in fuel value, is the third. The three worst—in a list of four hundred and thirty—are a yucca, a wild fig, and the giant sequoia.

The redwood made the genetic error of growing good lumber. The lumber of the giant sequoia is terrible. Be good for nothing if you want to live forever is the message of the giant sequoia.

The best of common firewoods are the ones that weigh upward of forty pounds per cubic foot. Sugar maple (43.08). White ash (40.78). Black locust (45.70). American elm (40.55). Beech (42.89). Scarlet oak (46.15). Northern red oak (40.76). White oak (46.35). Flowering dogwood (50.81). Shagbark hickory (52.17).

Eastern white pine weighs twenty-four pounds per cubic foot and burns like newspaper.

Harder than the others to ignite, or so it seems, is the black locust. Put it on a hot white fire and it burns with a low, steady flame and lasts for hours. While the rich burn lignum vitae, the poor can burn black locust. Amazing, ugly, weedlike tree, it grows as crooked as a bony finger and races for the sky at prodigious speed. Its early-year growth rings can be more than half an inch thick. Yet the wood is harder than concrete, dense and fibrous. Instant anthracite. Left lying on the ground for a decade, it refuses to rot. It makes the best fence posts, good coffins. It is enraging to split. The strongest wood that grows in the United States is nutmeg hickory (highest "modulus of rupture"). The second-strongest is torchwood. The third is black locust. The weakest is gumbo-limbo, which is even weaker than the giant sequoia.

> Elmwood burns like churchyard mould;
> E'en the very flames are cold.
> —ANON.

Fred Gerty, a New York State forester and colleague of Jerry Gotsch, found these couplets in the *Forestry Handbook*. He hands them out to woodcutters. Gerty and Gotsch subjectively agree that among the firewoods most abundant in Carmel the white ash is the best. Their second choice is red oak. Their third is red maple.

> Oak and maple, if dry and old,
> Keep away the winter cold.
> But ash wood wet and ash wood dry
> A king shall warm his slippers by.
> —ANON.

Wood was the main source of energy in the world until the eighteen-fifties, and it still could be. Roughly a tenth of the annual growth of all the trees on earth could yield alcohol enough to run everything that now uses coal and petroleum—every airplane, every industry, every automobile.

The fire starts to fade. Two logs will literally keep each other warm, radiate heat back and forth. One log alone loses so much heat it cannot keep going. Thermal radiation is red, white, and blue. A wood fire, in its core, in its glowing coals, could never be hot enough to be blue, but, at its hottest, it can be white, and orange-white. Subsiding, it becomes orange and orange-red and red and deeper red and dark red, until its light goes off the visible spectrum. The heat can be banked in ash, though, for eight, ten hours—long enough to last through the night and, in the morning, begin another fire.

Ranger

IN FRONT OF THE HOTEL ASTOR, some years ago, a policeman was doing what he could to improve the flow of traffic when a tall and youthful man stepped off the curb and approached him. "Excuse me, Officer," he said. "My name is George Hartzog, I'm a ranger from Great Smoky Mountains National Park." It is, of course, impossible to say what ran through the cop's mind at that moment, but something stirred there—perhaps a sense of colleagueship, however distant. Hartzog, for his part, feeling bewildered in this milieu, was attempting not to show his extrinsic fear. He had never been and never would be comfortable in New York. He gestured upstream into the river of metal that was moving south, one way, around them. "My wife is about to come down through here in a yellow station wagon," he said. "I told her I'd be waiting for her, and she should be here any minute. Would you help me get her out of the traffic?" "Ranger, you stand right here, and when you see your wife, point her out," said the cop. Two minutes later, the yellow station wagon appeared under the big advertising signs and moved past Lindy's and Jack Dempsey's and McGinnis of Sheepshead Bay and on into the zone of the Astor, where the policeman, paralyzing the traffic of the city, cleared out an acre of the avenue and guided Mrs. Hartzog to the curb.

When Hartzog was nineteen years old, he went to work in the law offices of Padgett & Moorer, in a one-story frame building on Jefferies Boulevard, in Walterboro, South Carolina. Padgett had died, and Moorer needed assistance. Hartzog, who knew shorthand, worked as stenographer, typist, and general clerk. Before long, he told Moorer that he would like to read law, and that he would like Moorer to be his law school. Moorer, a thin man in a black suit, made no immediate response, but finally took from a shelf the four volumes of Sir William Blackstone's *Commentaries on the Laws of England.* "They're in Old English," Moorer said, meaning that the s's would appear to be f's. "Read them. If you're still interested after that, I'll think about it." Hartzog read Blackstone, and Hartzog's aspirations somehow survived. So Moorer took him across the street to the Colleton County Courthouse, got out an enormous pile of deeds, mortgages, and probate papers, and put him to work on a land-title case. Moorer told Hartzog to copy everything as quickly as he could, and Moorer went off to play golf. It was a blazing August day, followed by a dense and unrelieving August night. Hartzog got the permission of the county clerk to remain after hours in the courthouse, and he sat there all night. "I did it," he said to Moorer in the morning, giving him a completed memorandum. Moorer showed Hartzog another lawbook, and talked over with him what he read there. He took him back to the courthouse and had him copy more papers. This went on for thirty-three months, and then Hartzog sat for and passed the bar examinations of South Carolina.

Hartzog, Director of the National Park Service, has on his office wall in the Department of the Interior a framed admonition from George Washington: "Do not suffer your good nature, when application is made, to say 'Yes' when you should say 'No.' Remember, it is a public not a private cause that is to be injured or benefitted by your choice." On a table beneath the quotation is a telephone console (a garden of square buttons, seventeen in all) through which application of one kind or another is made to Hartzog all day long—an office day that begins at 7:30 A.M. and almost never lasts less than twelve hours.

He sits beside the console in a leather armchair. He punches one of the buttons. "Yes, sir? . . . How are you? . . . Fine. . . . Put any kind of restriction on me you want to, and I'll come back for oversight reporting and all the rest." He punches another button. "Joe, it's cheaper than transporting 'em to jail. If it's good, why should you quit? And if it's good, why shouldn't you do it?" Hartzog lights a Garcia y Vega cigar. He uses a silver-trimmed walnut cigar holder, and the entire rig extends about twelve inches from his mouth. As he talks, he smiles and grins, as if his gestures as well as his language were going out over the line. All this smiling has put crow's-feet in the corners of his eyes. He is in his early fifties, and his face is still youthful, even delicate. The skin is soft. His eyelashes are long. His eyes are bright, and they do not move when he is talking. In Washington, he has become overweight to the point of medical concern. Most of the excess is concentrated in the space between the arms of his chair. His hair is thin, and he is growing bald at the temples. He wears a dark suit, a white shirt, a striped tie, and a shell-inlay Indian ring. Hartzog's deputies—his deputy for legislation, his deputy for operations—sit down with him at eight-fifteen. The Director expects everyone else to work as long hours as he does. They talk about a ribbon-cutting in Maryland, a photographic safari in Wyoming, exposure, publicity, and wilderness. "Is wilderness a zone of use or is wilderness a physical state?" Hartzog's voice is loud—signifying nothing more than animation, but to people who don't know him it can sound like anger. "Don't pass over my question," he says when someone changes the subject, but the question is really rhetorical. Wilderness, as seen from this corner of the Department of the Interior, is a zone of use. Hartzog puts down his cigar and lights a cigarette. The meeting expands into a conference room, where pictures of the Secretary of the Interior and the President hang side by side on a wall. The top of the Secretary's head is hung so that it is level with the President's chin. Twelve people, Hartzog's central staff, now surround the Director, and he lights another cigar. In all, some thirteen thousand people work for him, and these vary from Washington policemen to wilderness rangers, naturalists, historians, and men who pick up papers on the ends of sticks. Hartzog is the administrative overlord of one one-hundredth of the United States. His dispersed domains cover nearly thirty million acres. He has not only the national parks, and territories equally remote, but also parkland and other properties in Boston, New York, Philadelphia, and St. Louis, and eight thousand acres of the District of Columbia. He is the janitor of the White House. He runs the Statue of Liberty, and all the national monuments, cemeteries, seashores, parkways, battlefields, military parks, historical parks, and recreation areas. The clock above the door says 9 A.M. Hartzog picks up a paper

clip and bends it open so that it resembles a propeller. While
he talks, leaning forward, forearms against the conference
table, he spins the paper clip. "Justice wouldn't file the suit
because there was no money. I waited a year to have some
paper in your hand so you could agree with Justice."

"We have supporting data."

"That's what you told me last year. How's the pay cost?
Does it hurt or is it just annoying?"

"We can live with it."

"There's a disallowance of pay-increase values. If the sav-
ings didn't come about through lapses, we would have to have
a reduction in force. I just don't think you can get an item like
that through Congress. They're not going to give you any
Washington-office support costs. I want to get the thing to the
Office of Management and Budget, though. I don't see any
point in fiddling around with it. That's what stripped the gears
last week."

The National Park Service is more than fifty years old and
has had only seven directors. Hartzog is the second to come up
from ranger. His two principal goals are to maintain the park
system's vast existing apparatus and at the same time to give
it a new emphasis toward cities. Implementing his programs,
he attempts to inform, influence, entice, flatter, outguess, and
sense the mood of congressmen, senators, and various members
of the Administration, including his own overlord, the Secretary of the Interior. There is much laughter around his conference table, shot through with moments of high-pitched
intensity. The men seem to care a great deal about what they
are saying, and they apparently understand one another, although their language, to the laity, is unintelligible.

"Supplemental itself does not give you positions," the Director says.

"We'll understand it better when we get more feedback,"
says one of his deputies.

"The report has been surnamed. We'll know something soon."

"We want to get something down that's serious as a foundation for budget figures."

"A talking document."

"It will smoke out Management and Budget."

"Every time we try to do something, they ask for another study. They've been studying the hell out of me for seven years."

"You won't know anything if there's insufficient input."

"Or if you don't understand what the broad parameters are." Laughter.

"O.M.B. won't put up money for experimental programs."

"Are we the lead agency?"

"Yes."

"We'll need to supplement our in-house capabilities."

"Amen."

"Then we'll be able to monitor the full flow of the effort when it is in gear."

"We can tool up to do this by 1972, particularly if we reprogram it."

"We're spinning our wheels."

"Be careful," Hartzog warns. "If you send them a tentative figure for 1972, that becomes your ceiling, and at this stage we need that sort of thing like a Buick needs a fifth hole. Any more questions?"

Hartzog is a master of transitions, from subject to subject or meeting to meeting. He keeps a conversation in flight just as long as he feels it is getting somewhere, and then he puts it down. "Take the numbers out of the back of it," he concludes. "Put a new map with it, write letters, and say, 'Here it is.'"

The persons, populations, and places beneath these punch-card blocks of language gradually emerge. What these people have been talking about—among other things—are a group of islands in Lake Superior, certain areas of the City of New York, the south-Florida ecosystem, and Everglades National Park. The Park Service is making a national lakeshore of the Apostle Islands, an hour's drive from Duluth, three hours from Minneapolis. Local speculators, as is frequently the case, are gumming the procedure. The Park Service would like to establish a vast recreation area among beaches and islands around the entrance to New York Harbor. Problems there only begin with speculators. But the Apostle Islands and the gateway beaches of New York are near people—nearer, that is, than Yellowstone—and the park system needs to go to the people now. Yellowstone National Park was established in 1872 and was the first thing of its kind in the world. It set an international example. But Yellowstone is a long way from the East River, and another example is coming. Hartzog wants to clean up and, in a limited way, to develop big areas of beach and harbor front, and then to connect these places to Harlem and Bedford-Stuyvesant with a fleet of fast-moving boats that charge no fares. The plans are well along. Meanwhile, he has to protect what he already has. The Everglades are drying up, because something called the Central and Southern Florida Flood Control District—a project of the Army Engineers—is intercepting water and diverting it to agricultural use. For two days, Hartzog has been on the phone to senators who are holding hearings on the subject. Further threat to the Everglades appeared in the form of a stupendous jetport to be placed in the swamps near Miami. The Park Service and conservation groups—not always friends—joined to block the jetport, and they were successful, but, in compromise, a jet-training airport has been established instead, and it is now up to the Park Service, protecting the swamps, protecting the Seminoles and the Miccosukees, to monitor the various forms of pollution that come from the site, including noise.

"What is the psychological effect of noise on an Indian?"

"Who the hell is capable of doing that kind of research?"

"The University of Miami."

"It will be in the environmental plan."

"O.K. Photograph the draft and let the task force on Big Cypress have it."

Hartzog puts out a cigarette and unhurriedly lights another cigar. He is like a man with a rake, steadily burning leaves. Word of crisis reaches the room. The roof beams at Wolf Trap Farm have sheared. Wolf Trap Farm is in Fairfax County, Virginia, and there the Park Service is building a performing-arts center that includes a theatre big enough to accommodate more than six thousand people. Invitations have been sent to the First Lady, a large piece of Congress, various Cabinet members, and ambassadors from countries on all levels of economic development to collect at Wolf Trap for a ceremony focussed on the topping out of the roof, the beams of which—laminated, six feet thick—have just cracked. Joe Jensen, Associate Director for Professional Services, quietly explains to everyone what queen-post trusses are and how, under excessive strain, they may shear. Slowly—or so it seems —the import of what is being said comes clear in Hartzog's mind, and then he speaks rapidly and his voice is sharp and hard.

"Where are the sheared beams?"

"They're lying in the parking lot."

"And we're supposed to have a topping-out ceremony with the roof beams lying in the parking lot? You're not going to kid the press to the point of thinking you're having a topping-out ceremony in a building that has a structural defect so that you can't put a roof on it. You've got the First Lady involved. You don't involve her in a sham. Call her people and tell them we don't think we should go ahead with the ceremony." A man on Hartzog's right gets up and leaves the room.

"The structure is safe enough, George. You're not worried about anyone getting hurt, are you?"

"I'm not worried about anyone getting hurt, except politically."

The crisis is abruptly dropped.

"I need a superintendent at Chamizal like a Buick needs a fifth hole, but I got one, because he is locked into the budget," Hartzog says. "I don't want that to happen again." He raps his knuckles on the table. "Senator Bible is complaining about our slowness on the Craters of the Moon Wilderness Area. I want that tied into the next budget appeal. And we've got to move on Alaska. Alaska is hot right now. What is the list of the things we want?"

"Klondike Gold Rush International Historical Park, Wood-Tikchik National Recreation Area, the Lake Clark Pass, extensions to Mount McKinley National Park, Gates of the Arctic National Park, and the St. Elias Range—fifteen million acres in all."

"Before you assign someone to the theme study, I want you to touch base with Pat Ryan. Any more questions?"

The Park Service archeologist, smoking Kools, begins to talk about a Park Service underwater-salvage plan involving ancient shipwrecks off the Florida coast. He wears a string tie secured with a silver-and-turquoise shell-inlay brooch. Hartzog lets him talk for a while, then says, "Any more questions?"

"St. Catherines Island, on the Georgia coast—do we want it? The foundation that owns it wants to get rid of it."

"Do we *want* it? I don't know. It's not in the study plan."

"Yes, it's one of three we want."

"Any more questions?"

"You know about the arson at the Richmond Battlefield?"

"Yes. Disgusting. How much damage?"

"Thirty thousand dollars."

"When are the Connecticut River hearings?"

"Thursday. In Hartford."

"Nothing else? That's all, gentlemen."

Hartzog hurries back to his console, and moments later he is again on the phone, while his secretary orchestrates incoming and outgoing calls. He punches a button. "Senator, I want you to know I've gone the last mile with these people. Make a deal with them and it turns to ashes. We simply aren't going to have enough water. Not nearly enough water. . . . Yes. . . . Thank you. . . . Thank you, sir. I deeply appreciate it." Punch.

"Congressman, you and I have been through this sort of thing before, and we know that in a situation like this a lie goes around the world before the truth gets its britches on." Punch.

"Senator, I want you to know I've gone the last mile with these people. . . . Yes. . . . No. . . . Yes, I knew you'd tell me honestly, that's why I called you." Punch.

"Better hold off, Joe. I have the Secretary roiled up enough now, and I think if you were to throw a restudy in there at this time you'd kill it." Punch. A fresh cigar.

"No. It's very simple. The Indians have the government over a barrel. We can't force those Indian lands into this, because both tribes have now changed their minds and want to stay out. The Indians are listening to their white brother the real-estate speculator." Punch. Puff.

"Mr. Secretary, I appreciate your returning my call. It's about this photographic safari in Yellowstone. I'd like very much to give you this exposure. You would inaugurate it, then we'd take you off and bring you out." Punch.

An incoming call informs Hartzog that the White House feels it is too late to stop the ceremony at Wolf Trap Farm, because the invitations have all gone out. Hartzog, staring into the floor, is quiet for two minutes. "Then just don't call it a topping-out ceremony," he says at last. "Whatever you do, change the name."

It is noon. He gets up to leave, explaining to his assistants that the meeting he is going to is secret. "It's with the Idaho delegation," he tells them, "and it's so secret they won't even let their staff in on it. But when I come back, I may have a national park."

By the door is another framed quotation. This one says, "Great Spirit, grant that I may not criticize my neighbor until I have walked a mile in his moccasins."

For two hours now, Hartzog has been sitting in a boat on the Buffalo River doing the closest thing to nothing at all. He is fishing. Fishing is his only recreation. The Park Service stocks bass and bream in Prince William Forest Park, near Washington, and Hartzog sometimes goes out there for what he contemptuously calls "put-and-take," but the Buffalo, in Arkansas, is his idea of the real thing, and there is almost nowhere he would rather be. He says he feels he has to "stay close to the deck," though—to Washington, to Interior, to Capitol Hill, to the console—and so he allows himself to make such a trip only once every three or four years. The Buffalo River rises in the Boston Mountains. Wild and free-flowing, it drops to the east for a hundred and fifty miles through Ozark forest terrain. It is punctuated with rapids, and it has cut canyons five hundred feet into limestone. Infrequently, it passes small farms, which are for the most part abandoned, and in the river below such farms are islands of coarse gravel. Hartzog's boat is anchored in the stream just beyond the tip of a gravel island. The anchor is a two-foot piece of railroad track. Hartzog, casting rod in hand, cocks his wrist and flips a crawdad in a high, silent parabola. It falls, and splats near the riverbank—a skillful cast. He wears desert boots, white socks, a fading shirt and old gray trousers, a suède jacket, a baseball cap. He has a string tie with a shell-inlay clasp that was made by a Zuñi about a hundred years ago. After some minutes of silence, he says, "The gravel came from erosion from that hardscrabble farm. That was before we learned what contour plowing was about. And by the time we learned what contour plowing was about, the people had all moved to the city, and contour plowing was irrelevant." He casts again. Splat. More silence. Hartzog, who ordinarily holds intense conversations with at least a hundred people a day, appears at this moment to be drinking the silence. The fishing is terrible, but he doesn't seem to care. The river is full of twigs, leaves, and specks of forest trash. It is swollen four feet above its normal level, and only ten days earlier it was twenty-eight feet above normal and in savage flood. "She's perky. Oh yeah, she's real nasty," says Hartzog's boatman, whose name is Cal Smith. The boat is a johnboat, twenty feet long, narrow, flat-bottomed. Hartzog sits near the bow in a strapped-down director's chair, and Smith is in the stern beside a nine-and-a-half-horse Johnson outboard. Smith is a big man with heavy bones, frankfurtery fingers, lithic jowls. He grew up by a quiet stream in Missouri. His father used to tell him what the bullfrogs were saying to each other when they conversed in the night. "Come around, come around," said Mr. Frog. And Mrs. Frog's answer was "Too deep. Too deep." Hartzog laughs a big, shaking laugh at the story of the frustrated frog. So Smith tries another one—about President Roosevelt gettin' in trouble with a gal named Pearl Harbor. Hartzog's laughter has the same volume but is somewhat forced this time. Hartzog tells Smith about a moonshiner who took up counterfeiting and made a fifteen-dollar bill. He gave it to a country storekeeper, asking for change, and he was given two sixes and a three. Smith almost chuckles himself out of the boat. The silences between these stories are long ones, without a nibble. That flood really stirred up the river. The engine of another johnboat whines impa-

tiently several hundred yards downstream. This one contains
Hartzog's friend Anthony Buford, and Buford's boat is now
heading back upstream, apparently to rendezvous with Hartzog's. Buford is a middle-sized man with a leonine head, deep
facial wrinkles, and a gruff, gravelly voice. (A third boat,
beyond sight around a bend, contains Hartzog's two sons, one
of them under ten and the other in his twenties.) Like
Hartzog, Buford is a self-educated lawyer who grew up
against a rural background—in his case, southeastern Missouri, where he now has a big farm. Buford is an aggressive
man. He aggressively raises quarter horses. He aggressively
raises peerless cattle. He was an aggressive attorney, before he
retired. He was general counsel of Anheuser-Busch. Hartzog
and Buford got to know each other when Hartzog was the
chief Park Service ranger at the Jefferson National Expansion
Memorial, in St. Louis. It was Hartzog who took a set of plans
that had been lying dormant for fifteen years and built the
great arch of St. Louis. Those who know the story of the arch
say that had it not been for Hartzog there would be no arch.
Hartzog the Ranger is a hero in St. Louis, but at this moment
he is not a hero to Tony Buford. "God damn it, George, this
river is a mess. There is no point fishing this God-damned
river, George. The fishing is no good."
    Hartzog looks at Buford for a long moment, and the expres-
sion on his face indicates affectionate pity. He says, "Tony,
fishing is always good." The essential difference between these
friends is that Buford is an aggressive fisherman and Hartzog
is a passive fisherman. Spread before Buford on the bow deck
of his johnboat is an open, three-tiered tackle box that resembles the keyboard of a large theatre organ. Buford has fished
at least nine places while Hartzog has been anchored at the
gravel island.
    Hartzog flips another crawdad into the air. Splat.
    "God damn it, George, I think we ought to pull our lines in,

turn up the engines, and go for the White River. We could be near there by sundown, make camp, and be ready to fish the White in the morning."

A long period of quiet follows while Hartzog contemplates the tip of his rod. The quiet is so prolonged, in fact, that Buford becomes impatient and tells his boatman, Preston Jones, to move on and try another spot. "Under that cliff," he says. "Maybe that's where they're all hiding."

The cliff is a high limestone wall that has been striped by dripping water. Beyond the rim of the cliff is a forest of red oak, white oak, cedar, hickory. On the other side of the river, where the ground is lower, are groves of sycamore, locust, and willow. The strata of the limestone are level—flat lines reaching out beyond the peripheries of vision. Below them, and above the bend, is a run of white rapids.

"We've got to have this river," Hartzog says. He wants to make its entire hundred and fifty miles a national river, which means that the Park Service would buy the river and all the riverine lands necessary to—as he puts it—"protect its overview." The opposition consists of the Army Corps of Engineers, which would like to arrest the Buffalo with flood-control dams, and private owners who are against the intrusion of the government in any form; but Hartzog thinks he can get the river for the Park Service, and he will work to get it as long as he needs to. "It's just unspoiled," he says. "People haven't found it yet."

He stretches his legs a little and leans back, watching the tip of the rod. He would like to see the tip move in short, erratic arcs. That, after all—that brief, dactylic burst up there at the end of the fibre-glass rod—is what he is supposedly waiting for. He pushes his baseball cap forward on his head, as if he were about to catch a nap in a dugout. There are five eyes on his rod. He sights through the last one into a patch of flat blue among high mounds of cumulus. He finds a fragment of cloud loose in the blue and he frames it steadily in the fifth eye while he waits for the glass to bend.

From five hundred feet in the air, Jamaica Bay looks something like the Okefenokee Swamp—mud islands, dry islands, fringe vegetation, mottled marshland. Hartzog points to the hull of a wooden ship, its ribs protruding from the water. He points to a flight of geese descending toward a landing. He points to two men on horseback, cantering along a dirt road at the water's edge. In the background of the riders, wiggling in heat waves, is the Empire State Building. The aircraft is a big, boat-hulled Sikorsky helicopter borrowed (with crew) from the Coast Guard. Hartzog and members of his staff are flying over the proposed Gateway National Recreation Area. They came to survey the terrain and to discuss how best to bring a natural and recreational environment—offering light, air, and quiet—close to the masses of the city. But, just now, pointing is the only way Hartzog can communicate. Strapped tightly into a bucket seat, he is beside an enormous open doorway, and his ears are covered with heavy black plastic cups that appear to be some sort of audio headset but are connected to nothing. The headset simply blocks sound. Each person in the cabin is wearing one. Printed instructions warn that the plastic cups should be kept firmly in place "to minimize ear damage due to high-frequency engine noise." A little ear damage is apparently routine—all part of a day with the Coast Guard. The chopper circles, doing eighty miles an hour, and the pilot turns it on its side to provide an optimum view. There is nothing but a seat belt between Hartzog and Jamaica Bay. The open doorway—now beneath him—is so large that a mature camel could fall through it, let alone the Director of the National Park Service. On a map, Hartzog circles Jamaica Bay with his finger, indicating that he wants all of it for the Park Service—twenty square miles.

The helicopter moves across Rockaway Inlet and along the Breezy Point peninsula—first over Jacob Riis Park, then over the Nike bunkers of Fort Tilden, and on to Breezy Point itself. Breezy Point, the lower extremity of Queens, is the southernmost tip of Long Island. It reaches out into one side of the entrance to New York Harbor in much the way that Sandy Hook, New Jersey, reaches into the other. Together, Sandy Hook and Breezy Point are pincers in the sea that constitute a kind of gateway to the city. The Park Service would include the whole of each peninsula in the Gateway National Recreation Area, where twenty million visitors a year would find swimming beaches, surfing beaches, pavilions, restaurants, promenades, golf courses, tennis courts, playing fields, bike trails, hiking trails, surf fishing, pier fishing, campgrounds, picnic zones, amphitheatres for the performing arts, a museum of marine life, a cultural and educational center, "creative open spaces," "nature areas," and "walk and wander" areas for solitary ambles by the sea.

Hartzog points down to sand dunes. The outermost two hundred and thirty-two acres of Breezy Point peninsula have never been developed. Although they are an integral part of the City of New York, they are as pristine as they were when Verrazano discovered them. The chopper moves out over ribbed blue waves and flecks of whitecaps—New York Bay. Now framed in the open doorway—and two miles distant— are the flypaper beaches of Coney Island, three and a half miles of people. Hartzog's ferries—fast single-screw pontoon airboats, shooting around the harbor like waterbugs—would siphon people from Coney Island and spread them out into Gateway's twenty thousand acres. Hartzog holds in his hand a copy of the Gateway proposal, a map-filled booklet that flutters wildly in the breeze. He folds it back to show a map of the ferry system, trellising the harbor.

The chopper descends. Two miles south of the Verrazano-

Narrows Bridge, almost in the lane of the giant ships, are two small islands. The helicopter hovers over them. The northern one has three trees on it. It is called Hoffman Island. The other—Swinburne Island—has no trees at all. Only one New Yorker in, say, fifty thousand has any idea that these islands exist. Hartzog envisions, among other things, an outdoor restaurant there beside the sea lanes, the big ships slicing by. The chopper moves. A gust rips into the cabin and tears several maps from Hartzog's hands. Clutching the remaining sheaves, he writes on one of them, in shorthand, "There goes half my park."

"Any government agency has its own personality, and George knows his bureau. He knows what's happening here in Interior, he knows what's happening in Morro Castle, and he knows what's happening at Mount McKinley."

"The personality of the Park Service is changing as it becomes an organization that reflects Hartzog. The Park Service is vital, active, and on the ball today, and has great *esprit de corps*."

"He's very hard on his people. He cracks the whip. And he has a short fuse."

"He is too august, too removed a figure."

"He never asks the next guy to do what he wouldn't do himself. He's demanding, but his example is high."

"He has the *service* idea. His attitude is that people should be willing to move from one post to another. They should do what they're told. He inspires both respect and fear. This is true of any strong man."

"He is so politically inclined that he shuffles and changes things constantly. The poor old bureaucrats around here don't know quite where they're at."

"We used to be trying to catch up on development in established parks, but George is trying to find the needs of the seventies. Those who identify the natural scene as the true purview of the Park Service think of him as a renegade."

"He reacts emotionally to people. He's way up on them or way down. He snoops around the parks, and if everything is O.K. the superintendent is great. If not, the guy is finished."

"If it rains, it's the superintendent's fault."

"With his own staff, he will delegate, but the delegation is only good while the delegatee operates exactly the way George would operate if he were the delegatee."

"This building is loaded—it's stuffed—with people who are overridden by personal ambitions. But that is not true of George. I never have a fear that I'm being used and that when I'm used up I'll be discarded."

"Instead of being preoccupied with the process, he is preoccupied with the idea. I've never heard him discuss reasons why things can't be done."

Hartzog lights his seventh cigar. He says, "People, people, people—they're coming out of my ears." The door of his office opens and in walks the superintendent of Yosemite National Park. His name is Lawrence Hadley. He is in Washington to confer with the California delegation to Congress, and Hartzog has fifteen minutes to sift Hadley's thoughts before Hadley goes to the Hill. The superintendent of Yosemite is a young and strong-appearing man with dark features, dark hair, and a suggestion of melancholy in his face. He wears a silver watchband with turquoise inlay and a large silver-and-turquoise shell-inlay ring. He speaks softly and with an unpretentious air of absolute competence. He is Hartzog's idea of the Park Service personified—a man who does anything well and is ready to serve anywhere any time. Hartzog is confident that when Hadley and his wife are asked abruptly to change their personal plans and go to an airport to meet an official visitor, they will do so without pause or regret. Hadley grew up in Maine, where his father was the superintendent of Acadia National Park. The word is that Hadley may one day succeed Hartzog as director of the Service, and that Hadley will soon be transferred to Washington. Meanwhile, the problem of Yosemite Valley is the sort of thing he ought to be dealing with, for the Yosemite's problem is population pressure as expressed in the invading automobile, and if solutions can be found there, where the pressure is most intense, the solutions may be applied throughout the national-park system. Yosemite Valley has a flat floor and sheer granite walls. It is about six miles long, and has been penetrated by a roadway from the west. Driving into it is like driving up through a drain and out into an exaggerated bathtub. The vertical walls of the valley in places are three thousand six hundred feet high, and for an automobile there is only the one way in and out. With its pluming waterfalls, its alpine meadows, and its granite pinnacles, the Yosemite is in all likelihood the most exquisite cul-de-sac on earth, and each year about seven hundred thousand cars go in there.

"The automobile as a recreational experience is obsolete," Hartzog says. "We cannot accommodate automobiles in such numbers and still provide a quality environment for a recreational experience." Accordingly, Hadley will ask Congress for three hundred thousand dollars so he can close at least a part of the valley to automobiles and carry people through the closed area in chartered buses. Hartzog says that eventually he would like to block cars from the valley altogether and possibly build a funicular that would lower people into the Yosemite from the rim. To transport people around the valley floor, he contemplates the use of electric trains, which would run on rubber tracks. As Hadley and Hartzog talk, it becomes increasingly apparent that everything they are saying rests on the assumption that the visiting public has the right to be carried from place to place—that the right to vehicular transportation, privately or publicly provided, now comes under less question than the right to freedom of assembly or freedom of speech.

The Park Service tried elephant trains in Yosemite for a period of ten weeks. The valley was stuffed with cars, but people got out of them and spent twenty-five thousand dollars on the trains, at three dollars and fifty cents a ride. "People want some alternative," Hartzog says. "No more roads will be built or widened until these alternatives are explored. We want to give people a park experience, not a parkway experience. We need to limit access to parks and wilderness. We've simply got to do something besides build roads in these parks if we're going to have any parks left. We need controlled mechanical access. We can put parking lots outside the parks, then take people in with public transportation. When you get too many people, simply shut off the machinery. If we get rid of the automobile, we can have more people. No one knows what the carrying capacity of Yosemite is for human beings alone. I don't think you can stay bound up in this knot you've been in of roads and trails and more roads and more trails, Larry. You've got to end it. The beauty is that you can take a dynamite stick and blow up the pavement and then all you have is a hole there and you can fill up the hole. I'm not inflexible on anything except that I'm going to get rid of the damned automobile and I'm not going to get rid of people in the process."

Hadley, thoroughly coached, departs for Capitol Hill. As he goes out, Nathaniel Owings, of the architectural firm Skidmore, Owings & Merrill, comes in. Owings wearily says, "Hello, George," sits down, takes out a handkerchief, and wipes his brow. He is middle-aged, middle height, middle weight. He, too, wears a turquoise ring. He is, as it happens, chairman of the Advisory Board of the Park Service. Immediately, he says what he wants. He is redeveloping the Mall—the sweeping greensward that runs between the Capitol and the Washington Monument—and he wants to put a subway entrance in the middle of it. Hartzog's eyebrows rise. Some of Owings' ideas are untraditional; the Mall would not be everybody's first choice as a site for a subway station. Owings says, "The Mall doesn't have to be just for monuments, George. It can be for living. The subway station won't be junk and crappy, I guarantee. There is nothing that says we can't put the subway entrance where the people are."

"With that idea, Nat, we can start something new in planning," Hartzog says, with a booming laugh.

After Owings leaves, Hartzog begins assembling papers. He punches the telephone console and says, "Ed, just make sure of one thing. Whatever you do, just make sure there's no tree on top of that structure at Wolf Trap Farm." Papers in hand, he hurries out. He has an appearance of his own on Capitol Hill.

"I stay pretty close to the deck," Hartzog says as he rides across the city in a chauffeur-driven unmarked patrol car of the United States Park Police. "If the Congress of the United States is going to hold hearings on my legislation, I ought to be there to testify." He has only once permitted himself a trip to Europe, and that was just a fast tour of England, France, and the Netherlands with a governmental committee sent to study historic preservation. He will travel, though, to the remotest corner of any state in the Union to please a senator or a significant congressman. Remote corners of distant states can be, in a sense, integral segments of the deck. He once made a speech at the Cherokee Strip Living Museum, in Arkansas City, Kansas, for example, because Joe Skubitz asked him to go there. Arkansas City is in Skubitz's district. Skubitz is the ranking minority member of the House Subcommittee on

Parks and Recreation. Among other things, Skubitz promised Hartzog on this visit that he would arrange with Wayne Aspinall, the chairman of the committee, for a hearing on Hartzog's proposal for a Buffalo National River. Hartzog is tireless. He knows that in Washington the shortest distance between two points often includes a trip to Kansas. So he goes. He fears flying, but he goes. He speaks. He drinks. He grins. He guffaws. And he comes home with a hearing (or the promise of one) that might otherwise not occur. He travels, too, as an evangelist for his causes. Wherever something is up—Florida, Minnesota, Arkansas, California—he goes to talk to farmers, freeholders, Indians, or entrepreneurs and tries to show them what he wants to do, and why. "These things go slow," he says. "You don't make any converts at a big meeting. You have to get one man talking to one man. The opposition always has the advantage at first, because a lie goes around the world before the truth gets its britches on. You've got to get the facts out onto the table so the local people can see them."

Where the success or failure of all this effort is measured, of course, is on Capitol Hill, in hearing rooms, where Hartzog presents and defends his programs. Now he gets out of the car, tells the driver to wait, and, looking over his papers as he goes, hikes the long corridors of the Senate Office Building. In the hearing room are folding chairs, carafes of water, maps of the Everglades, and a raised platform where seven senators sit at a curvilinear table. "Each time I think I have agreement with the Army Corps of Engineers and the Central and Southern Florida Flood Control District, it turns out to be ashes in my mouth and papier-mâché," Hartzog tells them. He speaks strongly and colloquially, reviewing aspects of the training jetport and of the water system of southern Florida. He also talks about fifty-eight thousand acres of inholdings—private lands within Everglades National Park—that he would like Congress to condemn and buy. What he says is clear and is obviously well prepared, and this, among other things, has earned him the high regard of the men on the platform. They say that when he speaks he always knows what he is talking about, and that this puts him in something of a minority among bureaucrats making appearances on the Hill. Hartzog has friends and enemies in both houses and both parties, because, in the words of Congressman John Saylor, of Pennsylvania, "he's willing to stand up and fight—he has a healthy respect for Congress, not a callous disregard, but he's willing to stand up and fight. Some days I wouldn't trade him for anyone in the world, and some days I could kill him."

In 1969, when rumor spread that Hartzog was about to be replaced, congressmen and senators heated up in sufficient numbers to evaporate the rumor. They think he is the most industrious director the Park Service has ever had. They admire his effort to give new directions to the park system, and they feel that he has drawn into the Park Service people of very high calibre who might not have been attracted to it had he not been there. They are sympathetic to some of Hartzog's problems within the Administration. "Sometimes he gets clobbered by the Secretary or the White House," Saylor has said. "Sometimes he comes in here in a straitjacket. He is not always free to act as an individual. He is told policy. It takes a strong, strong man to overcome the political shenanigans that go on here in Washington. His is supposed to be a nonpolitical job, but it's not."

"George has too many irons in the fire," Aspinall once said. Aspinall is in his seventies and is covered with spikes, and from him this is uncommon praise. "George is a little too fast for his own good. He skips over details. He is a builder without considering the cost of the building. So I say to him, 'No,

George. Back up and start over.' He has the personality to be able to back up. He is a personable, lovable character, a very fine companion, a complete public servant."

Hartzog taps together his papers on the table before him, thanks the senators above him, and leaves the hearing room. He walks about thirty feet down the corridor, opens a back door to the hearing room, goes in, takes one of the senators aside, and says to him privately, "You really hit the sciatic nerve in there, Alan, and unless this committee gets with this thing we'll probably get the short end of the stick again."

When the Director of the National Park Service goes on a camping trip, survival in the wilderness is not at issue. His party on the Buffalo consists of nine people, four of whom are professional rivermen, paid to do all the work. One is a full-time cook, and he rides alone in the "commissary boat," which is crammed to the gunwales with food. Mornings, the cook runs on ahead, so that when lunchtime comes and the other boats catch up with him he has already set up a tent fly to create shade, a table and chairs are beneath it, and dozens of pieces of batter-dipped chicken are gurgling away in deep Ozark fat. At night, he fries multiple pork chops or big individual steaks and covers the meat with fried potatoes. His breakfasts compound cords of dark bacon with eggs and pancakes fried in bacon grease. The cook's name is Karl Hudson. He is not light on his feet. He has a mustache, and he seems to radiate anachronism. He could be a wax museum's idea of a cook in the Civil War. In fact, the whole campsite seems to be ready for Mathew Brady. The big iron skillet. The tall black coffeepot. The two wall tents. The folding cots. The canvas armchairs. The tent-fly kitchen. The heavy iron stakes. The sledgehammer.

The tents are pitched by the rivermen, who set up the cots and carefully line the sleeping bags with white percale sheets.

Tony Buford pours a drink. There are worse things in life than Scotch on the Buffalo. Buford has had his way all day, for he finally succeeded in disengaging Hartzog from the swollen river, persuading him to turn up the engines and shoot on downstream in anticipation of better fishing on the morrow in the White. Every so often, the Buffalo drops enough to make a rapid—to leap with haystacks, with gardens of standing waves. These rapids would give a feel of the river to people in canoes, but the johnboats go through the white water the way automobiles go across wet pavement—no pitch, no roll, no river. Now, at the campsite, young Edward Hartzog is fishing for big channel cats. He is using minnows. His father calls to him, "Try a wurrum." Edward reels in his line and tries a wurrum. He is in the second grade, and his brother and sister are in college. Friends say that when Edward was born Hartzog's age went down ten years. The family lives in an old remodelled farmhouse on a big lot surrounded by a rail fence, in McLean, Virginia. They raise chickens. A small brook runs through the property—a wet ditch, really—and Hartzog from time to time promises to clean it out and build a series of dams. The brook disappears into an uncut thicket known as the Bird Sanctuary. There is a burro as well. Hartzog hitches her to a two-wheeled cart and, with Edward at his side, races around his land shouting "Gee!" and "Haw!" "Many men are captains of industry, but when they get home they are mice," one of Hartzog's close friends has said while observing this scene. "George is the captain at home." His wife, Helen, is from Massachusetts, and is described by their friends as a Yankee trader. She sells real estate, and buys and sells antiques, which she stores in an unoccupied house next door. The two buildings stand very close to a county highway. Hartzog's front yard is mostly gravel and is barely large enough for the bug Volkswagen in which he drives to work. Inside the house, over a stone fireplace, is an oil painting that consists of a field of miscellaneous red dots traversed by a bulging black line, thick with dried paint. The title of this painting is "Nature." It was given to Hartzog in appreciation of, among other things, Hartzog's modern approach to the natural world.

Edward has caught a big channel cat. Hartzog is elated. "I told you to stop poormouthin' those cottonpickin' fish," he says to Buford. Edward draws the catfish into the shallow water. Sinister and spiky, it looks like a drifting mine. "Be careful," Hartzog warns him. "He'll fin the daylights out of you." The big cat occasions a series of stories told by the rivermen about even bigger catfish caught in the Buffalo, in the Ohio, in the Mississippi, in the Arkansas. And the catfish series, in turn, leads to a sequence of expanding stories about deer. Orville Ranck, who is tall, one-eyed, slim, and old, remarks that it was he who shot the second-largest deer ever shot in the United States. Preston Jones, brown and thin as a cowboy, looks away. Jones is working on a Coleman stove that he found a few hours ago, full of muck and sand. He knows who owned it—a couple who were camping on an island in the river when the twenty-eight-foot rise occurred two weeks ago. The couple climbed a willow and were clinging to its uppermost branches when the sheriff of Marion County came along in a search boat and made the rescue. "Their eyes were like a treeful of owls," Jones says.

"When you camp on these rivers, you've got to have land to your back," Hartzog comments.

"On the other hand," Jones tells him, "I've seen big bears come out of the woods here, fighting like hell." This occasions a series of stories by the rivermen about enormous bears they have known, and Hartzog throws in a story of his own about a bear in the Great Smoky Mountains. Two tourists were feeding this bear by the roadside when a Cherokee drove up.

(There is a Cherokee reservation just outside the park.) The Cherokee got out of his car, shot the bear, put the bear in the back seat, and drove away while the tourists stood there with their mouths open and popcorn in their hands.

Under Jones' meticulous attention, miraculous hand, the Coleman stove is sputtering with flame. Even its thinnest tubes were packed with the muck of the flood, but one of its burners is now blazing in yellow spurts. Gradually, Jones works down the flame to a hard copper blue. Looking up, finally, he says, "Orville, tell us about the time you shot the second-largest deer in the United States."

"I can't see too well. I have only one good eye. I lost the other to a fishhook," Ranck explains—and how this led to the second largest deer in the United States was a simple matter of optics: anything smaller would have escaped his attention. One fall, Ranck went to Meeker, Colorado, because near Meeker is a narrow mountain pass through which thousands of Rocky Mountain deer move on their annual migration. So many of them go through there, Ranck says, that they resemble driven cattle. They even raise a dust cloud. Ranck crouched on a ledge so close to the deer that he could almost reach out and touch them, and to improve his chances he had equipped his rifle with a large telescopic sight. All day, he sat there looking point-blank at the deer through the big lens, and finally he saw the great buck, the second-ever largest deer. Its tines were multiple and fine. Moving the crosshair across a wall of venison, Ranck stopped it just behind the animal's shoulder, and he fired. The buck turned the second-largest somersault ever seen in the United States, and it lay on the ground, its four legs kicking in the air.

"How much did it weigh, Orville?"

"Five hundred and twenty-two pounds."

Jones looks away.

Buford, who is unimpressed by deer of any size, says, "One thing that surprises hell out of me on this river is that we haven't seen any snakes."

"I saw twenty-four today," Jones says.

"You don't say. What kinds did you see?"

"Mainly moccasins. Some cottonmouths."

"I grew up with cottonmouths and rattlesnakes," Hartzog says. "Where I grew up, you never stepped *over* a log. You stepped *on* it, or you might wish you had."

In the Geechie section of the South Carolina coastal plain, streams had names like the Little Salkehatchie and the Hog Branch of Buckhead Creek; swamps were called Tony Hill Bay, Bull Bay, the Copeland Drain; and the big Edisto River, an entrail of continual oxbows, flowed through marshlands miles wide. On the higher ground were pinewoods, small cleared farms, dirt roads, and every two miles a church—Beulah Church, Bethel Church, Mount Olive Church, Tabernacle Church. Reaching into the pinelands on a single track, trains of the Hampton & Branchville Railroad stopped at hamlet crossroads and picked up turpentine and rough-cut boards and the produce of the small farms. One place they stopped was Smoaks. Hartzog was born in 1920, in Smoaks.

His father was a dirt farmer who worked about a hundred and fifty acres and also had a stand of loblolly pine. His grandfather had farmed the same land. The house the family lived in was paintless and weathered. A large porch wrapped around a front corner, and there was another porch off the kitchen, in back. There was a pump in the yard, between the house and the outbuildings—the smokehouses, the chicken houses, the barn. Hartzog's first school was a one-room building by the Edisto. Whenever he could, he fished the river for red-breasted perch, catfish, pike, and bream. At home, he learned early to "plow a mule," and he helped his father grow cantaloupes, cucumbers, watermelons, corn, green vegetables, and cotton. His father was also a hunter and a fisherman, and he had a big sense of humor. He could tell stories all day without repeating himself. He sent his watermelons to New York and his cotton to Columbia, and before the Depression the family had a "cash income"—apparently as good a one as any farmer's in the area, for George Hartzog, Sr., was the first man in that part of the country to own a Model T Ford. After it was delivered to him, he drove it without knowing how. He kept shouting "Whoa! Whoa!" at the car as it circled the farmhouse out of control. "Whoa! Whoa!" Finally, it wedged itself between two trees.

Hartzog always signs his name "George B. Hartzog, Jr.," although his father has been dead for many years. It is as if he were reluctant to add, however minutely, to the erasure of his father's existence, remembering, as he does with something just short of bitterness, how his father's relatively good life was suddenly knocked apart—his hope and eventually his health broken by the great economic depression. When Hartzog, Sr., shipped his watermelons to New York, the railroad sent him a bill instead of a check—freight costs for carrying produce that found no market. The price of cotton dropped to five cents a pound—a figure lower than the cost of picking and shipping it. So the Hartzogs' cotton was left in the field, where cattle, in their hunger, ate it. The family had no money at all. "For a dirt farmer who had been put out of business life became a very simple issue: Did we have something to eat or didn't we have something to eat? This was the poverty level of zero. My father became a severe asthmatic—a combination of pollen and nerves. He did odd jobs, farming. He tried to hang on, but he couldn't." One day when Hartzog came home from school, his father, his mother, and his two younger sisters were standing in the yard helplessly watching the house burn. A bed was all that had been removed to the yard before the intense heat stopped further salvage. While the house was burning to the ground, flaming debris fell on the bed and destroyed it.

Hartzog is walking on the beach at Sandy Hook. The big chopper is down and silent, but its high-frequency engine noise still rings in his ears. The wind is gentle, coming off the ocean. The day is warm. Coney Island was covered with people, but over here in New Jersey, Hartzog's party aside, there are only two on this broad stretch of beach. They are soldiers, sunbathing near their car, which has a Nebraska plate. The major part of Sandy Hook is a military base, Fort Hancock—a thousand acres reaching out into New York Bay. Its huge, curving beach is spectacular, with the open ocean in one direction and the skyline of the city in the other. Hartzog, in his black suit, black shoes, looks like a preacher, not a bather, and he starts to preach. "The selfishness of the military in terms of the recreational needs of people in urban areas is unbelievable," he says. "It is pointless to lock up an area like this when people need a little sun in their faces and water on their backs. Each of those soldiers over there has two miles of beach to himself."

Fort Hancock is prime duty. Soldiers bring their girls here, and the couples get lost together on the enormous beach. Officers live in houses designed by Stanford White. A Nike tracking site is here. The general in charge of all Nike installations from Boston to Philadelphia presumably could live anywhere he wished between the two cities, and he has chosen Fort Hancock. Ospreys nest in the telephone poles, and herons in rookeries among the dunes. The central landmark is the oldest operating lighthouse in the United States. New Jersey rents a small piece of the peninsula, at its landward end, from the Department of Defense. The rented area is called Sandy

Hook State Park and is the most heavily visited park in New Jersey. People press in there by the thousands, but the beach is quite narrow where it is open to the public, and the dunes behind it are green with deep growths of poison ivy. When the tide comes in, the ocean shoves the people into the poison ivy.

Hartzog, on the broad Army beach, continues. "We've asked the military to surrender these lands for recreational use," he says. "Beach land simply needs to be made available. The military usually claim that they have to have places like this for military recreation. They need it like a Buick needs a fifth hole." Sandy Hook is almost the least of Hartzog's ambitions toward military land. He wants Vandenberg Air Force Base. He wants the Aberdeen Proving Ground. He wants Quantico, Fort Belvoir, Eglin Air Force Base, the Naval Air Station at Floyd Bennett Field, and Forts Barry, Baker, and Cronkhite on the Marin Headlands of San Francisco. He wants at least a dozen other military principalities as well, all close to cities, and all, in his view, being now given a mistaken priority. He thinks he could get the Department of Defense out of Fort Hancock in two years. Other difficulties would remain, though. Reaching out as it does into the mouth of the Hudson, Sandy Hook catches a high percentage of what the river disgorges, and the beach near its tip is blemished with flotsam—plastic bags, plastic bottles, plastic buckets, rusted cans, little bits of Albany, the tenth part of Troy, and hundreds of acres of driftwood. When trees die in the Adirondacks, they go to Sandy Hook. Rangers could take care of the cleanup, but not on an hourly schedule, and all that plastic would have to be stopped at its source. The Park Service thus joins, as it has all over the country, the general fight against pollution, and not simply against things that float. The feasibility of the Gateway project depends on an optimistic view of what can be done about river and ocean pollution. Right now, when striped bass are caught in the waters of Sandy Hook they sometimes have fin rot, and cataracts over their eyes.

"In 1960, Congress said no to the arch. Any other Park Service ranger would have said, 'O.K. Where am I to be sent now? Back to the Great Smokies? Out to Alaska to count blankets?' But not George. He kept at it until funds were appropriated."

"George was a lawyer. That's why they had him in St. Louis. The Park Service had never built anything bigger than an outhouse before."

"When the arch was halfway up, the contractor was losing money, so he stopped work, saying the structure was unsafe. Two legs, three hundred feet high, were sticking out of the ground. Hartzog said to the contractor, 'Listen. I ordered an arch and I want an arch.'"

"In the pecking order of park superintendents, the superintendent at St. Louis is not very high. I just spotted him immediately as a good leader, a driving type, full of enthusiasm and interest. I met him on the Current River, in Missouri, in 1962. We were trying to make the Current a national river, and a group of us made a two-day float trip there. George went on the trip. He and I rode in the same boat, and I felt that in those two days I really got to know him well. It was a situation of utter informality, heightened communication. We went skinny-dipping at night. It was in September, and chilly. But this was a group of outdoor people, who were in their element. The Current was going to be the first national river. We hadn't done anything like it before. George knew all the arguments, all the facts, although the Current River is a hundred and fifty miles from St. Louis and the project was not part of his job. Later that year, I heard he had quit the Park Service, because he thought he had no future in it. I went to

St. Louis and looked him up and asked him if he would come back and if he thought being director was enough of a future. He said, 'Mr. Secretary, I surely do.' "

Hartzog is busy catching trout. This river—the White River —is everything Tony Buford said it would be. Cal Smith, the riverman, has to work hard to keep Hartzog's hook covered with corn. The bait is canned kernel corn. The boat is anchored in a broad patch of dancing water. The corn drifts down through V-shaped riffles and, almost every time, disappears into the mouth of a trout. The White River is the dream of thousands, who come from all over the United States to fish it. It is broad, cold, clear, shallow, and frequently broken by the aerated rips that seem to intoxicate trout. The White River comes out of Bull Shoals Dam, near Lakeview, Arkansas. The water impounded on the other side of the dam is so deep that it is very cold near the bottom, and it is this cold water that comes shooting out of the penstocks and forms the river, which is green and beautiful and as natural as a city street. The White River grows toward the end of the day. Around 5:30 P.M., people start turning on lights, heating up ovens, and frying pork chops in Fayetteville, Little Rock, Mountain Home, Memphis. The river rises. More people, more pork chops—the river goes on rising. Turbines spin in Bull Shoals Dam. The peak comes when one million pork chops are sizzling all at once and the river is so high it flows around the trunks of trees. Then it starts going down. While Arkansas sleeps, the river goes down so far that the trout have to know where to go to survive. At 6 A.M., a small creek is running through the riverbed, viscous with trout. Then people start getting up in Fayetteville, Little Rock, Mountain Home, and Memphis. The fatback hits the frying pans. Up comes the river, cold, clear, fast, and green. Trout are not native down here. There are no trout in the Buffalo. They can live in the

White River for a hundred miles below Lakeview because of the refrigerant effect of the dam. The trout are born in a federal hatchery near Norfork, where they are raised on dry meal. They are stocked in the White River—ninety-six thousand trout a month in the summer—creating what most of the sport fishermen who have been here would call a paradise. Smith strings corn like pearls on Hartzog's hook, one kernel after another, completely covering the metal from eye to barb. Hartzog flips the bait into the stream. Vapors rise from the cold river. The line and the rod vibrate. It is difficult to tell whether the vibration is from the strike of a trout or the pull of the current. Once more it is a trout. Hartzog reels the fish in. It flips once to the right, once to the left, and lolls by the boat as it is netted. The trout is nine inches long. With a pair of forceps, Smith takes the hook out of the fish's gullet. Then he re-beads the hook with corn while Hartzog tells him about Hazel Creek in the Great Smoky Mountains. "There hasn't been a stocked trout put in that creek in three hundred years," he says. "Mountain people have been fishing Hazel Creek since European civilization moved over here. And there's only been one kind of trout in there, ever, and those are wild trout. I fish for the fun of fishing, and there's a real difference between a hatchery fish and a wild fish. One good bass out of the Buffalo would be worth more to me than six hundred trout out of here. Tony and the boys can stay here if they want. I'm going back up the Buffalo."

Hartzog believes that he was the youngest preacher ever licensed in the state of South Carolina. ("The Lord has looked out for me all my life.") He began preaching when he was sixteen, and the following year—1937—he officially became a licensed local minister. He preached all over the area—in Smoaks, in Cottageville, in Walterboro—and for a time he was assistant minister at the Bethel Methodist Church in Spartanburg. He gave his sermons in Baptist churches, too. In that part of the world, a Baptist was defined as an educated Methodist.

Hartzog's family had moved into Walterboro when the farm failed at Smoaks. His father got a job as a ticket agent for the Greyhound Bus Lines, and his mother became county supervisor of W.P.A. sewing rooms. A tall woman, severe and serious, she seemed to believe fundamentally in work. "She worked hard. She pulled the family through. She believed you couldn't fail to achieve anything if you just worked. She encouraged me and instilled in me the responsibility for working." The law ultimately attracted Hartzog as a kind of practical replacement for his first ambition, which was to spend his life in the ministry. In 1937, he entered Wofford College, in Spartanburg, to study Methodist theology and become something more than an unpaid travelling preacher, but he had to drop out of college after one semester for lack of money.

He went home and worked at any jobs he could find. He cooked and washed dishes in an all-night beanery. He pumped gas at an Amoco station. He typed forms and letters for the National Youth Administration. He worked around the clock. At night, he was busboy and desk clerk at A. J. Novit's Lafayette Hotel. From 6 P.M. to 6 A.M., he watched the teletype machine for reservations coming in, and he carried bags when the people showed up. "In a service establishment, you learn a lot about human beings," he says. Novit paid him one dollar a night.

Hartzog had no idea that he was underprivileged. To the contrary, he felt lucky to have encountered people who opened doors for him, first to the ministry and then to the law. He went on preaching. No one in his congregations seemed to mind that a teen-ager was giving them the Word. He still preaches whenever he can, in churches around Washington, and to his congregations he has explained his work in the Park Service by saying, "I feel that I am performing a mission as necessary and constructive as a ministry."

Hartzog has never seen anything quite like the Silver Gull Club, Beach 193, Breezy Point, Queens. This wide, low structure rambles lumpily all over the beach and on piles out over the ocean. The Park Service has learned something peculiar about the way the people of New York use their beaches. On Coney Island, on Jones Beach, on Rockaway Beach, more than half the people prefer never to put a toe in the ocean. The Silver Gull Club caters to this majority. It lifts its clientele above the ocean, and even above the beach. The waves of the Atlantic lap helplessly at the club's cantilevered undersides. Abovedecks, there are three swimming pools, four hundred cabañas, and a cocktail lounge called the Crystal Palace. Families spend five hundred dollars per season to go to the Silver Gull, where they can be close to the ocean but free from contact with the wild sea, and free from contact with its gritty edges.

This is outermost Queens, the middle of the proposed Gateway National Recreation Area, and Hartzog's brochure indicates that the Silver Gull and everything around it will someday be cleared away. The streets in that part of the city are largely deserted in winter, and they are used as unofficial, illegal dumps, where trucks make deposits in the dead of night: rotting timbers from razed buildings, ash, smooth tires, shards of concrete, stripped and crumpled automobiles—tons upon tons of junk. "One of the greatest things that could happen to this country would be just to clean it up," Hartzog says. Detritus is nothing new to him. The national parks are for people, and people leave junk wherever they go. Park rangers become so disgusted they can't wait for the season to end, so the people will go away from the parks. People throw

trash over the rim of the Grand Canyon, the world's deepest
and widest wastebasket. So much trash goes into the Grand
Canyon that the view is smirched. For this reason, ranger
trainees are sent to Grand Canyon National Park to learn
mountaineering. They go down on ropes and climb back up
with the things that tourists throw over the rim. In Yellowstone, visitors throw junk into the thermal pools. The temperature of the pools is two hundred degrees. Rangers have to rake
out the junk. In Washington, D.C., people throw tires, washing machines, refrigerators, mattresses, and automobiles into
the Potomac and the Anacostia Rivers. The Park Service cleans
up the mess with a thirty-five-foot landing craft. The Park
Service has used a scuba team to collect all the junk that
tourists throw into the Merced River, in Yosemite Valley. Cans
and bottles retrieved from Lake Powell, in Utah, fill five
barges a week. "Learning how to pick up trash better than
anyone else is a significant achievement in itself," Hartzog
says. In his view, the most heroic achievers in this line are the
trash gatherers of Coney Island, and Hartzog from time to
time sends his superintendents there to give them a whiff of
the major leagues.

The skeletons of five six-story buildings and two fifteen-
story buildings stand on Breezy Point, above the trash. The
Wagner administration condemned these buildings when they
were under construction, because they represented an en-
croachment of high-rise upon a beach area. The Park Service
plans to finish the two fifteen-story buildings and turn them
into cultural centers and low-cost hostels. Beyond the skeletal
buildings, bent and twisted chain-link fencing topped with
barbed wire separates the developed wasteland from the
virginal dunes of Breezy Point. The ocean, pounding, is visible
through the fence. Hartzog, in a government car, says he is
allergic to chain-link fencing and barbed wire and can't wait to
get rid of it. The car swings around and into the Breezy Point

Cooperative—twenty-eight hundred small one-story houses on a compact grid of streets. A third of the houses are equipped for year-round use. The cooperative covers four hundred and three acres in all, and its future is a sensitive political issue. In Hartzog's brochure, the area now filled by the Breezy Point Cooperative is designated as "creative open space."

The car turns onto Cross Bay Boulevard and moves toward the middle of Jamaica Bay. "We're about out of the opportunity to set aside wilderness areas," Hartzog says. "What we need to do now is to set aside areas close to or in the cities. City people are dying of social pollution, and they need room to move in." Park Service projects like New York's Gateway are planned or are already under development in Washington, St. Louis, Los Angeles, San Francisco, Corpus Christi, Philadelphia, and Chicago. Rangers used to spend nine months of their one-year training period assigned to a national park; now they spend the same nine months in a city, and rangers and administrators throughout the system get a Lewis and Clark feeling whenever they contemplate asphalt jungles and urban skylines. Their enthusiasm to bring the national parks to the people may entail the removal of some people—such as, quite possibly, the people of Broad Channel, an island community in Jamaica Bay. Hartzog's car is cruising down the central street of Broad Channel, past Audrey Murphy's Lounge, the St. Virgilius Parish Hall, and dead-end streets that reach like fishbones into the bay. The people of Broad Channel lease city land. They and their predecessors have been there for over seventy years. The community has a population of five thousand now—in a thousand houses, most of which are covered with tarpaper decorated to resemble brick or stone. The outermost houses are on pilings. Sewage, untreated, goes into the water. Ultimately, the Park Service would like to depopulate Broad Channel altogether.

Adjacent to Broad Channel is the Jamaica Bay Wildlife

Refuge. Hartzog stops and takes a walk. "This is the world's only wildlife refuge that has a subway station," he observes, and this is true: the IND stops there. Moving along a sand trail with the midtown-Manhattan skyline in clear view, he sees egrets, bitterns, black ducks, ruddy ducks, a muskrat, rabbits, quails, and phalaropes. More than two hundred and fifty species of birds inhabit Jamaica Bay, and various kinds of mammals, and uncounted varieties of fish. Jamaica Bay embarrasses the ecological crisis. Jamaica Bay is in all likelihood one of the most polluted bodies of water in North America. It pulses with wildlife.

A ranger walking with Hartzog says, "Those fellows out in Yellowstone don't know what they're missing."

"They haven't learned that all the wilderness isn't in the woods," Hartzog tells him. "Good Lord, what's that?"

"That's a horseshoe crab," the ranger answers. "It's one of the oldest forms of life."

Hartzog slaps his way through a cloud of mosquitoes, then stops to watch two Canada geese land in a freshwater pond that is isolated from the saline bay by grass-covered hummocks. Twenty minutes later, he registers at the Hotel Taft and sends the ranger out for a pint of whiskey. They have a drink in Hartzog's room before going to Mamma Leone's for dinner.

Responding to the buzzer, Hartzog picks up his office telephone, speaks his name, listens, smiles, and the smile widens into a grin. He draws deeply on his cigar, No. 11 today, blows out a billow of smoke, and at the same time reaches for a fresh cigarette. He puts down the receiver, picks it up again, and asks his secretary to call various senators. "We won the Everglades hands down," he tells her. "Isn't that fabulous?" The Senate Public Works Committee has just put the mark of Cain on the Army Corps of Engineers.

Hartzog calls the Secretary of the Interior, tells him the good news, chuckles once, guffaws twice, wreathes himself in puffed smoke, and afterward says, "That man is saltier than fat pork." An architect from Louisville is waiting outside the door. "He's got some ideas on how I ought to run Mammoth Cave, so I'm going to let him come in here and tell me how to run Mammoth Cave," Hartzog says. "Send him in."

The architect is a tall man with a weathered face, and the distillate of what he has to say is this: "There's a commercial hub developing on your periphery down there, and it's all junk and crud."

The Park Service owns land in something like a five-mile radius around the entrance to Mammoth Cave. Near the property line—as on the edges of many parks—honky-tonk agglomerates. "I talked to those people down there about zoning," Hartzog says. " 'Zoning?' they said. 'Zoning?' I had the impression that I was in a foreign land."

Mammoth Cave is so mammoth that it reaches underground even beyond the boundaries of the park. The architect now tells Hartzog that surface pollutants from the junk and crud of the commercial hub are seeping down into the cave. Hartzog thanks the architect for this unattractive news, and for alerting Washington to still another threat to the environment—speleological pollution.

Three men from the General Services Administration come in, ushered by one of Hartzog's assistant directors. The General Services Administration is about to demolish the office buildings on Constitution Avenue that were put up as "temporary" structures during the First World War. The three men try to make a deal with Hartzog for a small piece of land they would like to use for a U-turn for trucks. "That's like trading a bucket of coal for two buckets of ashes," Hartzog says. "I gave that up when I left the Ozarks. I want a *quid pro quo*. If you

help me get the entire U.S. Congress off my back by opening
another access to the Key Bridge, I'll happily give you your U-
turn." When the office buildings go down, the Park Service
will take over the land they now stand on. The assistant
director says that lawns will fill the space. "The hell they will,"
Hartzog says. "Nat Owings wants to put rose gardens and a
restaurant there. The last thing we need in downtown Washington is more grass. We've got grass coming out of our ears in
this city, and in summer we let it turn brown. We're up to our
noses in horticulturists who don't know enough not to water
grass when it gets hot. We need more vistas like a Buick needs
a fifth hole. I don't think this is Paris. The strength and heart
of Washington is to reflect this country, which is virile and
informal and friendly."

Alone again, Hartzog punches a button on the telephone
console and says to his secretary, "I want a copy of the language that the Senate Public Works Committee passed today."

Representatives of the Student Conservation Association file
into the office. Hartzog settles into his armchair and lights a
cigar—No. 12, 7:20 P.M., the last working smoke of the day.
The Student Conservation Association is more or less a private, contemporary version of the Civilian Conservation
Corps. Its members labor for the Park Service, building trails,
building cabins. Hartzog watches them with a recruiter's eye,
looking for rangers. Most of them are in high school, and he
tries to nudge them toward his kind of curriculum. "I'm looking for social scientists, not just natural scientists," he tells
them. "It's not enough just to interpret the natural phenomena
of Yellowstone. I want people to staff big recreation areas near
urban ghettos." One thing that emerges in this interview is
that some members of the Student Conservation Association
are paid five hundred dollars a summer for doing the same
work as Park Service seasonal employees who are paid fifteen
hundred dollars. Hartzog explodes, picks up the phone, and

orders that a supplemental one thousand dollars be given to every student in such a situation. After the S.C.A. representatives leave, he blasts away at one of his assistants, who answers, "But I staffed it out with Management and Budget, the Bureau of Outdoor Recreation, the Department of Labor, and the Hill!"

"You're missing my point—I'm not articulating my point," Hartzog says. "I'm concerned about these youngsters. What they're trying to say to us, if they're trying to say anything, is that the Establishment is a bunch of hypocrites, and I kind of agree with them."

There is a buzz in the console. One of his calls to the Senate Office Building has gone through. He picks up the phone, and says, "Senator, I just called to say I deeply appreciate what happened on that south-Florida vote. I detected your fine hand in there, and . . ."

All afternoon, he has been on the Buffalo under five-hundred-foot cliffs, catching nothing and caring less. A hawk swoops across the blazing sun. It is a day of high, thin cirrus and pale-blue sky. "Look at that old buzzard sashaying around," Hartzog says to Cal Smith. "Now he's just a speck a-riding away. My Lord, what a beautiful place this is! We need this river real bad, and we're going to have to get it. There ought to be something around those bushes, Cal."

"Well, there sure had ought to be. This is a pretty deep pocket back down through here."

Smith puts a crawdad on Hartzog's hook, and Hartzog releases a high, soft shot toward the bushes. Splat.

Thirty minutes go by. Nothing whatever happens.

"There ought to be something where that little stream comes in there, Cal."

"Well, there sure had ought to be. There's always a pretty deep pocket in there by those little streams. There must be an old boy out there huntin' and makin' the rounds lookin' for crawdaddies. I just know it."

Another crawdad sails through the air. Splat. Thirty minutes go by. Nothing happens. Hartzog talks, almost to himself, about his parks. He talks about the big trees in Sequoia in the early morning, about the eerie moods in the rain forests of the Olympic Peninsula, and about rangers' airboats in the Everglades—the worst way to see the park. "You've got to be still, and in being still you see everything," he says. "The most beautiful thing I have ever seen in a national park is snow falling into the Grand Canyon. Reds, oranges, pinks, and browns come through the white snow. It falls quietly. It really helps you sort out all of life." He is silent for some minutes, watching the tip of his rod. "We're building a Museum of Immigration inside the base of the Statue of Liberty," he goes on. "Some of the things young people are protesting about are the very things that brought people to this country—personal involvement, achievement, commitment, the worth of the individual. We haven't perfected the system. It's a good system. A birthright. Youth today has its opportunity in perfecting the system, not rejecting it. 'Tear it down,' 'Burn it up' is the antithesis of what they are trying to say. The same things motivate them that motivated the people who established the system."

Slowly, the tip of his rod bends toward the river, then nods rapidly, four times.

"Snag?" says the riverman.

"No."

The line begins to run. Hartzog lets it go. He feeds it out through his hand, waiting, guessing, judging his moment. The line runs on. Then Hartzog, after five and a half hours of almost complete inactivity, makes his move. He stops the line, lifts the rod, and sets the hook. The line is taut and moves quickly across an arc of the river. It moves back. It moves in, and he reels the slack. It tightens, and the rod bends, throbbing, to a symmetrical U. The fish makes a final lateral dash, breaks the surface, and flies through the air—deep cordovan brown with a broad black tail, a two-and-a-half-pound wild bass.

Ruidoso

IN JUNE, 1973, a blue Ford pickup, freckled with mud, moved down out of the Ozarks, dragging a four-horse trailer. It crossed Oklahoma, and it crossed the Texas Panhandle. The weight of the horses—even though there were only three—was too much for the power of the motor. Miles came slowly in flat land, where the view from the cab—uninterrupted in every direction—ran over the curve of the earth. In the back of the truck was a big can of disinfectant and an even larger (ten-gallon) milk can full of gasoline. There was, as well, a cardboard box full of bottles and cans of vinegar, alcohol, Epsom salts, Bigeloil, Vaseline, Canada brace, flybait, Traileze, Louisiana leg brace, Absorbine senior. Eight hundred miles west of home, truck and trailer reached the beginnings of the Sacramento Mountains, in southern New Mexico, and the driver—Bill H. Smith, of Pea Ridge, Arkansas—had no choice

265

now but to gear down and crawl uphill. He had come out here on a kind of dare. There was a lot of jealousy in Pea Ridge, where Bill Smith was one among a thousand people. No dignity could be perfect in a town that size. About his horses, people liked to—as they say it there—gig him. "That stallion of yours, he isn't much, that old stallion, Bill." No one, on the other hand, was in any sense competing with him. If strangers came to Pea Ridge and asked, as they often did, for "the quarter-horse man," they could be asking only for Bill H. Smith. The semidesert fell behind, and the Ford slowly pulled the trailer up through the Hondo Valley—ponderosas rising from steep mountainsides, a clear stream flowing past cottonwoods and orchards (apples and apricots). Haciendas. Small wonder so much gunsmoke had hung there. With altitude, the temperature was markedly cooler. Four thousand, five thousand, six thousand feet. Smith intended to spend the whole summer up in the high country, so his horses would have ample time to get used to thin air. Gigs or no gigs, all of Pea Ridge was with him now, in his journey into the center of the quarter-racing world, where—fifty-six years old—he was still an unknown.

Bill's father was a horse-and-mule trader. In the nineteen-twenties, before the era came when horses and mules were shipped by rail or truck, Bill's father and other traders would make up a great herd of animals and drive them—"trail them"—for six months, from spring to early fall: "trail down plumb through the southern part of Arkansas into Louisiana, and then swing back into Texas, then up through Oklahoma." When Bill was eleven, twelve, and thirteen, he made the trip each year. Head to tail, fifteen animals would be tied together in a unit. Bill rode a horse at the head of such a unit. There might be as many as forty strings—six hundred head—on the move. The drive went from town to town, county seat to county seat, eighteen to twenty-five miles a day, trading animals all the way, camping by a stream at night. In every deal, the horse trader tried to "draw boot"—swap animals with a farmer and get some of his money to boot.

There was, of course, a chuck wagon, and tied to the back of the chuck wagon was a horse named Windmill. He belonged to Bill's father. As the drive approached a town, Windmill was taken from the back of the wagon and around to the front, where he was put in harness. Sometimes in the evenings Bill's father streaked Windmill's shoulders with peroxide so it would appear that Windmill had spent all his travelling days in the harness. Now the drive came into the town. People gathered to say hello, to talk, to stare, to look over the horses and the mules. "Windmill had a collar on him a size or two too large. Standing there in the middle of town, he would drop his head, and the collar would fall down on his neck. He'd let his lip go down. He'd drop his lower lip and hang his head. He just didn't look too good."

Sooner or later, somebody in the town would walk up and stand around for a while looking at all the animals and finally look Bill's father in the eye and say, "You got a race horse?" It was expected that a trader would carry a race horse.

Bill's father would say, "No." And he would look off down the street and not say anything more.

In time, the man might say, "Oh. I was hoping."

Smith senior would turn and just look at him.

In time, the man would say, "*I've* got a race horse."

This was known as "jumping the trader," or "bouncing the trader for a race." And there would be no immediate reaction from Bill's father. After a while, though, he would say, "Well, let's *see* your race horse."

A finger pointed at the town race horse. Every town had at least one. There followed a long look in its direction. Bill's father then pointed to the front of the chuck wagon. "Well, that old horse I'm a-workin' up there can outrun *him*," he would say.

"How much would you want to bet on that?"

"Not very much. But I'd run you four hundred and forty yards for twenty-five dollars."

("My dad's idea was not to scare him.")

"Hell, I wouldn't run my horse for twenty-five dollars," the townsman said, and spat off the curb into the dirt.

"Oh. Well. How much would you run him for?"

The crowd that had inevitably collected by this time was a small one, but interested, and crowd enough to get up fifty here and twenty-five there until as much as a thousand dollars had been assembled on each of the two sides.

Windmill, as it happened, was "a practically straight Thoroughbred horse," so close to pure that in this context the difference was irrelevant. He was "a big roan bald-faced horse," and in his lifetime he never lost a race. If the town was a county seat—Arkadelphia, El Dorado, Nacogdoches—it would have some sort of race track, and if there was no track the crowd headed out to the edge of a field, a section line. Bill—eleven, twelve, thirteen years old—was Windmill's rider, and all the horse had on him was a neck rope and Bill, wearing overalls and a homemade shirt. "Windmill had a nice personality until that neck rope went on him. He was a running horse—a typical modern quarter horse. He was heavy-muscled, yet he showed a lot of Thoroughbred." Bill was too small to stop him, and after Windmill had shot across the finish line he would run on for two miles for the sheer galloping joy of it. The Smiths owned him until he died.

The pickup and the four-horse trailer finally made it all the way up the valley, and far into Lincoln National Forest, near the edge of the reservation of the Mescalero Apache—among the tribes of the United States, the last to give up. At elevation sixty-four hundred feet, Smith came to his destination, where a big sign by the roadside said, "Ruidoso Downs, Home of the World's Richest Horse Race."

Smith turned his truck in at a drive marked "Horsemen's Entrance." He clattered downhill and across a trout stream into a broad spread of barns. He found the racing office and got an assignment of stalls, went to them, and sprayed them up and down from his can of disinfectant. Then he opened his trailer and took out his horses. One was a pony horse. The two others were quarter-horse colts.

In Ruidoso, at the end of the summer, ten horses would sprint a quarter mile in pursuit of seven hundred and sixty-six thousand dollars—this by far the largest purse in horse racing, any kind of horse racing, anywhere in the world. It was a sum almost twice as large as the combined purses of the Kentucky Derby, the Preakness, and the Belmont Stakes. The winner's share alone would be three hundred and thirty thousand dollars—awarded after a blur of a race, hard to follow, a flat-out cavalry charge that would last a third of a minute, start to finish. The quarter-racing horse was bred specifically for this kind of dash. At short distance, nothing equine can touch the quarter horse—not even the Thoroughbred. New Mexico is one of the few states in the United States where quarter-horse races and Thoroughbred races can be run on the same track on the same day, and the difference is considerable. After a race in which the quarter horses come cracking down the big straightaway, all bunched as they flash across the line, Thoroughbreds, making their plodded rounds, disconcert the observer. Furlong upon furlong, they seem to lope along, panting, and one wonders anxiously if they will make it to the end.

The setting is a small race track in big dry mountains that rise up to eleven and twelve thousand feet. Ruidoso is a linear town, stretched out along miles of highway in creases of the mountains, its wide streets lined with flaky plastic. Curio bins. Drive-in burgers. The same versatile hand that painted Las Vegas into the desert may have painted Ruidoso into the mountains. One has only to get on a horse and go sidewise, though, up into a canyon or onto a mesa, to see what beautiful country Ruidoso was built in and why the town is the retreat and playground of, primarily, Texans. Ruidoso is where Texans cool off. It is in the nearest mountain region to the plains of West Texas, and Texans have been going to Ruidoso in big numbers for many decades. Long before there was a track, the Texans on holiday were betting on horses. They brought their quarter horses with them, their "cow ponies." (The quarter horse is the horse of the cowboy—the roping horse, the cattle cutter unparalleled.) Conversations would develop roughly like the ones about Windmill.

"I'd run you four hundred and forty yards for twenty-five hundred dollars."

"Hell, I wouldn't *run* my horse for twenty-five hundred dollars."

"Well, then, how about twenty-five thousand?"

Match races were held in the shadow of Gavilan Ridge, on the only stretch of ground that approximated level, the place where the grandstand and barns of Ruidoso Downs were eventually built. They were gamblers at base, these vacationing Texans. If they had not had horses to bet on, they would have bet on frogs. The All-American Futurity, Ruidoso's big race, exploits that particular kind of horse owner right in the soul. When their horses are very small and not even far off the teat, owners start writing checks to Ruidoso Downs, each owner obviously picturing not the little stilt in the pasture but a champion quarter horse exploding out of the gate. They put in fifty dollars at first. ("My dad's idea was not to scare him.")

The first fifty dollars toward the All-American Futurity of

1973 was due on January 15, 1972, and money flooded into Ruidoso in the name of one thousand and seventy-two colts and fillies. The owners, for the most part, were Texans and Oklahomans. Cattle ranchers. Wheatland ranchers. Some oil people. Here and there a road contractor, a doctor, a film star, a lawyer. The almost common denominator of the owners was that they, like the owners of racing Thoroughbreds, were very rich. It was not completely unimaginable—but somewhere near it—that an unrich man sitting around having his coffee in a drugstore in a small town in Arkansas, as Bill Smith did every morning, might see himself as an owner equipped to enter the All-American, might hear once too often that his old stallion was producing not so many horses as dogs, and that if his horse and its get were really as good as he said they were then why didn't he enter those two new colts of his in that race in New Mexico? Smith said he figured those two colts had the bloodlines to do it, but he didn't want to be away from fishing that long. "*Do* it, Bill," said his friend Wayne Laughlin, a feed salesman. "You *should* put those two colts in the All-American."

"All right," Bill said. "I believe I will." And a hundred dollars went from Pea Ridge, Arkansas, to Ruidoso Downs.

On March 15, 1972, when a hundred additional dollars per horse was due, eighty-seven horses dropped out. But nearly a thousand stayed in, and that second payment added about a hundred thousand dollars to the pot. A third payment was due in June—a hundred and fifty dollars this time—and more than a hundred horses quit. The pot, though, moved up to over two hundred and fifty thousand dollars. October 1st, December 15th, March 15th, payments due went up in small, coaxing increments of fifty and then a hundred dollars, while the number of paid-up owners gradually grew smaller. Anyone who owned a two-year-old registered quarter horse that had not been entered in the All-American could buy eligibility for the horse with a penalty payment—on or before June 1, 1973—of six thousand two hundred and fifty dollars. Eight such penalties were paid. On June 15th, when the next incremental payment (five hundred dollars) was due, some three hundred and fifty horses stayed in. After rubber checks were deducted (there had by now been seventeen of them), the total pot accrued to date was one million thirty-one thousand four hundred and twenty-five dollars.

In order to determine the ten horses that would take part in the climactic race, to be run on Labor Day, all eligibles would race in trial heats a week before. In hundredths of a second, every horse would be timed, and the ten fastest, notwithstanding where they may have placed in their trial heats, would be the ten horses of the All-American. Their purse would draw seven hundred and sixty-six thousand dollars out of the pot. The horses that ran from eleventh to fortieth in the trials would run in other races and partake—in lesser substance—of the mother lode.

Twenty-five hundred dollars was the aggregate required for a horse that had been paid in from the beginning, but there was one more chance for a late horse to get into the field. Just chip in fifteen thousand dollars on or before August 15th, and join the group. Owners of twelve horses came forth with such money—a hundred and eighty thousand dollars. When everything was added up, including more than thirty thousand dollars in interest payments from the Ruidoso State Bank, the total pot collected for the 1973 All-American was, in round figures, a million five hundred thousand dollars. The track management, though, had decided to hold on to the excess over a million, and to apply it to still another race—for these same horses a year hence, when they were three-year-olds. All they would have to do to stay eligible would be to make a few additional, incremental payments.

There have been smaller pyramids. The man who, some

twenty years ago, developed and first promoted this hippic chain letter frenetically travelled the Southwest—the quarter-horse states—seeking out owners, selling his race, signing them up. He was, at the time, the owner of the track. Eventually, he had to watch the big race on television, if at all, because he was confined to a federal penitentiary for tax evasion.

One of Bill H. Smith's colts, Joy's Cutter, pulled up lame during his first workout at Ruidoso and was finished for the season, fit only to move slowly in circles on the exercise walker and to eat his daily hay, at up to seven dollars a bale—many times what it would cost at home. The other colt, Calcutta Deck, was a gentle bay with a small star on his forehead. He had the gluteal muscles of an eight-ton jackrabbit. His grandfather Top Deck had sired a great line of quarter horses. And his great-great-grandfather was Wilson's Yellow Cat, "the Iron Horse of Arkansas." The iron horse had once won two match races in a single day. All this—as quarter horses go—did not add up to aristocracy; but neither, on paper, was Smith a fool. He had not come a thousand miles with nothing. The breeding of the horse was not expensive, but it was not common, either. In the vernacular of the business, the horse had the license to win.

Bill called him simply Deck. "This horse right here," he would say, shoving the horse aside so he could muck out his stall, "this horse right here, you could take him off this track and in a month have him working cattle if you wanted to." Something similar might have been said of Smith himself. One look at him suggested a rolled smoke, a shivery morning, coffee in an iron pot, inseparability from the horse. He was a small, spare man, trim. He walked in a natural riding position. When he stood still, he bent forward as one would when brushing one's teeth. More often than not, he had a toothpick in his mouth, or a cigarette. When he spoke, he leaned right at you. This helped make his words emphatic. He had seven small diamonds in a ring on his right hand. The skin across his face was tight, and he had sharp brown eyes that moved quickly but without suspicion. He wore a long-sleeved shirt, Levi's, a big silver buckle from Ozark Downs. "Leading Trainer." Ozark Downs had folded five years before. "Race interest kind of left out down there." On his head was a Bulldogger hat—four-inch curling brim—and it came off virtually never. When it did, it revealed hair as black as shoe polish, beginning halfway back.

Smith was registered at the Horseshoe Court motel, hard by the main road of town, and when he was not down at the barns he was up at the motel sitting under a shade tree, a big cottonwood, playing dominoes and talking about his horse. He ate breakfast soon after five, lunch at ten-thirty, dinner at four. He moved his patronage a lot, the food in town was so bad. He washed his clothes in a coin laundry, and he missed his home, his wife, his boat, the fishing. As Labor Day drew near, he slept less and less. He weighed a hundred and fifty-five when he arrived in Ruidoso. In the course of the summer he lost fifteen pounds. He had companions. Jimmy Grimes, his assistant, his exercise boy, had made the trip with him. Wayne Laughlin, the feed salesman, who had retired, joined them there. Jimmy walked slowly as a result of polio. If Calcutta Deck hit it big, it was Smith's intention to use part of the winnings to pay for an operation for Jimmy. Money would go also to a crippled-children's hospital in Little Rock. All summer long, Smith never left Ruidoso, was never more than five or ten minutes away from his horse, with one exception, a short tour of the reservation of the Mescalero Apache.

The horse had a radio down in the barn and liked listening to it. He liked hard rock and country-and-Western. He liked the six-o'clock news. He was a neat horse. His droppings always landed in the same place in the stall, making it easy for Bill and his pitchfork. Bill walked Deck by hand, in a small oval outside the stall, or had Jimmy lead him with the pony; he never put the horse on a walker. Walkers were invented to reduce the high cost of grooms. A walker is a mechanized device that has four cantilevered steel arms, lead ropes attached, leading four horses in a circle. Many dozens of them were spaced among the barns. Horses have on rare occasions been electrocuted by walkers, which are powered by electric motors that gently coax the horses to move. Horses have tried to bolt away from walkers and have broken their necks.

Bill rubbed some of his own formula leg brace over the metacarpals of Deck. "The skill is with the feet and the legs," Wayne said. Wayne was a heavyset man with wavy gray hair. He, like Bill, was about as talkative as Jimmy Grimes was silent. "I don't think there's a man in the world who understands horses and horses' legs better than Bill does," Wayne went on. "He could have been one of the great trainers. But he just took his own horses. He don't like to be away from home."

"We're not rich people," Bill confessed. "These millionaires has tried to win the All-American years and years. Fellow out of Kansas City had ten entered once. The Old Boy upstairs has to help you. Somebody has to."

Larry Wilson, Deck's jockey, turned up shivering at the barn one morning at five-thirty. The temperature was fifty. Deck was going to go out on the track for a blow. Smith said, "It's colder than a well digger's butt. Look at Larry, there—hair standing up on his arms like the bristles on a hog." Larry was unusually tall for a jockey, blond, slender, fine-featured. He was thirty-one and was from Kansas, and had been riding quarter-horse races since he was sixteen. In the early-morning light, Wayne and Bill watched Deck gallop, Larry clinging for—if nothing else—warmth.

The track was a small oval, five-eighths of a mile around, the inside plowed by circling Thoroughbreds. Tangent to the oval was a straightaway as broad as a turnpike, where ten quarter horses could race abreast. The straightaway reached far back into the barn area. Quarter horses of various ages and classes dash three hundred, three hundred and fifty, four hundred, four hundred and forty, and sometimes five hundred and fifty yards. In the infield were two flagpoles, and a tote board about the size of a one-room cabin, and the graves of two quarter horses, and two small ponds, one in the shape of an R, the other in the shape of a D, with an R- and a D-shaped island in their respective centers. What was painted had been painted blue—grandstand, rail, filming towers, starting gate. Hanging limp from the flagpoles were the flags of New Mexico and the United States. They were wind indicators to the horsemen, who watched them closely. When the flags straightened out and whipped toward the east, as they often did, racing quarter horses had to dig through a direct head wind all the way.

By the standards of quarter racing, such a track had grandeur, for the old brush tracks of the type Windmill had run on were still in use as well. In Louisiana, for example, horses still run in clearings in woods, between rail fences set up as lanes—no starting gate, just ready-set-go. Riders race for cigars, for eggs. The practice has been called "folk racing." Within ten miles of Evangeline Downs—a quarter-racing track in Lafayette, Louisiana—are ten brush tracks. There are more than a hundred actual quarter-horse race tracks in the United States, and of these many do not have pari-mutuel systems— not Blue Ribbon Downs, in Sallisaw, Oklahoma, where Bill Smith first raced Deck, or Blue Stem Downs, in Emporia, Kansas, or Life Downs, in Laredo. Narrow Gauge Downs is in Durango, Colorado, Uranium Downs in Grand Junction. There are two tracks in Michigan, five in Ohio, and two in Florida, but most are in the West, and the preeminent ones are

Bay Meadows and Los Alamitos, in California, and, in New Mexico, Sunland Park and Ruidoso Downs.

"The horse is a gentleman this morning," Wayne said.

Bill explained, "He's on the track. He's a race horse. He knows what he's there for."

"He's broke just like an old horse, as if he had run a hundred times," Larry Wilson said when he brought Deck in from his gallop. "I think they're going to have to catch him here if they want to beat him."

Before travelling to Ruidoso, Bill tried Deck in four races, in Oklahoma and Kansas, and Deck won three of them. On two occasions, he ended the day with the fastest time of any horse on the program. ("We knew we had something good then.") Some years ago, Wilson had broken an arm in the starting gate, a dangerous place for sitting on a quarter horse. "You're glad to get out and away," he said. "You sure enough are. But this colt doesn't make any mistakes at all. You can relax on him and get ready to go. He puts his head right up there in the front and doesn't move."

When Deck came in from any kind of exercise, Smith washed off his legs and feet with a hose—no telling what he might have got into out there. Finished rinsing, he let Deck take hold of the hose and drink. When Bill forgot to do this, Deck bit him. Bill frequently sprayed the walls of the stall with disinfectant. "A horse can be well one day and a sick peckerwood the next," he would say. "There are so many viruses around the barn. I've got to take care of him. All of northwest Arkansas—that's their horse now."

Bill's farm in Pea Ridge is small. Or, as a Ruidoso Texan might say, "thirty-five acres would kill it dead." Smith has eight brood mares, and runs some cattle, and raises horses for rodeos as well as for racing. Bill himself rode broncos for ten years in rodeos, breaking ribs, fingers, tearing cartilage in his knees. He rode a bull once that got a horn inside his pants, tore them completely off, and stood there in triumph with the shredded Levi's hanging from the horn. Bill has raced his own horses for twenty-two years, mainly in Kansas, Oklahoma, and Missouri, and, before the track closed down, in Arkansas. He says he can tell early, even when a horse is still a "little old shaggy colt," if it is going to be good as a runner. "You can watch a colt in the pasture. See his action. You can tell if he's got speed or not. Say the mares are way up in the pasture. The colts are way down by the pond. The colts have a horse race getting back to the mares. The little cusses all race together, all coming for their mammy." Deck was a quick one getting back to his mammy.

The colt needed race experience at Ruidoso, and toward the end of July—although he had been there almost two months— he had still not been given a chance to run. There were racing programs four times a week, but races for two-year-old quarter horses were insufficient to include all the horses that had collected to prepare for the All-American. It was impera- tive that Deck run at least once. Bill felt he needed it badly. So he entered Deck in the one race he could get—of all things, a claiming race. For ten thousand dollars, in this instance, any- one who wanted to buy a horse running in the race had only to present a certified check at the track office beforehand. Then, after the race, the new owner would approach the old one and take the horse. Smith, as it happened, had offered to sell Deck for a thousand dollars when he was a yearling, but he obvi- ously figured him for a great deal more than ten times that now. The claiming device is a method of making a horse race, of finding a level for a field. Owners and trainers, in effect, classify their own horses. A horse will "buy no feed" when it is entered in a claiming race above its level. Theoretically, it will run last. So it must run at the level of its worth, and an owner should be content with the price if the horse should be claimed. There is an old simple saying about owners who bemoan the loss of horses in claiming races: "They can read and write." That is, they knew it was a claiming race; they knew the conditions; they entered the race. Bill Smith, for his part, knew exactly what he was risking, but he reasoned, "Deck never had run in this country. Nobody knew a thing about him. He was an unknown horse."

Deck drew the 1 hole, the inside position in the starting gate—the worst position as well. The quarter-horse straightaway joined what might be called the Thoroughbred oval about halfway through the race, and quarter horses coming out of the 1 hole had to run in the plowed furrows of the Thoroughbreds. The track was heavy from recent rain. Deck was good in mud, but the situation lacked promise. Yet he won, in the fastest quarter-horse time of that day.

As Deck was led back toward the saddling paddock, Bill, moving to meet him, was addressed by a man—a rancher—who was leaning against a post, looking down, potato-chip hat over his eyes. Never looking up, the man said, "Would you take ten thousand dollars for this horse?"

Relieved immeasurably, Bill said, "I don't believe so today."

Rich and John came in by air on the Sunday before the trials. Those were their nicknames—what everyone close around them called them, particularly their trainer, Jerry Fisher. Rich and John were California quarter horses bred, born, and raised, and they were accustomed to an elevation far lower than Pea Ridge, let alone the mountains of New Mexico. So Fisher started them at once on twice-daily rations of bottled oxygen. Their home was the Vessels Stallion Farm, near Anaheim, nearer sea level, and their owner, Frank Vessels, Jr., was a grandee of quarter racing, as his father had been. The Vessels family had a four-hundred-and-fifty-acre compound, which included their breeding farm, a golf course, five private homes (their own and Fisher's among them), and

Los Alamitos, their prodigiously successful quarter-horse race track. Since the inception of the All-American, in 1959, the Vessels family had been trying to win it.

Sometimes at Los Alamitos, to delight the crowd before the beginning of a night's racing program, Vessels stages milk runs. Brood mares stand by the finish line. Their foals, from a hundred and fifty yards away, bedazzled by floodlight, run to their mothers like condensed giraffes. John, in his time, was the star of the milk runs. He liked milk. He also liked Hershey Bars, Nestlé's Crunch, Mars Bars, and chocolate doughnuts. His favorite drink was Pepsi-Cola. He grew up on such stuff, living around a race track like that, and so did Rich. As John matured, he became a lazy horse, and began what would apparently be a life-long habit of spending much of his day lying down in his stall. When it came time for him to race, he would stop to rest on the way from the barn to the paddock. Still, he could outrun a bullet. Rich, for his part, had always been alert. Always looking around, always biting something. If anything moved near his stall, Rich would stick his head out to see what was happening—while John, next door, slept on. John's father was Father John. John, of course, needed a name of his own, and in the quarter-horse registry he was Go Fartherfaster. Rich's father was Aforethought and his mother was Chronometer, so they called him Timeto Thinkrich.

An overland drive was thought to be too punishing for these two; hence they were flown to Roswell, seventy miles east of Ruidoso. Fisher brought with him a bag full of candy bars and chocolate doughnuts. He bought local Pepsi-Cola. The candy, the doughnuts, the Pepsi, and the oxygen might see them through. On the day of the trials, he put muzzles on them. "When you muzzle them, they know they're going to run," he said. "These two colts are pretty good eaters. With the muzzle, they're not filling up. You want these quarter horses fresh. You want them high. With Thoroughbreds, they blow those horses out the day before. A lot of Thoroughbreds gallop the day they run. They don't want Thoroughbreds to be too fresh. These colts are nice colts. They're hard-knocking colts. Rich is always walking around, playing around. John, though, he don't get high. He rests a lot. He's down in his stall. When he is on the walker, he stands still. If he so much as shakes his head, he's feeling good. He acts like a saddle horse. He's just kind of a big old pet."

Fisher, as a trainer, was under his fourth millionaire. He had worked for several of the prominent farms in the business. Five times, horses he trained had run in the All-American, and the most successful of them had placed third. He had been a jockey—a brush-track rider from the age of ten, a professional from seventeen. He came from Meade, Kansas. Toward the end of the nineteen-fifties, he had found it "too hard to do the weight" and had become a trainer. Thirty-seven now, slim, shy, recently married, he looked ten years younger.

Frank Vessels, a ship captain of a man with rampant sideburns and a tan head, had paid thirty thousand dollars to give Rich and John a chance at the All-American. Vessels' approach was to ignore all the peanut payments, look over his crop of two-year-olds, decide which might win, pay the maximum penalty at the ultimate moment, and send the horses to Ruidoso. No horse from California had won the All-American in ten years. California quarter-horse people wanted badly to change that. A third California horse had also paid fifteen thousand to come in, and riding it would be the foremost jockey in quarter racing. The word among the Texans was that the Californians had come to Ruidoso "loaded for bear."

When the trials came, Rich drew the 7 hole in the fourteenth race. Deck unluckily drew the 1 hole, in the twelfth. Three horses were scratched only hours before, reducing the total number from the eleven hundred-odd that in one way or another were represented in the pot to two hundred and seven. To put them through trial heats, twenty-one races would be required, all in a single program, beginning in the morning and ending in gathered dusk. John drew the 8 hole in the twenty-first race, and could sleep through the morning and the afternoon.

Starting a quarter-horse race is extraordinarily difficult, for so much can be gained or lost in the first part of the first second. Human sprinters—diggers or floaters or whatever they may be in their various styles on the straightaway—are losers if they do not, at the beginning, find the rhythm of the gun. With Thoroughbred horses, the start of a race is important, to be sure, but Thoroughbreds have a lot of ground to cover, and they are in some ways like human distance runners, who, seeming to loiter in groups as they wait for the gun, do not even bother to bend over. Thoroughbreds, for all the difficulties they can cause in the gate, are mild in there compared with quarter horses. The least dispensable talent in Ruidoso belonged to Dean Turpitt, the starter.

Turpitt was an independent, freelance contractor, offering his crew and himself as a package to the management of the track. Far removed from grandstand and barn, his starting gate was his own principality, where his decisions were absolute, and he controlled there something that was like the isthmus of an hourglass, a point of transfer between disparate milieus—the grandstand on the one hand, the barns on the other. The grandstand—with its Jockey Club, its All-American Turf Club—was full of millionaires who looked like vaudeville cowboys in tailored jeans, their abdomens sparkling with platters of silver. Turpitt called them "Texas-buckled sons of bitches." He wore a plain business suit and a Knox panama. Behind him were the barns—long, quiet corridors, people around who looked like farmers, rare the owner who, like the trainers, was welded to the creatures in the stalls. There were fourteen hundred stalls. Loudspeakers there said, "Take your horses to the paddock for the twelfth race. Take your horses to the paddock for the twelfth race." And Calcutta Deck walked half a mile, through the complex of barns, around the beginning of the straightaway, and down a long path to the paddock, in the shadow of the stand. When the horses approached the gate, Turpitt was standing in a small tower, outside the rail, with an electric cord in his hand. His voice was soft and low, somewhat husky, but it carried successfully into the gate, where seven men in baseball hats did what he suggested.

"If the 8 horse gets a little bouncy, who's got him?"

"I do, Dean."

"O.K., Cotton. Just pick up his tail a little bit if he gives you trouble."

The horses were led, pulled, or crammed, one by one, into the gate—in this case, in numerical order.

"Kent, get that 3 horse's feet under him."

Some horses cause so much trouble in the gate that Turpitt has them kept out until the last minute and then stuffed in. Some other horses will freeze if they stand in the gate too long, or, conversely, relax so completely that when the gates open they just stand there and don't move. So they, too, are kept out until the last minute.

On a program in Turpitt's pocket were hieroglyphs beside the names of the horses in this race, reminders to himself of their inconvenient idiosyncrasies. When a horse might require some wrestling into line, there was beside his name an "H," for "handle." Where the program said "Bill H. Smith, Pea Ridge, Arkansas, owner, Calcutta Deck," Turpitt had written nothing. That horse in the 1 hole was all right. Turpitt had seen him before.

"That 10 horse is going to need tail, Gene."

They were all in the gate now—forty hooves, ten heads, ten jocks in their racing silks, seven crewmen.

At the back of the starting gate, on the ground, was a heavy steel bar that backed up all ten holes. It served the same purpose that starting blocks serve for a human sprinter. It was called the braking block. The quarter horses in the gate worked their hind feet back against it—the better to spring away.

"Johnny, hold the horse's nose down a little."

"I can't get hold of him, Dean."

"Well, *get* a hold. This bus is leaving."

"Hold it, Dean."

"Hold it."

"Hold it."

"Back him up, Cotton."

"Dean."

"Dean."

"No, Dean."

The entire gate, a steel structure ten feet high and more than twenty feet wide, vibrated from the activity within it—heads whipping, forced straight, bodies pushing against the steel walls. Heads should be straight, all four feet on the ground solid. Turpitt watched the feet, the heads, and waited for a moment of appropriate stillness. It came. He pressed a button.

Dirt flew thirty feet into the air. In no time, the horses were massed on the immediate horizon, their distant motion like a heat wave. Dean looked after them with real interest, absorbed in the outcome. "That was a good one, a good line break," he said. "It looks like the No. 1 horse from here. Of course, I'm not right very often. After all, I'm looking at their rear ends." Inside the gate, in the ground by the braking bar, were deep divots.

Deck's winning time was twenty-two and two-hundredths seconds—half a second slower than the track record. A fast first quarter turned in by a Thoroughbred might have read within a second of that, but Thoroughbreds are not timed, as quarter horses are, from a standing start. They are already doing thirty or thirty-five miles an hour when they trip an electric eye. The clock on these quarter horses was started by the button that opened the gate. The precise timing for each horse behind the leader was accomplished by photography.

On non-racing days, Turpitt spent a fair part of his time schooling young horses in the gate. "Quarter horses in the gate are more excited than Thoroughbreds. Excitable, anyway. Maybe a little more *tense* would be the word." So he walks them into the gate a few times, slowly—a mistake to do it too fast. "If you can keep colts where they're not scared and nervous in the gate, they got a lot better chance. Walk them in four or five times. Stop them. Open the gate by hand. Walk them out. Sometimes they'll just set up a little bit to see if those gates are open, but after that they just go. They learn fast. Thoroughbreds are slower out of the gate. These quarter horses are just like shooting a bullet out of there."

Certain bloodlines are rough in the gate, others calm, he says. Ask him which are which, and he won't say. "The owners would be all over me." Whether he has schooled it or not, he remembers any horse he has ever started. "I remember them. The good ones I don't remember in detail. You remember them better if they screw up a little. But once I've started them I'd remember them if I saw them on a street in Hong Kong, China." With a kind of reverence, he speaks of certain people in his field—Bill Mills, of Santa Anita; George Cassidy, of Belmont. "They are the great ones. I've met Mr. Cassidy."

Between races, Turpitt goes back to the paddock, and sometimes sits in the shade on the porch of the jocks' room. Fifty at dawn, the temperature will rise toward ninety by midafternoon. He kids with the jockeys. They tease him. He tells them, at the call, "Get out there and shut up." A time when he is almost sure to be there with the jockeys is after a bad start. Taking it all on himself, he seems to feel that he has let them down, and he seems to want to be among them, to absorb anything that may be said, to respond, if necessary. He was a jockey once himself. He grew up on a farm near Hemingford, Nebraska, and he started out riding in county fairs, long before the advent of the electric starting gate, when races were begun with a flag. There were gates as well at some places, but they consisted only of slots open in front. "You sat there and sawed on them reins and got that horse in there, and broke with him, too." So much for the pampered modern jockey, led into the gate, sprung out. "Get out there and shut up."

In the fourteenth race of the All-American trials, Rich lost, running second to Azure Teen. John, at the end of the day, walked slowly from the barn, rested on the way to the paddock, stood quietly through the saddling while the other horses snorted and pranced. His time, as winner of his heat, was twenty-two seconds flat, the third-best time of the day— third among two hundred and seven. Six colts and four fillies would be the ten finalists—four from Texas, two from Oklahoma, three from California, and one from Arkansas. Coca's Kid, the other California horse that paid fifteen thousand to get in, had the best trial time of all. Calcutta Deck's time was so good that two other horses in his heat got into the final as well. Rich, close enough behind Azure Teen, made it, too. Separating first from last, the difference in time among the ten horses who emerged as the qualified finalists for the All-American Futurity was one-sixth of a second.

Before 1973, the All-American Futurity was run at four hundred yards. After changing the conditions of the race (a

change that was announced, perforce, in 1971, long before any
money at all had been paid in), the track management explained that its motive was merely to tidy up—to extend the
distance to the classic measure for which the quarter horse
was named. Seems reasonable—but the news touched off a
smoky dispute. The classic distance, some owners said, should
be saved for older horses; these horses were too young. The
forty extra yards—ten per cent—might well increase proportionately the number of injuries and breakdowns suffered by
two-year-old horses, for the longer the sprint the more punishing it will be, and the bone structure of a two-year-old, being
incompletely formed, is particularly vulnerable. In the main,
though, what brought so much concerned attention to those
forty extra yards was the fact that somewhere not much
farther than a quarter mile comes the point where the Thoroughbred catches the quarter horse. Thoroughbreds, of
course, do not run in quarter-mile races. Their offspring do.

By the rules of quarter racing, only one parent has to be a
registered quarter horse. The other can be a Thoroughbred. Of
the ten horses set for the All-American final, five had Thoroughbred sires. John's father, Father John, was a Thoroughbred. All three California horses had Thoroughbred sires. All
quarter horses, without exception, have Thoroughbred blood
in them. It is not unusual for a quarter horse to be mostly
Thoroughbred, and with the lengthening of the big race it
would now become increasingly customary for a quarter horse
to be seven-eighths or fifteen-sixteenths, or even thirty-one
thirty-seconds, Thoroughbred—a dismaying trend, in the view
of some people, and one that seems to make less clear the
definition of the quarter horse as a type.

Thoroughbreds are Thoroughbreds, pure and uncompli-
cated, dam and sire, and to get onto a track they have to have
pedigrees that go all the way back to one or another of the
three foundation studs from which the breed descends—the

Godolphin Arabian (foaled in 1724), the Darley Arabian (1700), and the Byerly Turk (1685). Quarter horses go back, in a generic sense, a great deal farther than 1685. Quarter racing in England is traceable at least to the late Middle Ages, and horses were bred to the purpose even then. All horse racing in early America was quarter racing, and the fastest runners, as it happened, were descendants of horses brought to America by the Spaniards—Arabian in history, heavily muscled not only in the rear but also across the chest, fast off the start, uncatchable for four or five hundred yards but tending to fade quickly after that. When the cowboy came along, he made these horses forever famous. He chose them because they could stop on a dollar, turn on a dime, sprint faster than anything else, and cut out a heifer from a herd with an athletic knack that was known as cow sense. When the United States Cavalry went West to help protect (among other things) the expanding cattle industry from disgruntled aborigines, many a government horse became host to an arrow. To replace the dead and gone, a cavalry station would have a Thoroughbred remount stallion standing at stud. The remount stallions were bred, often, to local mares, cow ponies, producing the modern quarter horse: part Thoroughbred, part Spanish-Arabian, part streak of light. The horse had a definite conformation, a long list of physical characteristics that contributed to its talents and made it a recognizable type—notably the heavy musculature in the rear and the chest, a height of about five feet, a weight around twelve hundred pounds, small ears, wide-set eyes, a short muzzle. In 1940, a quarter-horse studbook was opened, as a result of a movement among ranchers to make a formal breed of the animal that had become the horse of the Southwest, the region where the greatest concentration of quarter horses could be found—where the cows and the cowboys were, and where so many remount stallions had been. Speed and appropriate conformation were the criteria for inclusion in the book. Standards were high, and many thousands of applicants were turned down. The book closed in 1962. So far so simple: any quarter horse born thereafter would have to be traceable on both sides to a horse listed in the studbook. In racing, though, the studbook seems to act only as a kind of fixed foot around which something else can swing. The rule that one parent need not be a quarter horse seems to defy logic, if not to defeat altogether the purpose of the studbook. The quarter horse is by definition a mongrel. Walt Wiggins, the editor of *Quarter Racing World,* has observed, "The question has been 'Is it a registry or is it a breed?' The years have proved that it is a registry."

Aestheticians who show quarter horses for their conformation are enraged by the expanding infusions of Thoroughbred blood. Meanwhile, racing owners adapt their breeding programs to the apparent requirements of speed alone. The rift in the quarter-horse world is a wide one now, and there are even sub-rifts among racers—those who tingle to the cowpoke story and the valued idea of the quarter horse as a unique breed, and those who don't give a damn. Speed, to the latter, is the controlling word, and with speed the truest definition of a racing quarter horse must virtually end. Most quarter-horse races finish up with differences—first to tenth place—expressible in noses and necks. In a major race last August, about a week before the All-American, a colt named Truckle Feature—by a Thoroughbred and out of a registered quarter-horse dam—took on nine other horses, representing the best competition alive at the three- and four-year-old levels, and crossed the finish line three *lengths* in front. The time over the classic four hundred and forty yards was twenty-one and eight-hundredths seconds, a track record. (There are no world records, because surfaces vary.) A quarter-running horse, as the animal is often called, is—what else?—a horse that has at least a few drops of blood recognized in the studbook and can run a quarter of a mile somewhere near the standard of that colt.

Secretariat won the 1973 Kentucky Derby in record time, running five quarters at an average speed close to twenty-four seconds flat. Hence Secretariat was cruising at about thirty-eight miles an hour, while Truckle Feature, in his big race, was doing forty-two. Secretariat, of course, was running for distance. Heaven knows what he might do if he were trained to sprint. "He would follow these horses down the track and then they'd have to get out of his way somewhere around the finish," Dean Turpitt said one day. "They would have to get out of his way or he would run right over them. Take Secretariat out for half a year or so and retrain him, and he could run with the quarter horses. You shorten him up and train him like a quarter horse, and I don't believe these horses could outrun him. He might even be able to do it without the retraining, he's such a superhorse."

Despite the advancing role of the Thoroughbred, quarter-horse sires are still dominant in their field. Nine of every ten horses that ran in the 1973 All-American trials had quarter-horse sires. As it happened, about half the total field were the offspring of just five major studs. Among these, the greatest was Go Man Go. A son of Top Deck, a Thoroughbred, and Lightfoot Sis, a quarter-horse brood mare, he was the foremost money-making quarter-running horse for three straight years in the nineteen-fifties, and his prepotency was such that his get had followed where he had been, winning more money and races than the colts and fillies of any other stallion.

Go Man Go stands at stud at Buena Suerte Ranch, in Roswell, New Mexico, his life an apparent idyll. Firm white fences surround his private paddock. His name is writ in gold on his private barn beside his own demarcated pastures. When the time comes for him to serve his purpose, though, he is led around to the clinic, where a group of mares has been prepared by teaser stallions. Handlers—halters in hand—hold the mares and hold the teasers. A teaser is not restrained as he moves close to a mare. He nuzzles her. He rubs against her. He makes deep sexual sounds. His heart pounds. His blood courses. Her blood courses, too. Nostrils flaring, he tries to mount. Forcefully, he is pulled down and away. He is dragged off to a corral. The mare has ovulated and is ready. Teaser stallions do not last long. In a matter of months, they break down psychologically.

Now, with fourteen or so mares teased up, Go Man Go is brought to the scene. He will not cover one love in a pasture, but fourteen mares in a clinic. One of them is presented to him and, without preliminaries, he mounts. A vet stands beside him. At the ultimate moment before penetration, the vet diverts Go Man Go into an artificial vagina. A heavy leather tube, lined with plastic, it is about two feet long and has a suitcase handle. In its outer walls are two valves, one for compressed air and the other for water heated to a hundred and sixty-seven degrees. Injected hot water bubbles with air, giving Go Man Go a sense of grand reception. ("He doesn't know what is happening," the vet explains. "He thinks he is inside the mare.")

A bottle in the artificial vagina catches the sperm and semen, which are immediately placed in a spectrometer. Fifty million sperm are counted off, and syringed into a teased-up mare. Fifty million more go into the next mare. One ejaculation will more than cover the entire group. Go Man Go is led back to his private pasture, dragging behind him his shattered metaphor: Go Man Go, standing at stud.

The stud that resides next door to Go Man Go is known around the farm as a bad horse, because he recently went after the vet, bit him, shoved him around, and sent him off to the hospital for nine stitches in his arm. The name of this hero is Tony B Deck, property of Anthony Buford, of Caledonia,

Missouri, and it is explained that Tony B was spoiled when he was racing and that he is now "schizo." Tony B Deck was happy when he was racing. He was a big winner, a flying horse. Now—great stud—he must play his role with a fake vagina made from the hide of a cow. And he is considered insane because he took a piece out of the vet.

Tony B Deck's father, who stood in Perry, Oklahoma, was murdered in his stall there on an August night in 1971. Three men, reported to have come from Colorado and to have been hired for the job, spent several hours in the horse's stall gradually dosing him with barbiturates through the jugular vein. His name was Jet Deck. After certain litigation, the American Livestock Insurance Company paid the full face value—three hundred and twenty-five thousand dollars—of a policy on his life. His actual value when he died was almost two million. He was clearly one of the great quarter horses of all time. Winner of twenty-two races in thirty-one starts, frequently setting records, he was the best runner of the early sixties, and some said the best that ever ran. At stud, he sired about six hundred colts and fillies, and their statistical record was so impressive that one did not have to extrapolate far to see that Jet Deck would before long surpass Go Man Go as the greatest sire of all time. He was killed, though, and he left only seven crops of foals, the last of which would come into racing, as two-year-olds, in 1974. His name is cited in any discussion that calls in question the wisdom of artificial insemination, for without it his progeny would number only a hundred and fifty or so. Possumjet, winner of the All-American in 1972, was a Jet Deck filly. Flaming Jet, winner of the seventh trial heat and now a finalist in the 1973 All-American, was a Jet Deck colt. The murder of their father was never solved. It is said that the owners had suspicions about who planned the killing, and why, but no accusations were ever made. Meanwhile, in the Ruidoso barns, with the big race near, human beings stayed with the horses around the clock. Jimmy Grimes slept in the barn with Calcutta Deck. Mike Wilson, a young assistant to Jerry Fisher, slept beside the stalls of Rich and John. Dozing beside Wilson was a German shepherd.

Bill Smith had not gone to a breeding farm to have his mare mated to a celebrity. Unique among the owners of the ten finalists, he owned both the dam and the sire. Calcutta Deck was bred, born, and raised in Pea Ridge. One of the other owners was a horse-and-cattle auctioneer from Henderson, Texas, a man of unspectacular wealth. Most of the rest were millionaires. On the day of the post-position draw, Wayne Laughlin was already brushing up a lather of excuses. He said, looking mournfully at Smith, "You can see what the odds are for an old poor boy hitting this deal."

It had happened, though. On the edge of Norman, Oklahoma, is a milkshake-hamburger drive-in called Jonesy's, not far from a pasture where Jonesy keeps his horses. Jonesy won the All-American in 1967 with a filly named Laico Bird. Possumjet, winner in 1972, was owned by a man named Jack Byers, who drove a county bulldozer around Blanchard, Oklahoma, and, before his horse won, had never owned an automobile, only pickups. A horseman by avocation, he had bred a mare to Jet Deck, and had trained the resulting filly himself. Stud fees in the quarter-horse business are not forbidding. Jet Deck commanded three thousand five hundred dollars. Go Man Go gets seventy-five hundred. Artificial insemination keeps the price low, putting the great studs within occasional reach of the poor. This, among other reasons, is why Thoroughbred stallions must actually cover their mares. Fewer can be served, so the price can be kept high—as high as fifty thousand dollars. Thoroughbred conception, though, is not a liaison in a sea of bluegrass. The mare is hobbled, to reduce chances of injury, and is kept firmly in place by handlers.

The draw was held in the All-American Turf Club, a posh loft of the grandstand, where many owners maintain permanent box seats. Bill Smith missed the draw, because he did not know where the All-American Turf Club was. He was hunting for it while numbered pills were being shaken in a red plastic bottle and dropped out, one at a time, to be matched to the shuffled names of horses. Rich drew the 3 hole. John drew the 7 hole. Azure Teen the 1 hole. Dancer's Queen the 4 hole. And so on until the last pill, numbered 9, matched the last name, Calcutta Deck. Smith finally found the Turf Club, just in time to be jolted by the network man in charge of the television coverage of the race, which would be broadcast to about three-quarters of the United States. The TV man lectured the assembled owners on the importance of making a good appearance on national TV, told them to be sure to dress nicely and to prepare something interesting to say—at all costs to avoid what happened last year. On a monitor, he showed clips of what happened last year. Jack Byers, the winning owner, stood there in the winner's circle in a hat that had lost its Western brim curl, an open green shirt with a T-shirt visible at the throat, and bluejeans that had no belt, let alone a Texas buckle. When he talked, he seemed confused with excitement, and he did not use impressive grammar—and he was as interesting and true to self as anything ever seen on the home screen, but that was unacceptable to the network, whose representative now again reminded the owners to dress and behave not as they ordinarily would but within the margins of a "perception" that TV wanted them to project. He urged them, too, to thank the advertisers. The owners, for the most part in Western hats and Levi's, their millions hidden up their legs somewhere, were amazingly docile, heifers to a man, nodding assent to the electronic master. Bill Smith felt scared. He remembered Jack Byers' telling him that while he was facing television his mouth had been so dry he could not roll a cigarette. It occurred to Smith that he might well find himself standing in the winner's circle with television looking at *him*. He worried that he might faint.

Toward the back of the room sat a tall man with large bones, dark hair, a big grin, and youthful eyes. He was fifty-five and appeared to be forty. His clothing made him look like a rich cowboy, which, in a sense, he was. Across the small of his back, brass studs, embedded in his belt, spelled out his name, Vernon Pool. He had put millions into the All-American. Over the years—since 1959, when the race began—he had paid up nearly sixty horses; he had not yet had a winner. He came from Shawnee, Oklahoma, and his profession was the building of airports, dams, roads—long stretches of Interstate 40, Interstate 35. In the middle nineteen-fifties, he had begun vacationing in Ruidoso, renting a cabin in the mountains, finding rest and relaxation at the fifty-dollar window. It was not at all unusual for him to go there and buy ten tickets on a single horse in a single race. In fact, his betting range ran from fifty to a thousand dollars a race, depending on mood and the vagaries of the program. "The philosophy of gambling," he once explained, "is: Never change your way of betting. If you're a two-dollar bettor, stay there. If you're a fifty-dollar bettor, stay there. Don't try to catch up. Bet the same on each race all day long. You break about even. Always bet them to win. If they're not going to win, they're not going to get nowhere." He once bought ten hundred-dollar tickets on a 7–1 shot and exchanged the tickets after the race for eight thousand dollars.

Pool formed a friendship, early on at Ruidoso, with Audie Murphy, who owned quarter horses, and one day in 1959 Murphy called Pool in Shawnee to ask his help with the purchase of a four-hundred-and-fifty-thousand-dollar breeding farm that was for sale. Murphy got lost somewhere in the negotiations, and Pool bought it all himself—fifty head of horses, including eleven prime brood mares (one of which had been the quarter-running champion a few years before) and, to boot, almost the entire first crop of Go Man Go. Pool, in his life, had not owned so much as one colt until a few months before, and now, with a single signature, he became the premier owner of running quarter horses. To complete this conquest, he bought the remainder of the first crop of Go Man Go. His brother said to him, "You remind me of a man who bought a bottle of beer and liked it so well he bought the brewery."

Pool moved the horses to Shawnee and established his farm on four hundred and twenty acres running in an L shape along two sides of the Shawnee Country Club. His home is there now, and so is the home of his daughter and his four grandchildren. His son-in-law minds the Interstates for him when he is in Ruidoso. Jerry Fisher had once worked for Vernon Pool. Pool's trainer now was William Thompson. Pool's horses had run in the trials for every All-American, and five had been finalists. Two had been in a final together. A horse of his had been the favorite in 1972. The best he had ever done was third.

After the death of a major quarter horseman not long ago, there had been much speculation in the business over who might become the new owner of Vansarita Too, a great brood mare he had owned. While others maneuvered and planned formal offers, Pool saw the owner's widow at Ruidoso, sat down beside her, and said, "Neva, I'd like to buy your horse."

Neva said, straight back, "You couldn't afford her, Vernon."

Pool said, "Why?"

"Because I'd want a hundred thousand dollars for her," Neva said, and Pool reached into his pocket, took out a check, and wrote it. When he went to Pawhuska, Oklahoma, to pick up the mare, he noticed her filly Gotta Go Too. For forty thousand dollars more, he took the filly home as well. To the

1973 All-American he had brought four horses. In the trials, one broke down. Another had sore legs and faded away. The third simply did not run fast enough. The fourth was the filly Gotta Go Too, who qualified for the final.

Pool had lately acquired a semi-silent partner in his horse ventures, a rich private eye from Dallas. His name was Grady Hopper, and he was a dark-haired studious man with an excited manner. As an investor, he had tried Thoroughbreds for a few years but had now gone in for straight speed. He deferred unequivocally to Pool. He was having, above all else, a lot of fun; and at the All-American draw, when Gotta Go Too's number appeared and the horse drew the 10 hole, Hopper got so excited he turned a cup of coffee upside down. "Now, take it easy, Grady. You'll have a heart attack," Pool told him. Later that day, Pool and Hopper went over to a yearling sale that is held annually at Ruidoso, and bid on a brown filly who was a half sister of Truckle Feature. She had twelve pink carnations on her mane, one on her forehead, and two on her tail. Pool kept nodding at the babbling auctioneer as if he were listening to a long story. He bought the horse for a hundred and twenty thousand dollars—the highest price ever paid for a yearling quarter horse.

Bobby Adair flew in for the All-American on the eve of the race. He had been racing in California. He travelled a lot, as the best of jockeys will, coining money. Ten per cent of a race was his, and if he won this one he was going to get thirty-three thousand dollars. Like an airline captain, he would not have a drink with his dinner tonight, for he was flying tomorrow. "Having a drink the night before could slow a person down," he said. "And I sure don't want that." He would turn out his light at eleven and try to sleep for twelve hours, if possible, but such a feat was unlikely, because the race meant too much to him and lately he had not been sleeping well. "It's difficult to explain the feeling a rider has about a race like this," he said. "It's money, but it's prestige, too." For much of a decade, Adair had been the established leader among quarter-horse jockeys. He had won hundreds of thousands of dollars and almost every big race there was, but never an All-American. Four times before, he had been in the All-American final. He had lost by a neck in '71, by part of a nose in '66. He had run fifth in '70 and ninth in '67. He had long been in a position to pick the horse he would ride. Any owner who got him was lucky. He was a student mainly of bloodlines, but when he looked over a colt or a filly he also took into account the racing conformation. His horse this year was Coca's Kid, a filly that had previously run seven times, winning five, placing twice. Her time in the All-American trials—running under Adair— had been the best among the two hundred and seven horses. Sired by a Thoroughbred, Coca's Kid was a California horse. Her owner, a medical doctor named Edward Allred, had paid the penalty fifteen thousand dollars to bring the horse late into the eligible field. The Doctor's specialty was human abortion— "a hundred a day, the biggest in California"—and the jockey helped him invest the proceeds. The two sat side by side at yearling sales. Of late, the Doctor had become nervous, upset, cranky, and irritable, Adair said, and so had he. The pressure of this big race was so great. "The horse, though—she is like a child's pony, a nice, quiet filly. But she's high-strung, too. She changes into a bomb on the track. The farther she goes, the faster she gets. If others are in front of me for a while tomorrow, I don't feel I should panic."

Slender and not short, with blue eyes and curly blond hair, a diamond ring on his finger, Adair was Nordically handsome, and he spoke in a soft, cultured voice. He had grown up in a small town less than a hundred miles from Ruidoso. His father, a schoolteacher, insisted that Bobby get off his horse and study, and finish high school before disappearing into racing. Bobby started out by doing chores at Ruidoso Downs, sleeping in the tack room, looking for someone who would allow him to gallop a horse. The horses were too valuable, though, and for a long while no one would let him get on one. Finally, he got to know an owner who allowed him to take a horse to the track for an exercise gallop. Adair moved on with the owner to the track at Raton, three hundred miles to the north, his only chance to gallop horses, and then on to Denver, where he galloped Thoroughbreds for two dollars a run. He lived on free-lance galloping. He got his license. In September, 1961, he rode his first pari-mutuel race, came in second, and felt confident at once that he would one day win the All-American.

When he was a young rider, what impressed him most about quarter-horse dashes was that they seemed to be over before they started. There seemed to be no time for strategy, or even fleeting thought. He had ridden a thousand races a year for many years now, and his perspective had greatly altered. A race now came in parts, spaced along distinctly in his consciousness. There seemed to be plenty of time, with much going on. "I feel now, during a race, that I have time for coffee and a doughnut. You get your horse out of the gate—standing ride, feet under him, clean break. You maintain as straight a course as you can. You don't lug him in. It costs you ground, which you can't afford to lose in a quarter-horse race. You don't override him. If you hit him right-handed, he might duck to the left. If you're running second and you hit the horse, he might resent it and drop to fourth. If left alone, he might do it on his own. I won't whip this filly. She likes to do it on her own. I'll holler in her ear to keep her from being put off by the roar from the grandstand. I used to think I'd retire if I ever won the All-American, but I'm not an old man. I'll be thirty next month. I figure I'll be good for another ten years. If I win, they'll have to beat me again. I love the quarter horse. I like the looks of the horse and what you can do with him. A race rider is a race rider, quarter horse or Thoroughbred. We don't make anything like Shoemaker or Pincay—but why do that when here I'm king?"

The All-American was the twelfth race of the day and the last of the summer, run in the late afternoon. At five in the morning, while Bill Smith was having his breakfast biscuits, he said, "I went to bed at ten-thirty last night, and I slept awful good until one-thirty. I was up at fifteen to two." He had not slept beyond three-thirty for more than a week. Now, this morning, he had been patient for an hour and then had awakened everyone else at two-forty-five—his wife and daughter, who had joined him for the finish, his friend Wayne, a few others from Arkansas. He went down to the barn before dawn and fed Deck his usual grain, but only about two pounds. Water would stop at noon—a sip or two, no more, after that. The night before, worried about sabotage, he had written the horse's name in huge letters on the stall-front wall over an arrow that pointed to another horse.

As the day brightened and warmed, not a cloud appeared. "I've been doing a rain dance, and nothing has happened," Smith said. "This horse runs that mud."

Another horseman, looking on, said, "The clouds may build up, Bill. And in the afternoon you'll get an overcast, and a little wind will come up, and you'll have a little mountain storm."

"That would do just fine."

Long rows of stalls were empty now. Horsemen packing to leave would stop by for a word, a wistful look at a finalist. They helped chip away at the minutes—five hundred minutes until post time.

"When he drew the 1 hole in the trials, they said he couldn't win," Smith said. "They said you'd have to have a horse that could outrun the others by two or three lengths. Well, I guess I've got that horse."

"That's for sure. You've got that horse."

"As we say at home, I guess an old Arkansas hog has found his acorn."

He took Deck out of his stall, put an old and partly shredded cooling blanket over him, and led him out into the sunshine. Deck stood quietly, tranquilly, almost asleep on his feet. He dropped his head. He let his lip go down. He just didn't look too good. "He'll wake up soon enough," Smith said. "The horse is ready. I gave him a good bath last night. He bucked and kicked." Smith had "put a light breeze in him" five days before—a short gallop on the track. Since then, the horse had walked a little, but that was all. Smith gave the halter to Nancy Roller, his daughter—a young woman as trim and alert as her father, and, at home, his colleague in the training of the horses. He took his pitchfork and went into the stall to muck it out.

"How many millionaires are mucking out their horse's stalls right now?"

"Not too many of them."

"They're getting over those cocktails they drank last night."

"What did you drink last night, Bill?"

"Milk."

Wayne Laughlin was suddenly full of stories about things that could happen to a horse in the days and hours before the race. "People with a jackknife could poke a blade into his front leg muscles," he said. "They could shoot the horse with a needle. They could beat on his cannon bones with an iron pipe. If they would do that for fifty dollars—as people will—or for fifty thousand dollars, how about for a purse like this?"

"Anything can happen."

"He can break down in the race."

"This is a breakdown track—the surface is hard under the dirt. The other day, two horses broke down in one race."

"I remember three in one day."

"All destroyed."

"That's just part of it—part of racing."

"This track is like Russian roulette."

"Bill, they called home. The whole town's up. They're waitin' and hopin', they say. They just know Deck's going to win. Everybody's a-talkin' it."

"You need race luck," Bill said. "The horses are all winners. You need race luck."

In the afternoon, Smith put on a clean shirt, which was as close as he would come to knuckling under to television. He had bought striped breeches, too, for the occasion, but he vetoed them now and stayed in the blue ones he had been wearing all summer.

"You'll look good, Bill, in the winner's circle, with that camera pointing at you."

"That camera looks like a cannon to me."

By four, Deck was thirsty and on edge. Smith gave him a sip of water. The horse licked his lips, to miss nothing. A blacksmith came and tightened his shoes. Jim Grimes cleaned each foot with a steel brush, then covered the foot with Absorbine Hooflex hoof grease. The radio was turned up high—many banjos and guitars. The horse stood still. Jim and Bill brushed his forehead, combed his mane, and gently rubbed his whole body, like two men in a driveway on a Sunday polishing a car. Four-thirty—another sip of water.

The horse's legs had been wrapped overnight in an iodine mixture of Smith's formulation. Now he rinsed the cannons with cold water. "Do you see any pebbles on him?" he said.

"I never seen better legs," said Tom Warren, whose horses

had been stabled next to Smith's. "I want to see that trophy right over here, Bill."

"O.K. We'll put it here and you can look at it."

Slowly, Smith wiped Deck's whole face with a cool wet cloth. The call came from the loudspeakers: "Attention in the barn area. Take your horses to the paddock for the twelfth race. Attention in the barn area. Take your horses to the paddock for the twelfth race."

"You could try for a hundred years and you could never bring one horse here and qualify for the All-American," Smith said. "Now that we're here we don't want to be hoggish. We just want the top end of it."

Dean Turpitt looked at his program and reviewed the horses in the twelfth race. The only one that might present a problem was Vernon Pool's horse, Gotta Go Too. "All right, let's pay attention here," he said as he approached his crew, ten of them today, milling behind the gate. "Who's got the one on the outside?"

"I do."

"She'll rare up pretty high. Make sure we stay with her. She needs handling. If she gets to bouncing too high, pin her down." In each man's hip pocket was a pair of ear tongs.

Timeto Thinkrich, he remembered, had been fine in the gate, a horse that seemed to know why he was there. The other Frank Vessels horse, Go Fartherfaster, was hardly a problem to anyone but himself. He had a tendency to sit down on the tailgate. Coca's Kid, the favorite—the one Bobby Adair was riding—would require two men with locked arms to lift her into the gate. Otherwise, she would not go in. She would bounce a lot when she was in there, too. "Don't jam up the 3 horse," Turpitt said. "Just go to pettin' on her a little there." And he moved off toward his tower. The horses were on the track and were parading before the grandstand. With the exceptions he had noted, there should be no problems. They were, for one thing, two-year-olds, and, for another, they had class. "If a two-year-old is good and sound and he isn't hurting, he may be greener than older horses but he won't get mean in the gate. Least of all this group. Some people may think I'm a liar about it. They think a horse is a horse. But in my estimation higher-class horses seem to have more sense—to be more sensible. They're calmer and sharper, maybe. I don't know, by the time you get to bragging on them sons of bitches they throw a fit." A television camera would no doubt examine Turpitt in his tower, and he was, beyond argument, elegant today, in a tailored tan suit that was lined with silk, a subdued gold panama banded in pastels. That he happened to be bone-tired did not show through his face or clothes, yet he had barely slept at all. Worry or excitement was not what had kept him sleepless, though. As he was about to go to bed, "some son of a bitch" had run over a huge skunk on Route 70, just outside his mobile home.

The horses were approaching the starting gate. A few small clouds had appeared from the southwest, but the day was clear and warm, the track was fast, and chances of rain had long since gone to nil. The sun was low, and broad shadows reached out from the grandstand, which, from the starting gate, looked like an ocean liner about to sail from a pier, with fifteen thousand people—half in big Western hats—leaning out and waving goodbye, their necks, limbs, fingers, and belts shining with enough turquoise and silver to refinance Texas. The sound of the crowd crescendoed as post time came closer—information scattering like neutrons, out of one hat, into another. Those California horses were not here for nothing, and that bay colt was even faster than he was lazy. Frank Vessels owned two of the great quarter-horse studs in racing—Tiny Charger and Duplicate Copy—but to get these colts he had gone off his own breeding farm and bred his mares to Thoroughbred sires. Of all the colts he had at his place, only these two had made it. Azure Teen was the product of a frank program to infuse Thoroughbred blood and win races. Her father, Azure Te, was a Thoroughbred with extraordinary early speed, and a syndicate had bought him for the purpose of putting quarter-horse mares under him. The 7 horse, Go Benny Go, was the aristocrat of the group. He went to old King Ranch Thoroughbreds on both sides. His mother, Ruby Charge, was by Depth Charge by Bold Venture. His father was Go Man Go. That was as royal as you could get. For quality breeding—known performance on both sides—he was the best horse. Flaming Jet might just be the last Jet Deck colt that would ever run in an All-American. His owner, Joe Kirk Fulton, knee-deep in horses ever since he was a kid, had been handed a million dollars by his father when he was twenty-one years old. His daddy made it, and his daddy handed it to him. How did a horse from *Arkansas* get in here? He had won only three thousand dollars in his life, so he had never been far out of Arkansas. His presence was good for the business, showed it was not a closed door. For that matter, how did Dancer's Queen get into this race? Her father earned forty-three hundred dollars, lifetime total, on chipped knees. Mr. Hay Bug? This pot didn't get to be a million dollars on one class of people.

The horses were at the gate. Near the top of the grandstand was a light that Turpitt watched while the horses slowly moved in a circle. The light went out. "All right, bring 'em," Turpitt said, from his tower. One by one, in post-position order, they were brought into the gate. First Azure Teen, then Bobby Adair on Coca's Kid, then Rich.

"Make sure each horse has his feet in front of the braking bar," Turpitt said. "Larry, bear down there."

The flags of New Mexico and the United States hung straight down.

"Jimbo. Don't jam up that mare."

Dancer's Queen was dragged in, resisting. So was Flaming Jet.

"You want a tail on him, Cotton. Step down and tail him."

Mr. Hay Bug moved into the gate.

John, 7, ambled in and sat down.

The crew rubbed the heads of the horses, lightly, gently; they stood calm. Go Benny Go. Calcutta Deck. Gotta Go Too. The gate was full. Heads started whipping.

"All right. Quiet down in there."

The sound from the grandstand increased, and became a concentrated scream.

"Pin him down, Ugh."

Ugh was a Cree.

"Bear down, Gene. Watch your horse, Kent."

"No, Dean."

"No. Dean. No."

"No, boss."

"Hold it, Dean."

"Hold it, boss."

Suddenly there came a moment when the gate was still. Heads were straight. Feet were solid.

As soon as the horses were gone, Turpitt jumped down from his tower and looked at the divots of Go Benny Go. The aristocrat had stumbled a little. Otherwise, it had been a clean break. The horses, already over the finish line, were invisible in dust.

In twenty-one and fifty-eight hundredths seconds, Rich won by half a length. John was fourth. Rich and John together earned three hundred and seventy-five thousand dollars in the race. Flaming Jet, the Jet Deck colt, was second. Bobby Adair ran third on Coca's Kid. Vernon Pool's horse ran ninth. Bill Smith, who watched the race from a point about halfway down, was so hemmed in that he had only a glimpse of the horses flying by. He thought he saw Deck in the lead.

When Smith read the four numbers that came up on the tote board, he got into his pickup and went back to the barns. He filled a bucket with water. His friends began to collect. He moved around a lot, trying to grin. He asked, "Did you find out where he run?"

"He ran eighth."

"Oh, mercy," he said.

Smith picked up a sponge and the bucket and started for the test barn, where Jimmy had taken the horse. Beside the test barn was a corral, where Smith could get away from other people, and he seemed to welcome being in it, with the horse and no one at all. Carefully, he bathed Deck's shining skin, and cooled him down, and the horse moved close to him for more, and eventually Smith covered him with the same cooler he had worn in the morning. Tests over, they walked back to Deck's own barn, where the Arkansas people waited.

"Money talks," Wayne Laughlin was saying. "This old boy told me yesterday that if he gets a dry track this Timeto Thinkrich could outrun anything, but if you had a half inch of mud he couldn't do nothing. Money talks. They gambled fifteen thousand dollars on a dry day."

"They said that No. 1 hole was hard as a dirt floor today."

"Money talks."

"The inside of the track, you can't dig your heel into it, it's that hard."

"I tell you, it would have taken a hell of a horse to outrun that horse out there today."

Smith was not listening. "In the trials, we outrun the horse that won," he said. He filled a hay bag with a great deal of hay and carried it into Deck's stall. He stirred some mash. He tried to joke. He struggled for control. "I wish now I'd had my 1 hole back," he said. "In the trials, we outrun the horse that won."

"Did he pull up sound?"

"He pulled up sound."

Wayne said, "This old boy told me yesterday that if he gets a dry track this Timeto Thinkrich could outrun anything, but if you had a half inch of mud . . ."

"I wish I'd had my 1 hole back," Smith said.

He began assembling and packing his tack. Under some bottles and cans he found a pair of trousers. "There's my fishing britches," he said. "I'd better not lose *them*."

His daughter said to him, quietly, "Mama sold your boat."

He put an arm around his daughter.

She said to him, "I didn't think we'd win, but I didn't expect so many to outrun us."

In this richest of all races, every horse had shared in the purse, and Deck's share was thirty-one thousand dollars.

"I was wanting it to come a rain," he said. "I wish I'd had my 1 hole back. I was wanting it to come a rain."